MW00782692

ANABOLIC
MUSCLE MASS

The Secrets of
Anabolic Reinforcement
Without Steroids

ANABOLIC MUSCLE MASS

The Secrets of Anabolic Reinforcement Without Steroids

by Dennis B. Weis and Robert Kennedy

A MUSCLEMAG INTERNATIONAL PUBLICATION

Copyright © 1995 by Dennis B. Weis and Robert Kennedy

All rights reserved
including the right of reproduction
in whole or in part in any form.

Published by MuscleMag International
6465 Airport Road
Mississauga, Ontario
L4V 1E4

Designed by Jackie Kydyk

10 9 8 7 6 5 4 3 2 Pbk.

Canadian Cataloguing in Publication Data

Weis, Dennis B., 1945-
    Anabolic muscle mass: the secrets of anabolic
reinforcement without steroids

Includes index
ISBN 1-55210-000-6
    1. Bodybuilding-Training. I. Kennedy, Robert,
1938-II. Title.
GV546.5.W47 1996   646.7'5   C95-900921-3

Distributed in Canada by
CANBOOK Distribution Services
1220 Nicholson Road
Newmarket, Ontario
L3Y 7V1
800-399-6858

Distributed in the United States by
BookWorld Services
1933 Whitfield Park Loop
Sarasota, Florida 34243
800-444-2524

Printed in Canada

— WARNING TO THE READER —

The Instructions and advice contained within the pages of this book are intended for informational purposes only and *are not* intended as a substitute for medical counseling.

This book contains explicit information on many different exercises, training techniques and associated programs, that, depending on your current physical condition and present health, may or may not prove harmful to you. Therefore, as is usual with all exercise programs, we suggest that you consult your doctor prior to following any of the suggestions or information contained within.

Due care should also be given to the exercises, techniques and programs described because, if performed improperly, they may have the potential to cause injury. If you feel discomfort or pain associated from any of the exercise procedures, *do not continue.*

The authors and publisher of this book disclaim any and all liability in connection with the exercise concepts described. The user assumes all risks while performing the exercises, techniques and programs. Use of this book constitutes a covenant not to bring any lawsuit or action for any injury caused whatsoever by following its contents.

CONTENTS

Andreas Munzer brings new meaning to the word shredded.

Vince Taylor

Bill Pearl and John McDermott at "The Event" in San Diego, 1991.

Acknowledgements

A heartfelt "thank you" to my very close friend John McDermott, the artist who illustrated this book. The graphic drawings are superb.

A very special "thank you" goes out to my buddy, the late Don "The Ripper" Ross, for it was his own prolific writing on the concepts of the total-body workout which inspired me to colaborate with Bob Kennedy in writing this detailed treatise.

Contributing Photographers

Josef Adlt, Jim Amentler, Al Antuck, Garry Bartlett, Doris Barrilleaux, Caruso, Columbus, Paula Crane, Davey, Ralph DeHaan, Mike Deitz, Denie, Steve Douglas, Irvin Gelb, Bob Gruskin, Kevin Horton, Robert Kennedy, Ledford, Chris Lund, Jason Mathas, John McDermott, Mitsuru Okabe, Jon Running, Shigetomi, Taylor, Norbert Torriente, Verdugo, Dennis Weis, Art Zeller.

Special dedication
to my friend, Bill Pearl...

You are a legend and an inspiration to all who admire a powerful muscular physique, but more than that you are universally admired by those who know you for your genuine modesty and sincerity.

Yours in lasting friendship,

Dennis B. Weis

ABOUT THE AUTHORS

Author Dennis B. Weis is a former bodybuilding and physique champion and is now a feature writer and researcher for such worldwide bodybuilding journals as *MuscleMag International, IronMan, Muscular Development* and *Powerlifting USA*. He is the recognized co-author of two critically acclaimed hardcore bodybuilding books, *Mass!* and *Raw Muscle*. For the past two decades he has been a hard-hitting, uncompromising writer in the fields of bodybuilding, powerlifting and nutrition. Through his unique insights into the methods of exercise and nutrition (and no anabolic steroids!), he has personally accomplished many remarkable and lasting results in strength and muscle growth. Even today at age 50 he is able to barbell back squat (375 X 10), deadlift (470 X 8), barbell preacher curl (160 X 8) and 45° leg press (850 X 12), all at a bodyweight of 212 pounds. Other accomplishments include: Being a featured guest on select radio talk shows; Waldenbooks autograph parties and window displays for *Mass!* and *Raw Muscle*; Dennis has received meritorious service awards in Los Angeles for his contributions as a "muscle writer". He has been an accomplished professional fitness and bodybuilding instructor worldwide for the past two decades.

Co-author Robert Kennedy is legendary in the bodybuilding world as the publisher of *MuscleMag International*, a monthly magazine for male and female bodybuilders that he started in 1974.

Like Dennis Weis, Kennedy has trained for many years and has competed successfully in both weightlifting and bodybuilding contests. He was born in England in 1938 and emigrated to Canada at the age of 30. Robert Kennedy has written dozens of books on bodybuilding, including best-sellers *Hardcore Bodybuilding, Beef it! Pumping Up!* (co-authored with Ben Weider) and *Reps!* He was trained as an artist, specializing in oil painting and stone carving and to this day keeps up with both. He has had one-man art exhibitions in London, England; Salzburg, Austria and Toronto, Canada. His passion for bodybuilding, a sport he still practices today, has made him one of the most knowledgeable and respected authorities in the field.

Shawn Ray ascends Mt. Olympus.

CHAPTER ONE

Genetic-Superior Bodybuilding

A Question on Anabolic High-Volume Training

Suppose a bodybuilder is doing an average of 12 to 15 sets per muscle group with medium training intensity and decides to follow briefer but more intense workouts.

Will the muscle group atrophy for a period of time after the initial cutback in training because of the fact that it has grown somewhat dependent on the 12 to 15 sets, but later adapt and even gain in muscle size and strength with the briefer but more intense bodybuilding workouts?

This is an excellent question. We don't believe that there will be significant atrophy when a bodybuilder reduces his *anabolic volume load* of training. We base this on our knowledge, research and experiences in the areas of anatomy, exercise physiology, and nutrition as they relate to bodybuilders and powerlifters.

We have interviewed and observed literally hundreds of amateur and professional bodybuilders who trained with high-volume strategies and then back-cycled to a lower volume of training. The one revolutionary training effect was that in every case these individuals maintained their previous levels of hard-earned muscle mass and in many cases even increased it.

One group of biomechanical researchers in the iron game have gone on record as saying that the body has an *excercise setpoint* and that once you adapt to a particular workout intensity, such as anabolic volume training, and then back off to a lower volume of fewer sets, then muscle gains will stop increasing.

Sonny Schmidt – 1995 Masters Olympia winner.

This statement alone could be a reason for most bodybuilders to overtrain because they fear that atrophy is lurking around every corner. They're afraid that they will lose all their hard-earned muscle gains if they do less exercise. We have always respected the training wisdom of Bill Pearl and Vince Gironda, and they in particular have spoken out on the subject of anabolic volume training as it relates to the maximum-muscle-gain theory. Here is what they have to say.

There has to be a limit to this. There is no set answer. I know guys who can train three or four days a week, 45 minutes a day, and make very good progress, and other people who don't grow at all. I myself would never do more than 20 sets per muscle group three times per week. It's just not worth the effort. You're going to end up spending your whole life in the gym. A lot also depends on how long you have been training. I have trained for so many years that I am sure I could do 25 sets per muscle group, but it gets to the point where you are

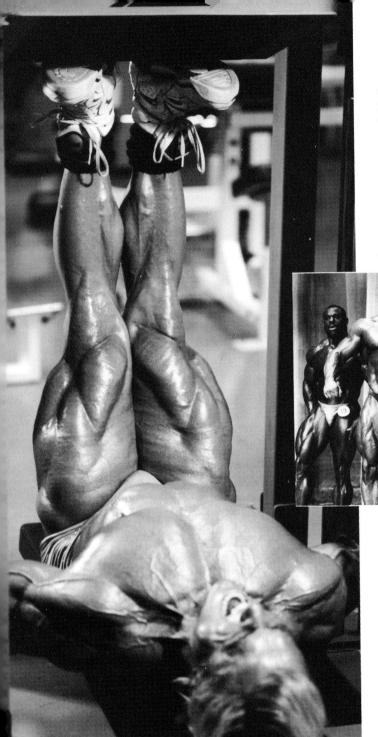

Achim Albrecht, Chris Cormier and Thierry Pastel.

literally wasting a tremendous amount of time. It's like trying to get six gallons of water into a five-gallon bucket. You can't do it because a gallon will spill over the side.

You can only put so much into a particular effort and get results out of it. If you haven't been training that long, then six to eight or 12 sets per muscle may be just as good for you as 20 sets would be for me. You've got to realize the length of time you have been in bodybuilding, how much of a background you have, and how mature your muscles are. All these factors have a big bearing on your training.

I am sure that if I do fewer than 20 sets per muscle group I'm not even going to maintain what I have, let alone make gains. Most people are like that. The longer you have been in the sport, if you want to continue to improve, you've got to spend more time at it. This is what is meant by the overload principle of training.

Tom Platz redefines the Pillars of Hercules.

Bill Pearl feels that this is a hypothetical question. He says, "If a bodybuilder is not responding on 20 sets per muscle group — for instance, five sets each (six to eight reps) of four exercises — three times per week for a total of 60 sets per week, then, believe me, five times that much is not going to do it for you.

You can get muscle overload in three different ways. The first is through your intensity or how hard you train. The second is the length of time you spend at training, by doing more sets or exercises. A third way is by using set-extending techniques such as forced reps and cheat reps. The longer you are in the sport of bodybuilding, the more you've got to follow one or more of these three methods or a combination of these three, to keep your body responding to training. Basically, your body can handle everything that you are doing to it now and still stay looking the same. If you want yourself to look worse, do less. If you want yourself to look better, do more.

You can never build a 20-inch arm with a 15-pound dumbell. You might do it with a 100-pounder, but never with a 15-pounder. Tom Platz couldn't have built his legs on 135-pound squats. Five hundred yes, but 135 pounds no! Just remember that your body at all times tries to adapt itself to whatever workload it is put through.

Bill Pearl's comments on anabolic volume training tend to support the exercise setpoint theory, but listen to what Vince Gironda has to say. "I don't know how anyone can get an honest workout doing high-volume sets for each bodypart because, depending on your power of concentration, your sets can vary from just one or two up to as many as 15, and anything over this is what produces overtonus (where the body shuts down insulin production and the amino acids can't get into the muscle cell for restorative anabolic activity)."

Jack London blasts his armour-plated pecs as Gary Strydom assists.

Tom Platz – contest-ready as always.

These are some very thought-provoking training comments from two of the most respected names in bodybuilding. What we are going to do now is give you a descriptive overview of anabolic volume training and outline some typical high-volume programs based on a three-way split. We will then go on to prove that you can, in fact, back off your training volume and still make sensational gains in maximum muscle mass.

Many of the bodybuilding champions are able to do 20 to 30 mega sets of anabolic high-volume training for each muscle group (and more in some extreme cases — for example,

Serge Nubret, who at the age of 55 is still banging out as many as 50 to 60 sets per muscle group on a day-to-day basis) because their nerves (that is, their basic chemistry at the muscle cell transfer point) are not easily chemically fatigued. For the average trainer this is different.

Serge Nubret knows how to stay peaked for decades!

To organize a plan of high-volume training (HVT), the champion will first select one or two exercises per muscle group. Each exercise is done on an average of 5 to 10 sets, depending, of course, on the training technique chosen. A champion's hard power rep sets can vary from blast singles to doubles and triples, or an ultimate big six power reps, with an occasional mix of maxi-pump reps. The exercises are performed on a frequency of at least once, preferably twice, and sometimes three times per week, usually on nonconsecutive training days.

From this power "base," many of the top amateur and pro bodybuilders will *slowly* add one or two additional sets for a muscle group (in the form of isolationary exercises) every few days or each proceding week until they are doing 10 to 20 additional mega sets, or whatever the greatest number of sets they can comfortably recuperate from.

The number of exercises they do can range from singles to as many as four to six. The *rep factor* for shape-training exercises is structured towards the development of a number of major mechanisms within the muscle. The first mechanism is *mass density* and most generally refers to the thickness of the myofibrils in the various aspects of a muscle group (or groups). This is accomplished by doing hard work sets within a rep range of 10-12, using 70 to 80% of your current unfatigued maximum single effort (MSE).

A second major muscle cell mechanism that the pro bodybuilder will work towards developing is *capillary mass,* which refers to the number of the oxygen-rich blood vessels in a muscle. One of the best ways that the champs have found to create a maximum muscle-flushing effect in this mechanism is to utilize a rep range of 15 to 30-35, using 30 to 60% of MSE, when either doing *warmup sets* prior to the hard work sets (mass density) or the *pump-out sets* afterwards. Rest pauses of one to one and a half minutes are usually taken between sets unless otherwise indicated.

When the champion bodybuilders do 20 to 30 mega sets per muscle group they know that physiologically they could not endure the battle of training nine muscle groups in a total-body workout without coasting at either the beginning or at the end of their workout. Even if the willpower held out the energy wouldn't.

The plan of attack then is to train only two to three muscle groups each workout session. The training frequency for these muscle groups is twice and, in some cases, three times per week. On a four-day-a-week frequency the pecs, lats, thighs and abs could be trained on Monday and Thursday. On Tuesday and Friday the delts, upper arms, calves and forearms are trained. When a pro bodybuilder is looking to train various muscle groups three times per week he would train for six days and might do the following. Delts, upper arms and neck are trained on Monday and Thursday. The thighs, calves and abs are hammered for mega sets on Tuesday and Friday. Finally, the pecs, lats and forearms are trained on Wednesday and Saturday.

When looking at the overall scope of each of the above workout frequencies the four-day-a-week offers three days of total rest and recuperation as opposed to only one in the six-day training week. Most of the champs we interviewed opted for the four-day-a-week frequency during the off-season, especially when doing mega sets.

The anti-stress groupings of major and minor muscle groups are not mindlessly thrown together, but are planned with a distinct structure. To explain this in detail we are going to share with you Larry Scott's opinion on anti-stress groupings when training major and minor muscles.

Chris Cormier

Rich Gaspari achieved bodybuilding stardom in his early twenties. Many feel he was responsible for ushering in a new level of contest conditioning.

"Deltoids and arms (biceps and triceps), for me, are extremely hard workouts so I don't want to do them on the same night. Yet I need something to warm up my arms, so they must be done second. The lat workout is excellent for warming up the elbows and lower biceps connector, so I combine lats, arms and neck on the same night. That leaves delts, thighs, calves, forearms and abs.

Deltoids are hard and nothing will really warm up the shoulders except light shoulder work, so I do them first while I'm full of energy. I could combine calves with deltoids, but after I'm through with delts, I'm a little tired from having fought the pain zone. So, for some, the battle with calves and the extra extreme pain associated with them may not go well with delts.

Paul Dillett boldly grows where no man has grown before.

▲ *Start*   *Finish* ▼

Shawn Ray blasting out reps in the Olympic-style high-bar squat.

I find myself withdrawing a little from the pain of high reps on calf raises if I have already drained a lot of my reserve of pain-withstanding tolerance while doing dumbell presses, heavy dumbell laterals and bent-over dumbell laterals. For me, the combination of delts and thighs works best. Thighs are hard but the reps are short and I like the exhaustion of heavy thigh work better than the long agony of calf work, so I combine delts, thighs and forearms.

That leaves pecs, calves and abdominals, which act like members of the same family.

Pecs are low pain, calves are high pain and the abdominals are not compromised with arms (biceps and triceps). That seems to be one of the best anti-stress groups I have come up with; but as always, it is constantly changing and a month from now I'm sure something will be different."

Continuing on with our discussion on high volume training (HVT), suffice it to say that the pro bodybuilder will actually put quite a bit of thought into planning out their programs. For developing Herculean muscle size and strength they will use the following five muscle density techniques.

CHAPTER TWO

Muscle Density Secrets

Six-Week Rapid Muscle Mass Technique

This training technique uses a fixed poundage, percentage of maximum unfatigued single-effort concept. The percentages of maximum and corresponding poundages increase only once every seven days, over the next six weeks. Here is an outline of the six progression training levels that many bodybuilders in both the amateur and pro ranks will use in their quest for behemoth muscle mass and power.

**Monday and Friday
or... Tuesday and Saturday**

LEVEL ONE
After a couple of light specific warmup sets perform five sets of ten maxi-pump reps with 65% of a current unfatigued maximum single effort (MSE).

LEVEL TWO
5 sets x 8 maxi-pump reps with 72% MSE

LEVEL THREE
5 sets x 6 power reps with 79% MSE

LEVEL FOUR
5 sets x 4 power reps with 86% MSE

LEVEL FIVE
4 sets x 3 power reps with 93% MSE

LEVEL SIX
1 set x 2 power reps with 100% MSE

Hold that pose, Dorian, until the bronze foundry workers arrive.

Clash of the Titans:
Paul Dillett, Nasser El Sonbaty,
Vince Taylor.

Aaron Baker, a.k.a. "Batman."

Big Six and Ten-Set Magic

On this particular mass and strength phase the high-bar Olympic-style squat, supine bench press, conventional deadlift, barbell bent-over rowing, barbell behind-the-neck press and the two-hand barbell curl have been chosen because of their pronounced anabolic effect on the major muscle groups of the body.

The following program is very intensive and the pros have found it best to do only four of the six mentioned exercises in any one workout. One of the best approaches is to do squatting, deadlifting and rowing-type movements on one day and the bench press and curling movement on another — or perhaps presses behind the neck and curling.

Begin each exercise with a warmup set with approximately 60% of the maximum poundage that you will be using on the initial two to three "barometer" hard-work sets. Do eight continuous reps with this relatively light poundage. Rest three and one half to four minutes. Now begin your first "barometer" set

Billy Smith performing seated horizontal rows for densifying his lats.

▲ *Start*   ▲ *Finish*

Within the structure of the progressive training levels two through six only the "barometer" hard work sets are listed. Regardless of the training level the champion bodybuilder is training at, a couple of light specific warmup sets are always done prior to the "barometer" sets.

All the repetition selections listed in each progression of training level are within the maxi-pump (medium poundages) and power-rep (heavy poundages) guidelines set forth in the Percentage of Max Rep Chart listed in Chapter Nine. The body will usually need from three and a half to four minutes to as much as ten minutes in the rest-pause state between sets, especially if you are looking to push some big poundages in exercises like the big three, squat, bench press and deadlift.

with a poundage which will allow you to do six continuous reps and absolutely no more. Rest one minute and then begin your second set with the same poundage and perform another six reps if you can. Rest another minute. Now perform your third set with the same poundage for an all-out effort. You may only get five reps but that is fine. Your only concern should be when you bottom out at four reps or less per set. When this happens (and most generally you will first notice it on the third or fourth set) *reduce* your poundage by 10 pounds for the next set, *but only* when you bottom out at four reps in a particular set. Continue on in the manner described. Do a set, rest one minute, etc., until you have completed 10 sets. After giving this program a run through you will probably notice that the eighth, ninth and tenth sets will be working your muscles to their absolute capacity, so here it would be a good idea to take two or three very deep breaths between each rep.

The Davis Set

This is a six-week mass and strength microcycle periodization training concept popularized by former AABA Mr. California, IFBB Mr. World and one of the world's most symmetrical bodybuilders, Steve Davis. On two nonconsecutive workout days during the first two weeks of training Davis suggests using the *one-rep principle* in which a weight can be handled in a strict positive/negative contraction. The idea is to do 10 continuous *one-rep* sets, decreasing the poundage just enough to grind out one more single rep till ten reps are completed.

Steve Davis, pioneer of the "New Breed" bodybuilding movement.

Hack slide squats are a cinch when you're Tom Platz.

There is no rest between each of these one-rep sets except to remove plates from the barbell for the next rep. Davis says that this program will really up one's power.

During the third and fourth week of training ten sets of maximum *triple reps* MTR are done with no rest other than the time it takes the lifter, or training partner, to remove just enough weight to accommodate three more continuous reps. Continue on in the manner described till all ten sets of three reps are completed. On this two-day-per-week workout cycle, new muscular size will become very evident.

On the final weeks (five or six), ten sets of seven reps are suggested. This should develop some very meaningful muscularity. Use the same training style and procedure as described for weeks one through four.

The *Davis Set* methodology lends itself quite well to the use of the master exercises which work the major muscle groups such as high-bar Olympic squats with heels on a block, hack squats, low-angle bench press, close-grip barbell bent-over rowing, seated press behind neck, braced barbell curl, lying barbell EZ-bar

Sue Price, Dave Fisher – the husband and wife pro bodybuilding team.

curl, French press and palms-up wrist curls. For the minor muscle groups master exercises such as leg curls, stiff-leg deadlifts and braced barlell reverse curls can be easily structured into the Davis Set concept.

Some strength coaches may argue that the Davis Set incorporates a fatigue factor (no rest between sets) into the size, power and muscularity equation. This may be true, but who is going to argue this point when such a great gain factor is so evident from doing the Davis Set?

Eastern Bloc Training System

One of the best-kept training secrets for acquiring brute size and strength is the Soviet Percentage System training methodology. The idea behind this vigorous training system is to take a poundage which is 65 - 85% of your one-rep maximum. Determine what your maximum reps are in this particular percentage range and divide them in half. Then do six to eight sets resting only 30 seconds to a minute and a half between sets.

A four-week training cycle would appear as follows:

Week No. 1 — 70%/max 8 sets x 3 reps
Week No. 2 — 75%/max 8 sets x 3 reps
Week No. 3 — 80%/max 6 sets x 3 reps
Week No. 4 — 85%/max 5 sets x 2 reps
Week No. 5 — test for a new max single.

The success of this program and others where you train by the percentage system will require you to base all your poundages on your actual current one-rep maximum and not on a supposed, or assumed projected max. One of the most efficient methods to test for a *new max single* is to do it under mock contest conditions where you take the correct corresponding warmup set poundages and rest-pauses between these sets prior to your first attempt. We will assume that the first attempt (of three) in the squat will be a poundage that you know without a doubt can be executed for a maximum triple set MTS. Let's assume it to be 400 pounds. Take your first specific warmup set 15 minutes prior to your first attempt (400 pounds). Execute five continuous reps with 50% of that poundage (equals 200 lbs.). Rest three minutes and then perform a second set of three reps with 70% (equals 280 pounds). Rest another three minutes then do a third set for two reps with 75% (equals 300 pounds), rest two and one half minutes, and then do a fourth set of one

Chris Cormier carves out coconut delts with some presses behind the neck.
Start

Shawn Ray/Lee Labrada – two proponents of "Mass With Class."

It has been an interesing observation of many bodybuilders that they can execute a single attempt with 16 to 21 percent more weight than they can do for five reps, 14 to 16 percent more for a set of four reps, and four to five percent more than they can do a set of two reps with. Using your new current max single

Michael Francois blasting out some high-bar Olympic-style barbell back squats.

rep only with 85% (equals 340 pounds), rest another two and one half minutes and then take a final warmup with 90-95% (equals 360-380 pounds). Rest four minutes and then take your first attempt with 400 pounds for one rep. Since this was a poundage that you could triple, you can now expect to lift somewhere between 10 and 13 percent more. So, jump halfway by increasing your poundage five to six and one half percent (420 to 426 pounds) on your second attempt. For your third attempt take another five to six and one half percent jump. This should take you 10 to 20 pounds beyond your mathematically projected *new max single*.

effort sample, adjust your training poundages to the percentage of max used in the proceeding cycle.

Week No. 6 — start a *new training cycle*.

Use the above four-week training cycle often throughout the year on your high-volume training sessions for the squat, bench press and deadlift only. There is a variant to the above training program and it goes something like this:

Week No. 6 — 70%/max 8 sets x 3 reps

Week No. 7 — 75%/max 8 sets x 3 reps

Week No. 8 — 80%/max 6 sets x 2 reps

Week No. 9 — 85%/max 5 sets x 2 reps

Week No. 10 — 80%/max x 1 set x 2 reps
                         85%/max x 1 set x 2 reps
                         90%/max x 1 set x 2 reps

Week No. 11 — test for a *new max single*.

Specific warmup sets are not included in the above 11-week program.

During the weeks six through eight rest two minutes between each set. On week nine rest three minutes between sets and on week ten be sure to rest five minutes between sets.

Finish

These rest periods allow for the central nervous system to function at its maximum capacity (or output) after one to two minutes of rest. The Eastern Bloc Training Percentage System may give the impression that it is a rather easy system to cruise through with its seemingly paltry triple- and double-rep sets. Don't be fooled by this. It is true that the stress within the muscles under this type of training will be somewhat submaximal in nature, but it is intended to be this way so that you can concentrate fully on doing the reps explosively (applying maximum force to whatever percentage of maximum you are using). There is no doubt that you will find some exacting demands on your cardio-respiratory system

Craig Titus – big and vascular!

Penny Price – truly one of the pioneers of the women's bodybuilding and fitness movement.

that will be way beyond anything you have ever experienced. This is especially true during the first four-week cycle, where you only take a rest/pause of perhaps 30 seconds between each of the six to eight sets.

Kevin Levrone and Vince Taylor compare their horseshoe triceps.

There is another variant to the Eastern Bloc Training System that is a favorite of many. It is called the Russian Competition Peaking Cycle and here's an outline of it.

18

Russian Competition Peaking Cycle

	Monday Wednesday	Friday	
Week 1	SQ — 70 x 2, 75 x 2, 80 x 2 x 6	DL — 70 x 2, 75 x 2, 80 x 2 x 6	SQ — 70 x 2, 75 x 2, 80 x 3 x 6
	BP — 70 x 2, 75 x 2, 80 x 2 x 6		BP — 70 x 2, 75 x 2, 80 x 3 x 6
Week 2	SQ — 70 x 2, 75 x 2, 80 x 2 x 6	DL — 70 x 2, 75 x 2, 80 x 3 x 6	SQ — 70 x 2, 75 x 2, 80 x 4 x 6
	BP — 70 x 2, 75 x 2, 80 x 2 x 6		BP — 70 x 2, 75 x 2, 80 x 4 x 6
Week 3	SQ — 70 x 2, 75 x 2, 80 x 2 x 6	DL — 70 x 2, 75 x 2, 80 x 2 x 6	SQ — 70 x 2, 75 x 2, 80 x 5 x 6
	BP — 70 x 2, 75 x 2, 80 x 2 x 6		BP — 70 x 2, 75 x 2, 80 x 5 x 6
Week 4	SQ — 70 x 2, 75 x 2, 80 x 2 x 6	DL — 70 x 2, 75 x 2, 80 x 5 x 6	SQ — 70 x 2, 75 x 2, 80 x 6 x 6
	BP — 70 x 2, 75 x 2, 80 x 2 x 6		BP — 70 x 2, 75 x 2, 80 x 6 x 6
Week 5	SQ — 70 x 2, 75 x 2, 80 x 2 x 6	DL — 70 x 2, 75 x 2, 80 x 2 x 6	SQ — 70 x 2, 75 x 2, 85 x 5 x 5
	BP — 70 x 2, 75 x 2, 80 x 2 x 6		BP — 70 x 2, 75 x 2, 85 x 5 x 5
Week 6	SQ — 70 x 2, 75 x 2, 80 x 2 x 6	DL — 70 x 2, 75 x 2, 80 x 6 x 6	SQ — 70 x 2, 75 x 2, 90 x 4 x 4
	BP — 70 x 2, 75 x 2, 80 x 2 x 6		BP — 70 x 2, 75 x 2, 90 x 4 x 4
Week 7	SQ — 70 x 2, 75 x 2, 80 x 2 x 6	DL — 70 x 2, 75 x 2, 85 x 5 x 5	SQ — 70 x 2, 75 x 2, 95 x 3 x 3
	BP — 70 x 2, 75 x 2, 80 x 2 x 6		BP — 70 x 2, 75 x 2, 95 x 3 x 3
Week 8	SQ — 70 x 2, 75 x 2, 80 x 2 x 6	DL — 70 x 2, 75 x 2, 90 x 4 x 4	SQ — 70 x 2, 75 x 2, 100 x 2 x 2
	BP — 70 x 2, 75 x 2, 80 x 2 x 6		BP — 70 x 2, 75 x 2, 100 x 2 x 2
Week 9	Rest	SQ — 70 x 2, 75 x 2, 80 x 2 x 2	
		BP — 70 x 2, 75 x 2, 80 x 2 x 2	

SQ = Squat   BP = Bench Press   DL = Deadlift

Where's the beef? One would have to be legally blind not to see it here.

Deciphering the Formula

Note: Read 70 x 2, 75 x 2, 80 x 2 x 6 as follows: 70 and 75 percent of your current single max for two reps, one set each, and 6 sets of 2 reps at 80 percent of your max for that week.

Monday is considered a light training day for the squat and bench press while Friday is considered heavy. With regard to the intensity progressions listed in the Friday workout, consider weeks one through four as the volume phase and weeks five through nine as the intensity phase. During the first five or six weeks do assistance work and flexibility work!

A lot of exhaustive research and experimentation went into rather unique Soviet training concepts and we must give credit where it is due. Our sincere and heart-felt appreciation is extended to Ed Coan (the Arnold Schwarzenegger of powerlifting, and the

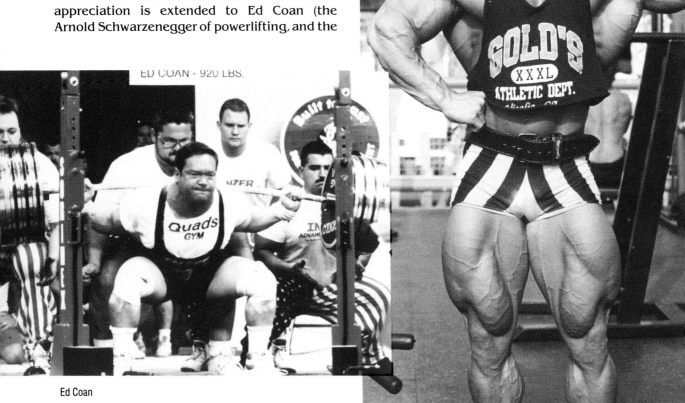

ED COAN - 920 LBS.

Ed Coan

Paul DeMayo obviously has the blueprint for garnering big guns and all his other muscle groups as well.

lightest strength champion to ever total more than 2,400-plus pounds. At a bodyweight of 219 pounds he squatted 959 pounds, bench pressed 545 pounds and deadlifted 898 pounds.), Louis Simmons, a trainer of powerlifting champions worldwide, and finally to "Dr. Squat," Fred C. Hatfield, PhD.

The "Wave" Program

The "Wave" is a program that was developed and written about in the magazine *Powerlifting USA*, May 1991, (Vol. 14, No. 10) by Dyke Naughton, C.F.C.S. of the Cutting Edge Sport Sciences. This state-of-the-art program varies the volume and intensity of training loads throughout the year without ever losing the feel of really heavy weights (golgi-tesdon readiness) and, most importantly, without overtraining.

Shawn Ray repping out in the flat barbell bench press.
Christa Bauch

Roland Cziurlock — brutally huge almost beyond belief.

Each wave (be it single, double or triple wave) base begins with three to five sets of five to eight reps, and peaks out at six to eight sets of one to three reps. We have just barely touched on this system of training but we hope it will perk your interest enough to write or call: Cutting Edge Sport Sciences, 189 Old Loudon Road, Latham, New York 12110, phone (non-collect) 1-518-785-8096, for additional information on the "Wave" programs.

So far, we have discussed five of the most potent and popular muscle-mass and strength-gaining programs that many of the pro bodybuilders use in the first phase of anabolic high-volume training. We must now give some attention to various shape-training techniques. Enter phase two.

Christa Bauch

CHAPTER THREE

Sculpture Blasting

Shape Training

It is of the utmost importance to the pro bodybuilder that, within the structure of an anabolic volume-training session, at least 50 percent of the training modality utilizes a variety of shaping or isolationary exercises which stress different aspects of the muscle (upper, lower, inner, outer, peak, etc.). This will have a two-fold effect. First you will become very aware of the resistance curve (which is how the weight feels) and then of the strength curve, or the hyper-contraction of tension within the muscle at the different joint angles of the movement itself.

As you gain more of an understanding of the significance of these physiological functions you will instinctively be able to select the right amount of weight and the exercise necessary to place stress on the aspect of the muscle you wish to shape. There are three

proven techniques the bodybuilding pros will use, time and time again, to accomplish this.

Technique No. 1
Super Flushing Technique

The basic form of this technique suggests that a bodybuilder should do flushing, or feeder workouts, where a variety of exercises are used with light weights of perhaps 20 to 30 percent of a one-rep max for sets of 20 to 30 repetitions. Joe Weider, the trainer of champions, upgraded the training value of this technique when he suggested that a bodybuilder could "train past the burn" by incorporating a cumulative/rotating giant set and rep mode. Generally, four to six exercises are selected. Here is a super flushing technique for the calves suggested by Joe Weider:

1. Seated calf raise (soleus)
2. Donkey calf raise (gastrocnemius)
3. Seated toe pullbacks using a Dard machine (tibialis)
4. One-leg calf raise (gastrocnemius)
5. Standing calf raise on machine (gastrocnemius)
6. Calf rockups

Aaron blasting his diamond-shaped calves. *Start*

Finish

The Master Blaster, Joe Weider, celebrates with his Mr. Olympia friends Lee Haney, Rich Gaspari and Lee Labrada.

The basic idea is to do one set for exercise number one, two sets for number two, three sets for number three, four sets for number four, five sets for number five and six sets for exercise number six. You can perform each exercise individually for the number of sets suggested if you wish, but if you are looking to up the intensity factor and the quality of your calf-blast workout, then the workout should be done in pure giant-set fashion — with no rest between exercises. Do one set of exercises one through six nonstop, then take a 30-second to one-and-one-half-minute rest. Then begin a new cycle by doing one set of all exercises two through six. Take another rest and continue on in the sequence described.

With regard to the rep schemes, there are many to choose from within the content of this book. Always remember to use a series of reps which will stimulate the muscle to a maximum and *not* overwork it. Rotate your rep selection from exercise to exercise and from workout to workout. This completes your first super flushing workout for the calves. The rotation for the next several workouts as it applies to the super flushing technique is as follows:

23

WORKOUT NO. TWO	WORKOUT NO. THREE	WORKOUT NO. FOUR	WORKOUT NO. FIVE	WORKOUT NO. SIX
Exercise				
No. 2 = 1 set	3 = 1 set	4 = 1 set	5 = 1 set	6 = 1 set
3 = 2 sets	4 = 2 sets	5 = 2 sets	6 = 2 sets	1 = 2 sets
4 = 3 sets	5 = 3 sets	6 = 3 sets	1 = 3 sets	2 = 3 sets
5 = 4 sets	6 = 4 sets	1 = 4 sets	2 = 4 sets	3 = 4 sets
6 = 5 sets	1 = 5 sets	2 = 5 sets	3 = 5 sets	4 = 5 sets
1 = 6 sets	2 = 6 sets	3 = 6 sets	4 = 6 sets	5 = 6 sets

Achim Albrecht, Vince Taylor and Flavio Baccianini on Judgment Day.

As you will notice upon looking back at the chart, beginning with the seventh workout the rotation has come full circle to the original sequence of workout number one. For those of you who are not acquainted with the seated toe pullbacks or dorsiflexion, it is the flexing of your ankle so that the front of your foot moves up, towards your shin — and plantar flexion, which is flexing your ankle so the front of your foot moves down, away from your shin. This is best done using a Dard machine. For a detailed description of this, and the calf rockup exercises, we suggest that you read the book *Maximum Calves*, written by the Health For Life people. For details of each call 1 (800) 874-5339 to order your copy.

Technique No. 2 — Double Antagonistic Supersets

The following double antagonistic supersets were a favorite sculpture-blasting technique that former IFBB Canadian bodybuilding superstar Jean-Charles St. Mars used on his biceps and triceps (antagonistic muscle groups) to create maximum blowtorch intensity training.

He would begin by performing a heavy strength-building exercise such as the rapid-pump seated barbell curl for eight reps (just one rep less than to positive failure). The reps were done with a moderately fast rhythm and without shutting the tension off between reps. The barbell was lowered to within two inches of the top of the thighs in the negative stretch contraction phase of each rep. This keeps maximum tension on the biceps. The only time the bar might touch the thighs is at the completion of the set.

He would immediately go from this heavy muscle-bulking biceps-building exercise to a light shape-training movement for the triceps. This would be either triceps pushdowns on the lat machine or a peak-contraction movement such as the two-dumbell kickback for 10 to 12 reps. Without a rest he would then do a set of face-forward incline (45 to 50-degree) peak-contraction dumbell curls for 10 to 12 reps (upper body resting against the padded surface of the inclined seat).

Start

Finish

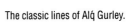

The classic lines of Alq Gurley.

Tonya Knight shows flawless technique emphasis on triceps pushdowns.

From here he would finish off the double antagonistic superset series by lying back on a 45-degree incline bench and do some barbell triceps extensions (lowering the bar just behind his head). This heavy triceps-bulking movement was done for eight solid reps. All four of the exercises are done in a non-stop series. He would go through this series three more times. A rest of up to three minutes was taken between each series.

Sue Price – Dave Fisher's better half.

Start   Finish

Tom Platz, going for that final rep, as only he can.

We know of some bodybuilders who have given this particular arm-training system a try and found that a rapid, kneeling, cheat barbell curl to be an excellent substitute for the seated tension barbell curl. This exercise is done where you are in a kneeling upright position with the end of a flat exercise bench against your lower abdominal region. You curl the barbell from the bench surface to your chin and then lower it down, lightly touching the bar to the flat surface of the bench each and every rep.

The program can be modified whereby the heavy muscle-power exercises for the biceps and triceps (rapid, kneeling, cheat barbell curl and barbell triceps extension, etc.) are performed to double and triple positive failure before going on to the shaping movements. To initiate this technique, begin with a poundage in either one of the two exercises and do six full cheating reps. Immediately reduce the poundage by 20 percent and do the exercise for eight more reps in a semi-cheat manner. Again, with no rest, reduce the poundage on the barbell by a final 20 percent and focus on executing eight reps in an ultra-strict manner. On paper this technique variation of the *double antagonistic superset* appears as follows:

Rapid seated barbell curls

or...

Rapid kneeling cheat barbell curls
   Cheat — 200 pounds x 6 reps
   Minus (–) 20 percent
   Semi-cheat — 160-pounds x 8 reps
   Minus (–) 20 percent
   Ultra-strict — 120-pounds x 8 reps

Then go on to:
Triceps pushdowns (on lat machine)

or...

Two-dumbell kickback, strict — 10-12 reps

Then:
Incline (45 to 50-degree) prone peak-
contraction dumbell curls strict — 10-12 reps

Finally:
Lying incline (45-degree) EZ-curl triceps
extensions
Or (substitute)...
Vertical-angle parallel bar dips
(On this exercise be sure to use a vertical
dipping bar and hold extra poundage
between your legs.)

On either one of these final triceps
exercises, do the double- and triple-positive
failure technique outlined above. The 20
percent decreases are always applied to the
original starting weight being used within the
technique. Though the biceps and triceps
muscle group of exercises have been used to
illustrate the double antagonistic superset
technique, be assured that this technique can,
with a little thought, be structured to accommodate other antagonistic muscle groups as
well.

John Brown shows yet another use for safety straps.

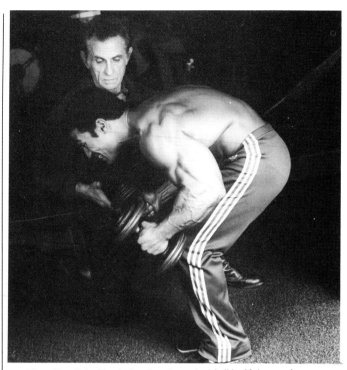

Vince Gironda barking instructions to pro bodybuilder Mohammed Makkawy.

Technique No. 3
Staggered Sets and
Staggered Volume Training

This system was originally known as the Weider
Staggered Sets Principle and was designed to
stimulate optimal new muscle growth. It was
used to minimize mental and physical fatigue
on the body by integrating one or two sets of a
high energy expending exercise between other
muscle groups. For example, the genetically
superior bodybuilder may find heavy leg and
back work in the form of squats and deadlifts
to be quite energy depleting, especially when
those exercises are done in consecutive sets.
The way to solve this problem is to alternate or
stagger one or two sets of say, barbell Olympic-
style squats after completing all the required
sets for another muscle group. This concept is,
of course, all relative to the number of muscle
groups being trained during a particular
workout. Some bodybuilders will use staggered
sets as a means of specialization within the
various muscle groups themselves, but usually
they will be used with low-energy isolationary
muscle-shaping exercises.

A good example of what we are talking about is to use staggered sets on abdominal exercises. After each set of an exercise for the chest, a set of crunches for the abs can be done. This alternating one-to-one ratio might go on for three or four sets then perhaps another abdominal movement might replace the crunches. Obviously if a bodybuilder is doing high-volume training where two or three muscle groups are being trained for 20 to 30 sets each, he may adjust the ratio of abdominal exercise sets from a one-to-one ratio to

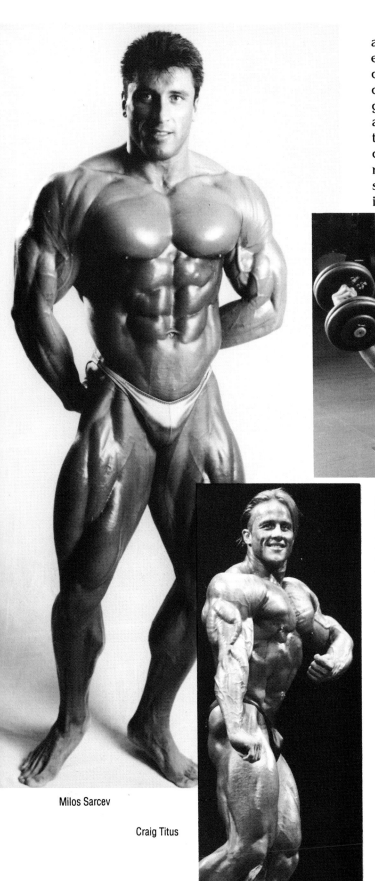

Milos Sarcev

Craig Titus

Dumbell incline flyes stretch Shawn Ray's upper pecs to their outer limits.

perhaps a three-to-one to spread the volume of staggered sets out over the entire workout rather than just pound the abs unmercifully.

This is the basic concept behind staggered sets. Recently, however, this training technique has been upgraded through the research of Dr. Douglas M. Crist, Ph.D. He has documented his research in a book titled *Growth Hormone Synergism.* Basically, the book explores what Dr. Crist terms, ''Staggered Volume Training'' (SVT). This system incorporated working antagonistic muscle groups (e.g. chest and back). As an example, if 18 mega sets were selected for the chest and the same number for the back, the total number of sets would be equally divided into six subgroups of three sets each. An example of staggered volume training, using the two muscle groups mentioned would be as follows:

Begin by doing three sets of flat bench presses. Use a system of increasing the poundage and decreasing the reps. Your reps for these three sets might be 12, 10 and eight. Next do three sets of wide-grip pullups. You can do them either to the front or the back-of-the-neck. Choose whatever you prefer for reps of ten. Repeat the cycle as described. Now go on to low incline (30 to 40-degree) bench presses with either dumbells or a barbell, and do three sets of ten, eight and six reps. If you elect to use a barbell, lower it to the neck, not to the upper pecs.

Next up is wide-grip pulldowns to the upper pecs for three sets of ten reps. Use the same poundage on each of these sets rather than pyramiding them. Frank Zane says that these two exercises in particular exert a broadening effect on the upper body. Repeat the cycle.

Next do dumbell flyes for three sets of twelve, ten and eight reps. You can do them either on a flat, an incline, or a decline bench, depending on which aspect of your pecs need the work. When these three sets are finished begin doing one-arm dumbell rowing for the

Mike Quinn shows the proper way of performing one-dumbell rows for the lats. **Start**

lats. Do ten reps per set. *Don't* repeat the cycle as you have done with other exercise combinations but go on to single-dumbell pullovers while lying lengthwise on a flat bench. This serratus-developing exercise should be done for three sets of twelve reps. Finally, finish off the staggered-volume training with leverage T-bar rowing for the lower and central lats. Do three sets of ten reps.

Alternating these subgroups in a push-pull sequence helps to delay the onset of localized muscle fatigue and thereby gives a bodybuilder maximum focus for the stimulation of muscle mass growth. There are endless combinations of subgrouping antagonistic muscle groups. If twelve sets are to be done, then it could be divided into two sub-groups of six sets each. A system we will describe later called "Series Training" would be one of many logical choices for subgrouping. If eight sets were planned for each muscle group, a subgrouping of four sets each would adapt to Vince Gironda's famous 10 (50%M) - 8 (75%M) - 6 (100%M) - 15 (35%M) routine. Percentages are based on a six-rep maximum.

Another option would be to use the "Division of Sets Technique." This training principle is described in Chapter Eight.

Finish

Last point: If six sets were selected for two antagonistic muscle groups, they could be divided into two subgroups of three sets each. The DeLorme-Watkins three-set progression program could be done for two cycles here. Read Three Sets of Ten Reps-Plus in Chapter

Aaron Baker smiles his way to a top placing.

exercises (pushing) could be done for a pre-determined number of subgroup sets and then an abdominal movement (pulling). Or how about working the delts, traps and lats by doing the barbell press behind the neck and then lat pulldowns behind the neck? The choice is yours.

All of the examples we have used to explain the concept of Staggered Volume Training (SVT) are some of the best combinations of push-pull super-sets you will find anywhere.

Staggered sets or, if you wish, staggered volume training, can be a bit more intricate in its application than we have explained thus far. We suggest you purchase a copy of Dr. Crist's book *Growth Hormone Synergism* for a more detailed explanation of this muscle-igniting

Ron Coleman — a former powerlifting great, now an achiever as a bodybuilding pro.

Serge Nubret doing stop-pause lat pulldowns behind the neck.

Ten for more information.

It is not uncommon for some bodybuilders to perform staggered-volume training on two nonadjacent muscle groups. For example, calf

training concept. It can be purchased by sending $42.95 (postage paid) to DMC Health Sciences, P.O. Box 23190, Albuquerque, NM 87192-1190.

CHAPTER FOUR

Overview of Anabolic High-Volume Training

The mass and strength exercises will most generally include the big six and those mentioned in the Davis Set, in Chapter Two. This, however, could be expanded upon to include those listed in the Exercise Selection Chart under the subtitle: "General Size and Power" in our book, *Mass!* (Contemporary Books Inc., Chicago 1986). This will allow you the option of choosing a replacement exercise every few weeks which will target the same muscle group but from a different stress angle. These exercises will most generally stimulate the surrounding muscles while causing minimum trauma to the joints.

Meryl Ertunc – looking good!

Use no more than 1 or 2 of these mass and strength exercises for a muscle group when performing multiple sets (base of 1 to 3, to an

Achim Albrecht, Vince Taylor and Flavio Baccianini – three's a crowd!

average of 5, to a high of 10 sets), and where the rep grid range varies from a low of 1 to 3 to an average of 4 to 6 to no more than 8 reps.

Intensity within the structure of this phase of training will be 70-90 percent of a current one-rep maximum. Rest between sets is up to you. It can go from 30 seconds to 90 seconds or more or, if you choose, you can work through with no rest at all.

Sharon Bruneau and Sonny Schmidt mug for the camera.

The dynamic structure of isolationary (muscle-shaping) exercises incorporates those recommended by Vince Gironda in his unique "A Muscle Has Four Sides" concept of training as well as those incorporated within the anatomical self-analysis chart summary in the Steve Davis book, *Magic of Symmetry*. (This book can be purchased from *MuscleMag*

International at a cost of $5.00.) Our book *Mass!*, also contains an expansive selection of these muscle-shaping exercises.

Four to six exercises in a mix of isolationary shaping and size-and-power movements are used in this part of the anabolic high-volume program for 10 to 20 total sets with a minimum rep scheme of 10-12 to 15-30, although, on occasion, they may go as high as 50. The percentage of one-rep maximum used will be between 40 and 80. Rest goes from absolute zero in some techniques to 30 seconds, to an absolute one-and-one-half minutes between sets, or cycles.

The number of muscle groups trained in a particular workout session will generally be two to three with a frequency of one (Eastern Bloc Training System) to an average of two and sometimes three workouts per week. Without going into a discussion on the typical three-way split, etc., you can be sure that many of the pro bodybuilders are doing anywhere from 60 to 90 sets for each muscle group each week with this procedure of anabolic high-volume

Lean beef – Nasser El Sonbaty, Ron Coleman and Vince Taylor.

training. The bottom line is that the pros are after continuous muscle gains and they will only use such a program until the gains stop. Their next training strategy is to reduce the frequency of training per week and reduce all poundages 15-25 percent and all sets by 20-25 percent. Here's how they do it.

The "push-pull system" is very popular among bodybuilders today so this will be the selected program model, and begins in the following chapter.

CHAPTER FIVE

Push and Pull of Power

Start ▲   Michael Francois bombing and blitzing his hams.   ▲ Finish

Modified Push/Pull System

"A" WORKOUT Quads, Hamstrings and Calves		
EXERCISES	**SETS X REPS**	**REST BETWEEN SETS (SECONDS)**
Superset: Leg extension	5 x 15	15
Leg curl	5 x 15	15
45-degree leg press	7 x 10-15	60
Or...		
Stiff-legged deadlift (non-lockout for hamstrings beginning just below knees to 3/4 lockout)	5 x 10-15	60
Donkey calf raise	3 x 25	60-75
Seated calf raise	5-7 x 12-15	15
Standing one-leg calf raise (dumbell in one hand)	5-7 x 12-15	15

Start   Finish ►

Leg extensions are a mainstay in quad shaping for Shawn Ray.

Start

Christa Bauch knows that dumbell laterals give the illusion of dramatic delt width.

Finish

Charles Clairmonte, from England, hits an imposing side chest pose.

"B" WORKOUT
Chest, Delts and Triceps

EXERCISES	SETS X REPS	REST BETWEEN SETS (SECONDS)
Barbell/dumbell bench press	5-7 x 10-15	60
Dumbell 35-degree incline press	5-7 x 10-15	60
Dumbell decline flye	4-6 x 12-15	15-30
Dumbell low incline flye	4-6 x 12-15	15-30
Dumbell press (seated)	5 x 15	60
Dumbell lateral raise	5-7 x 15	15
Dumbell front raise	5-7 x 15	15
Dumbell bent-over lateral raise	5-7 x 15	15
Close reverse-grip bench press	5 x 10-15	45
Barbell lying triceps extension	5 x 12-15	30
Triceps pushdown	5 x 15	30

34

"C" WORKOUT
Back, Biceps and Abdominals

EXERCISES	SETS X REPS	REST BETWEEN SETS (SECONDS)
Wide-grip lat pulldown (to back of the neck)	5 x 12-15	30
Lat pulldown to chest (pull to sternum using underhand grip)	5 x 10-15	60
Dumbell bent-over row (one arm)	5 x 12-15	Nonstop, rt/left
Seated horizontal pulley row	5 x 12-15	30-45
Or...		
Prone hyperextension (use your own bodyweight)	5 x 15-30	15-30
Standing barbell curl (EZ-curl bar)	4 x 10-15	30-45
Incline 45-50-degree dumbell curl	3 x 10-15	30
Or...		
Barbell preacher curl (EZ-curl bar or sub/dumbells)	3 x 10-15	30
Reverse barbell curl (standing or on Scott bench)	3 x 12-15	15-30
Barbell wrist curl (palms up)	3 x 15-20	15-30
Hanging knee pull-in (substitute hanging leg raise)	3-5 x 15-30	15
Or...		
Incline leg raise	3-5 x 15-30	15
Crunch	3-5 x 15-30	15
Reverse crunch	3-5 x 15-30	15

Edgar Fletcher smiling his way through some heavy, heavy one-arm dumbell rows. **Start**   **Finish ►**

The above program is a modified push/pull concept which has been structured into a typical three-way split. This program in particular contains a nice blend of general size and power and isolationary exercises which, due to the structuring of moderately high reps and very brief pauses, lends itself almost purely to muscle shaping.

The frequency of workouts on this modified push/pull training system can be approached from a number of different angles. Many of the pro bodybuilders tread the fine line of over-training and make a six-day routine out of it by performing workout "A" on Monday and Thursday, workout "B" on Tuesday and Friday, and "C" on Wednesday and Saturday — leaving Sunday as their only rest day.

In an attempt to compensate for the over-training factor, they will incorporate the heavy and light training principle. On Mondays (workout "A") all the poundages and number of sets are to be at 100 percent maximum capa-

Tonya Knight, the blonde bomber of pro female bodybuilding.

city. They always try to add some extra weight or reps on any muscle group functioning at 100 percent capacity. On Thursdays ("A") they reduce all their training poundages by 15 percent and reduce the number of sets by 20 to 25 percent.

During Tuesdays (workout "B"), all poundages for the chest are at 100 percent, while for the deltoids and triceps they use only 75 percent of the poundages they are capable of. Therefore, they reduce the number of sets by 20 to 25 percent on these latter two muscle groups. On Fridays ("B") they reduce training poundages on chest work by 25 percent and all sets for this muscle group are reduced by 20 to 25 percent.

Thierry Pastel punching out an awe-inspiring ab shot.

Jeff King – huge and freaky in the mid 1980s.

Dorian Yates and Shawn Ray relaxing in the lineup at a recent star-studded Mr. Olympia.

forearms. You may wish to try the above out for yourself. We assure you it is effective.

Jeff King, the 1983 AAU Mr. America and NABBA Mr. Universe title winner, took the heavy and light training principle one stage further. His version was a 16-day cyclic pattern of three training days on and one off, where the training poundage levels for a given number of sets for a muscle group(s) was varied. Many of you who have followed Jeff King's phenomenal bodybuilding career have heard that he followed very heavy, concentrated workouts to develop his herculean 220 pounds of ripped-to-the-bone muscle size and proportion. This is true, but not at every training session. It's here where Jeff's intensity manipulation factor came into the bodybuilding equation.

Jeff would follow a 16-day cyclic pattern where each muscle group receives one all-out training session, two sub-maximal (moderate) and one sub-maximal (light) training session. To clarify this more in detail, he would use 100 percent to 105 percent of the poundages he could handle in a proper exercise form for a complete range of movement (stretch and contraction). This he did for the assigned number of sets and reps for the muscle group(s). For the next workout on the same muscle group(s), he would use light poundages of 75 percent while for the two proceeding workouts he would follow up with sub-maximal (moderate) poundages of 90 percent and 85 percent respectively and in the order listed. Using the previously mentioned modified push/pull training system, a 16-day cyclic pattern would appear as follows:

The Wednesday (workout "C") follows suit by reducing all training poundages and sets for the back by 25 percent. All biceps and forearms sets and poundages remain firm at 100 percent of capacity. On the Saturday ("C") they reverse the procedure for the back, biceps and

	(100% - 105%)				(75%)		
Day 1	Day 2	Day 3	Day 4	Day 5	Day 6	Day 7	Day 8
A	B	C	Off	A	B	C	Off
	(90%)				(85%)		
Day 9	Day 10	Day 11	Day 12	Day 13	Day 14	Day 15	Day 16
A	B	C	Off	A	B	C	Off

Lee Labrada, the originator of Mass With Class, doing a most-muscular.

The effectiveness of the 16-day cyclic pattern is that it helps muscle recuperation while decreasing the overtraining factor — all of which guarantees a maximum in muscular overload.

If the pro bodybuilder feels that the frequency of this "72-hour split routine" is not allowing for maximum muscle, central nervous system and adrenalin recovery, he will structure a sequential push/pull system into three distinct and separate microcycles.

Larry Scott, the big-arms dude from North Salt Lake City, looking good at 50 and beyond.

The first **microcycle** is a five-days-a-week program. This particular program requires the bodybuilder to approach workouts on a continuing basis rather than by the week. The main difference between this cycle and the previous six-day training program (72-hour split routine) is that you won't be using Saturday as a workout day. In this respect it will require you to borrow one day from the next week in order to train the entire body twice. Larry Scott calls this a "double series."

Michael Francois doing stiff-legged deads like those mentioned in the Finnish Deadlift Program in Chapter 10.

Start

Finish

A second microcycle that also does not compromise bodybuilding gains is the two-on-one-off system. This is a very popular training approach with superstar bodybuilder Lee Labrada.

Finally, a third microcycle would be one on/two off/one on/three off. If there is a compromise within the structuring of this last microcycle it could be that there are too many rest and recuperation days between workouts and also the total body is not being worked even once in a seven-day week. Actually, of the three microcycles, this last one may be the best for a hard gaining anabolic steroid-free bodybuilder. From the standpoint of total recovery, the rest and relaxation days will allow for all of the bio-chemical processes and reserves to normalize after a maximum stress overload on the muscle group. This cannot help but induce maximum muscle growth!

With regard to the total body not being trained even once per week, rest assured that the muscle groups that are trained during a particular week will create an indirect stimulus to those not being trained. If this is not reassuring enough to you, then do as the champs do — modify the second workout of the two to include at least one, but not more than two flush sets of 20-25 rapid but controlled reps with 30-45 percent of a current unfatigued maximum single effort of a select exercise for the muscle group not trained on a particular week.

Suppose, for example, it will be a whole week before the back receives any direct stress overloads. Then the deadlift (which developes both the spinal erectors and traps) would be a good partial workout exercise to do. It would give slight stimulation to the lower back until it can be fully trained the following week. If used as a stop gap, the deadlift should be done in a measured movement style where it is pulled rapidly from just below the knees to a lockout

The late Don Ross grinding out some upright dumbell rows. They are fab for giving width to the medial (side) delt aspect.

position and then lowered down quickly to the starting point. This concept is explained in the Finnish Deadlift Routine near the end of Chapter Ten.

So that you will have a clearer understanding of the three microcycles, we are including the following Dynamic Frequency Chart. The previously outlined modified push/pull system (workouts "A," "B" and "C") will serve as illustrations on the chart.

Many of the top pro bodybuilders will take the push/pull system into a fourth dimension of hardcore training with a unique counter-split approach. With this system they will train the muscles with similar functions two days in succession.

Within the structure of the counter-split, the heavy muscle-bulking exercises are performed on Monday (pushing) and Thursday (pulling). Muscle shape-bulking or isolation movements are done on Tuesday (pushing) and Friday (pulling) with Wednesday, Saturday and Sunday as total rest days.

Power reps for an average of four to six reps will be used on Monday and Thursday, and maxi-pump reps of 12-15 will be done for the

		MON.	TUES.	WED.	THURS.	FRI.	SAT.	SUN.
Dynamic Training Frequency Chart								
Cycle 1								
Wk. No.	1	A	B	C	A	B	Rest	Rest
	2	C	A	B	C	A	Rest	Rest
	3	B	C	A	B	C	Rest	Rest
Cycle 2								
Wk. No.	1	A	B	Rest	C	A	Rest	B
	2	C	Rest	A	B	Rest	C	A
	3	Rest	B	C	Rest	A	B	Rest
	4	C	A	Rest	B	C	Rest	A
	5	B	Rest	C	A	Rest	B	C
	6	Rest	A	B	Rest	C	A	Rest
	7	B	C	Rest	A	B	Rest	C
	8	A	Rest	B	C	Rest	A	B
	9	Rest	C	A	Rest	B	C	Rest
Cycle 3								
Wk. No.	1	A	Rest	Rest	B	Rest	Rest	Rest
	2	C	Rest	Rest	A	Rest	Rest	Rest
	3	B	Rest	Rest	C	Rest	Rest	Rest
	4	A	Rest	Rest	B	Rest	Rest	Rest
	5	C	Rest	Rest	A	Rest	Rest	Rest
	6	B	Rest	Rest	C	Rest	Rest	Rest

Lou Ferrigno – 300 pounds of huge and ripped-beyond-belief muscle.

An important point to remember when doing shaping exercises is that not all aspects of the muscle require the same amount of stimulation. For example, if the serratus muscles on the ribcage are weak in development, do an honest workout using a burning pump technique such as **ten sets of ten reps** (taking five to ten deep breaths between sets), while decreasing poundage every two sets by 10 pounds. Choose just one exercise, such as Parrillo dips or Gironda "V-bar" dips, or one-dumbell pullover, and concentrate on the upper end (or peak contraction) range of the exercise. This way the weakest part of the muscle gets the most work.

isolation exercises on Tuesday and Friday. The abrupt changes in the cycling of the reps from four to six to 12 to 15 within the weekly workouts will "shock" the body into greater adaptation rather than going from four to six reps to just eight or ten.

On Monday and Thursday the "10-set magic" (Davis set plus Eastern Bloc training system), could be used; or perhaps a three-two-one power rep system could be used where three sets of three reps are performed, then three sets of two reps, and finally six sets of one rep are done. Don Ross explains this particular system in his best seller *Muscle Blasting!* (Sterling Publishing Co., Inc. New York).

It goes like this: On Tuesday and Friday workouts it is important to use a variety of muscle shape-bulking exercises to fully stimulate the muscle. This is best done from several different angles in the beginning, mid-range, and end range positions so that both muscle shape and mass are fully developed.

John Hansen – It's easy to smile your way to a contest victory when you're anabolic steroid free.

John C. Grimek, two-time Mr. America, Mr. USA and Mr. Universe (undefeated throughout his entire bodybuilding career), used to do a slightly different version of the ten sets of ten reps technique. He would perform one set of ten reps doing ten different exercises and used at least five different exercise apparatus. If you want to train in this manner, do the following exercises in sequence: two-hands barbell curl, alternate dumbell curl, kettle-bell curl, expander cable curl, swing-bell curls (a sleeveless dumbell bar with weights loaded centrally on the bar with a collar placed securely on each end of the bar to hold the weights in place), dumbell Scott curl, lying flat bench curl on lat machine, standing (or lying) curl on Universal

The great John Grimek shown in photos taken in his prime – strong and massively symmetrical!

Paul DeMayo shocking his huge vein-choked biceps with alternate dumbell curls.

machine, dumbell hammer curl, and finish up with fulcrum or leverage dumbell bar curl. Use a poundage on each exercise which is approximately 80 percent of a current unfatigued maximum single effort. Rest 20 seconds between each exercise. This arm-pumping blueprint, which incorporates a multi-angular (four sides to a muscle) concept, was known as the "copycat system" back in the mid 1960s.

Continuing on with our discussion of the unique counter-split workout approach, the muscle group sequence for the Monday/Tuesday "push" workouts should include quads, chest, delts (anterior and lateral) and triceps.

On Thursday and Friday (which is "pull" day) the hamstrings, back, traps, lats and spinal erectors, rear delts, biceps, forearms and calf muscle groups are trained. The neck, forearms, abs and calf are considered neutral by some bodybuilders and can be included within any of the anti-stress (major and minor) muscle groupings.

This unique counter-split pushing and pulling requires a 50-50 division of movement for heavy muscle (bulking/power) and shaping. It is, therefore, important that whatever strength and muscle-pumping techniques are chosen, they will be dictated by your individual muscle tolerance to accept such a strenuous technique. Some muscles have a low pain tolerance and others high. Some muscle groups respond well to training and others are slow and stubborn to grow. Champion bodybuilders realizes this and will design workouts with different intensity factors for different muscle groups. However, they always spend more time and intensity on the slower, least responsive areas.

Earlier, at the conclusion of the **Overview of Anabolic High-Volume Training,** we mentioned that the push/pull system is very popular among modern bodybuilders. While this is true, the pro bodybuilder will amost by instinct make minor changes in his workouts every couple of weeks and major changes every eight to 12 weeks. One of the major changes is to abort the push/pull system in favor of what is called the **Conjunctive Muscle Principle.** The chest, back and delts

Gary Strydom resting between brutal sets at Gold's Gym in Venice.

are worked on Monday and Thursday and on Tuesday and Friday the triceps, biceps and forearms are worked. Finally, legs are worked on Wednesday and Saturday. The idea behind the anti-stress grouping of these exercises is to keep the blood in one area to achieve a maximum pump.

This grouping can be worked out using the listed **Dynamic Training Frequency Chart.** A **conjunctive counter-split** is used from time to time as well as following the information provided above (Mon. - Tues. = chest, back and delts, Wed. - Thurs. = triceps, biceps and forearms, Fri. - Sat. = legs).

Chris Faildo obviously has trained for diamond-hard cuts but hasn't forgotten at all about muscle bulk!

When selected muscle groups are trained back to back, two consecutive days in a row (Don Ross, a professional bodybuilder and associate editor for *Muscular Development* magazine refers to this as double-blast training), a bodybuilder is performing what is known as a two-step split program. Training days planned for given muscle groups are divided into major and minor workouts.

For example, your major workout on Monday for the muscle group of the delts will consist of doing two-thirds the number of total sets planned for the two back-to-back training days. On Tuesday a minor workout will be the order of the day for the delts. During this "finishing off" workout the exact same exercises and rep pattern is used as was on Monday. The number of sets varies in that only one-third the total number of sets is performed on this training day. Here is an example of how this procedure works: Assume that 15 total sets are going to be done during the Monday and Tuesday workouts for the delts. On Monday a bodybuilder might begin with the seated fore and aft barbell press for three sets of six reps each. This exercise is performed by taking a false-grip handspacing that will allow the forearms to be perpendicular to the biceps and upper arm when the bar is being pressed from the base of the neck. Take a deep breath and press the barbell up from behind your neck until it passes just over the top of your head. Now lower the barbell to the clavicle area of your upper chest. Repeat by pressing it back up over the top of your head and lowering it down to the base of the neck. This constitutes one completed rep. More instructional technique will follow in another exercise program relating to pressing heavy poundages from behind the neck.

When you have completed the assigned sets and reps, take a rest and then begin doing seated dumbell lateral raises (for the medial or side deltoid) for three sets of eight to 12 repetitions. In order to gain the most effectiveness from this exercise, we offer you the following Mr. Olympia training tips from Larry Scott.

Ron Love in action at a top bodybuilding show.

44

These top pros show their amazing physiques to good advantage.

Begin by loading up two dumbells with the appropriate poundage, using seven-and-a-half, five and two-and-a-half-pound cast-iron plates. With all four parts of the dumbells touching, reach down and grasp each one with an off-center hand spacing so that the little finger side of each hand is firmly against the inner face plate of the dumbells. While seated, come to a position where you are leaning forward at the waist 15 to 30 degrees. The dumbells should be hanging at arms' length with the hands in a neutral or palms-facing-in position. Slowly, with the arms bent slightly at the elbow joint (relieves tension on elbow joints and biceps tendons), and with a pivoting action of the deltoids, lead with the elbows and raise the arms out from the side in an arc to a point two inches past the ears. Keep elbows rotated back.

During this phase of the movement you will simultaneously rotate the top of your wrist and thumb down in a clockwise motion so that, as you reach the top of the movement, your wrists will be lower than your elbows. As you reach the top of the lateral raise, dip the upper torso six inches further forward. This subtle action, when done in combination with the rotation of the wrists and thumb, will neutralize the traps and frontal delts, keeping them from controlling the movement and thus allow the medial or side delts to contract maximally. Lower the dumbells in the reverse manner described and begin another rep.

After you have finished this exercise it's time for another rest. Finish off your delt program with prone (face down) incline dumbell lateral raises or perhaps some seated bent-over dumbell lateral raises for three sets of twelve reps each.

Finish

On the prone incline dumbell lateral movement, the angle of incline can range from 30 degrees to as much as 70 degrees. Lee Labrada, for example, favors a 30-degree incline on the bench while others will use a 45-degree incline and on some occasions an extreme 60-70-degree incline.

If you favor the seated bent-over dumbell lateral raise, it is important to assume a position where your upper torso is parallel to the floor with the chest in contact with the frontal thighs.

To promote the maximum in muscular definition in the delts, especially the side and rear aspects, a bodybuilder can utilize the **"60-second variable-speed (timed) reps set"** and the sustained contraction secret. The 60-second set was devised by Joe Roark and follows this holistic rep-speed theory.

The start and finish of prone incline dumbell laterals for delts that stun.

Start

60-Second Variable-Speed (Timed) Reps Set

Rep No.	Positive Contraction (seconds)	Negative Contraction (seconds)
1	1	1
2	2	2
3	3	3
4	4	4
5	5	5
6	5	5
7	4	4
8	3	3
9	2	2
10	1	1

The above 60-second time grid works most effectively when a barbell is used.

Pro Tip: Do first half of reps of a set where each positive contraction takes five seconds and each negative six seconds. On second half of reps, spend one second in positive phase and two seconds in the negative phase.

46

The **"sustained contraction secret"** is a two-level optional training system which utilizes a ten-second measured movement isometric stop-pause rep at the conclusion of a set, and an isotension technique between sets. We are going to introduce you to the 10-second measured movement isometric pause rep concept by first explaining how to do the one plus one-half system of reps.

Of the four delt exercises that we mentioned previously, the tracking pattern for the seated dumbell lateral raise was the most descriptive. This exercise will serve as one of our main reference points as we describe the **one plus one-half system** and then combine it with the 10-second measured movement isometric pause rep.

Our dialogue on these various training systems will make numerous references to the positive and negative muscle contraction phases within a rep. For bodybuilders who are not familiar with these two terms, the following information should be helpful.

A positive (concentric) muscle contraction is when the muscle contracts and shortens as it overcomes resistance (weight) by lifting it upward by either a pushing or pulling motion. A complete range of movement in the positive muscle-contraction phase accounts for 50 percent of each full rep completed. The positive phase consists of two parts:

First half of the positive phase (beginning or first quarter of full rep) — This consists of the starting point and extends to the mid-

Shawn bombing, blitzing, blasting and shocking his delts into fresh new growth!

range phase. It equals 25 percent of a total rep.
Second half of the positive phase (second quarter of full rep) — This begins at the mid-range phase and extends to the contracted (finished) position. It also equals 25 percent of the total rep.

The negative (eccentric) contraction is where the muscle stretches or lengthens as the external resistance (weight) is lowered from the contracted (finished) position of the positive phase down to the pre-stretch starting point. This complete range of movement as described accounts for the remaining 50 percent of each rep completed. The negative phase also consists of two parts:

Shawn Ray — the man with the ebony-diamond physique.

First half of the negative phase (third quarter of full rep) — This phase of the rep takes over from the contracted (finished) position of the positive phase and extends down to mid range. It equals 25 percent of the total rep. The second half of the negative phase of the rep (fourth quarter of full rep) takes over from the mid-range point and terminates at the starting point of the positive rep phase.

We will be using the above-described terms (positive and negative phases) frequently as we describe exercise technique. For the sake of simplicity, we will use the following four symbols when speaking of the dual phases of positive and negative muscle movement.

Positive Symbols
(1/P) = First half of positive movement
(2/P) = Second half of positive movement

Negative Symbols
(1/N) = First half of negative movement
(2/N) = Second half of negative movement

Okay, let's walk through a set of seated dumbell lateral raises using the one plus one-half system. Begin the rep(s) by moving the dumbells in an arc from the positive phase starting point to a level just two inches above horizontal (1/P and 2/P). Hold this position of positive muscle contraction for a split second, and then lower the dumbells down from this position through the 1/N stretch-contraction phase to a point where your arms are 15 degrees or approximately two inches below shoulder level. Immediately, without hesita-

Lee Priest

Paul Dillett, Nasser El Sonbaty and Vince Taylor show the contrast in their total body development at a recent pro show.

tion, smoothly reverse your direction of movement from the 1/N phase back into the 2/P contraction phase, again moving the dumbells up to 15 degrees above the delts, or two inches past the shoulder horizontal position.

Contract and squeeze the delts maximally again for one second while in this position. Lower the dumbells slowly through the 1/N and 2/N phases of the rep to the starting point. The rep sequence of 1/P plus 2/P then 1/N and 2/P and finally 2/N and 1/N equals one and one-half reps, but only count it as one rep.

Chris Cormier and David Dearth.

Continue on in the manner described and do nine to eleven more reps. Most bodybuilders who use this system will do the reps in a consecutive manner without any rest whatsoever, while others have found that they can use slightly heavier poundages if they take a rest interval of up to ten seconds (about three or four deep breaths through pursed lips) between each completed (one and one-half) rep.

Ten-Second Measure Movement and Isometric Stop/Pause Rep:

Assuming that you are finishing up the final rep of the set and are getting ready to lower the dumbells through the 1/N and 2/N phases, don't, but rather lower them from two inches

A great pic of Lambert Bohm's amazing muscularity and muscle size.

49

Here are a couple more brief examples of select exercises which illustrate each of the two parts in the positive and negative phase of a total rep.

Barbell press behind neck:

Positive Phase:

1/P — From base of neck to top of head

2/P — Top of head to an arms locked position

Negative Phase:

1/N — Arms locked position to top of head

2/N — Top of head to base of neck

Barbell pump curl:

Positive Phase:

1/P — Leaning slightly backward, curl bar from a dead hang at the thighs to navel area so that back of forearms are parallel to floor.

2/P — With upper torso vertical (by now leaning forward) curl barbell from navel to chin. During the last half of this positive phase (mid-point between navel and chin) lean forward slightly further — 10 to 15

Ronnie Coleman is a physique star who personifies muscle bulk to an extreme degree.

Start

past the ears down in the 1/N or perhaps 2/N phase range to where you personally feel the absolute in peak muscle contraction. Hold this position for ten seconds in an isometric or pause (stop) rep style. The ten-second time frame is usually divided up in a manner that allows for two seconds to build up to a maximum contraction, six seconds to hold it, and two seconds to gradually release the muscular tension as the dumbells are lowered through to the starting point. Gradually, over a number of advancing workout sessions, the six-second maximum muscle contraction time frame could be increased to an absolute maximum of ten seconds but no more.

degrees). This tracking pattern will cause a maximum peak contraction on the upper aspect of biceps.

Negative Phase:

1/N — Lower the barbell, reversing the sequence of instructions given in 2/P above.

2/N — Continue lowering the bar, again reversing the sequence of exercise protocol given in 1/P.

Many bodybuilders who combine the one and one-half rep system and the ten-second isometric pause on the final rep in the negative stretch-contraction phase find it creates maximum muscle growth.

While this procedure works very well for most exercises where the starting point begins in the positive phase, what about squatting, leg presses, bench pressing variations and flyes where the starting point begins in the negative stretch-contraction phase?

If you combine the one and one-half rep system with the ten-second isometric stop pause on the final rep of a set within any of the four mentioned above, your rep sequence will be just the opposite of what we have described for the seated dumbell lateral raise, barbell press behind the neck and the pro pump curl.

On squatting, bench pressing, etc., you will find yourself doing the 10-second isometric stop pause somewhere within the first (1/P) and second (2/P) positive phases of the movement. Most bodybuilders we know prefer to do the 10-second stop pause in the negative phase of an exercise movement. If you wish to do this with squatting, leg pressing, benching and flyes, you have a number of alternatives.

The first option you have is to begin these particular exercises in the lower starting point of the positive movement enlisting the assistance of a couple of spotters. Knowing full well that this is not a practical or convenient solution, you must consider the second option.

Paul DeMayo doing pro pump curls with shut-out concentration.

Midpoint

Finish

That is to do a full range of negative (1/N and 2/N) and positive (1/P and 2/P) movements which are then followed with a half upper negative (1/N) and concludes with the half upper positive (2/P) phase to completion.

With this formula you can do the ten-second isometric pause (stop) rep within some sector of the full-range negative on the last rep and finish up with the half negative and half positive phase of the rep. However, we do not recommend this at all for a couple of reasons. Upon completion of the ten-second pause (stop) rep you would have to continue the completion of the remaining negative phase and the full positive phase plus a half negative and positive movement to meet the criterial of the one and one-half rep system.

This would be too demanding physically on most bodybuilders, so your best bet would be to do the ten-second isometric pause within the final upper half or negative phase on the final rep. The problem we find with this is that this upper area may not be in the range of movement where you feel absolute peak muscle contraction. This leads us to the third option. Do not do the one and one-half rep system on your final rep. Lower the weight in negative style to an area within the upper and lower phase where you feel peak muscle contraction and then hold it for ten seconds before pushing on the completion of positive contraction.

These are three options you have at your disposal if it is your desire to perform the ten-second isometric stop-pause rep within the negative phase(s) of the exercise movement.

There are, of course, other ways by which you can use the combined advanced bodybuilding techniques one and one-half system and the ten-second measured movement isometric stop-pause rep. You can do lat pulldowns, deadlifts or pullups, etc., for one-half positive and negative rep, and then one full rep.

To avoid loss of hormone depletion and muscle tone, you should not do more than three sets per exercise using the one and one-half system and only one of these sets should

Craig Titus

Start

Finish

Start

▲ The "Golden Eagle" Tom Platz doing some huge-beyond-belief deadlifts with eight wheels.

Finish

◄ The incredible Vince Taylor in a recent pose!

include the ten-second measured movement. You might consider reducing your training poundages when you are required to do eight to twelve reps per set for the three deltoid lateral exercises mentioned, or any exercise, for that matter where a minimum and maximum rep range is suggested. For example, on the first set do eight reps (using the one and

one-half system), then decrease the weight and do ten reps on the second set. Finally, decrease the weight just enough so that you can grind out twelve reps on your third set.

When you are not using the above combined training techniques you might do isotension movements between your workout

This photo shows ample evidence why Frank Zane was a popular three-time Mr. O.

sets. These will really enhance muscularity and density. They are done by contracting and tensing the muscles very hard in a variety of positions for eight to ten repetitions for between five and ten seconds each rep.

Frank Zane, a three-time IFBB Mr. Olympia superstar has been known to perform isotension techniques for up to 30 seconds at a time on just one mandatory muscle pose. However, duration of time for most bodybuilders is not as important as intensity and the latter is more a factor of the proper mind-to-muscle link.

You will do well to study the various posing routines of the champions by attending bodybuilding contests, reading the bodybuilding periodicals or purchasing videos on posing. One of the best videos on posing we have seen which will help you formulate your isotension techniques is Russ Testo's *Posing the Extra-Ordinary Way.* Russ goes all out to show the proper way to do mandatory poses and, once you learn this, the isotension techniques become even more effective. This 90-minute video can be purchased for $69.95 by contacting Russ Testo at 3 Oxford Road, Troy, NY 12180, or by phoning him noncollect at (518) 274-0952.

The 60-second variable-speed rep set and the sustained-contraction secret (two-level optional training system) as described, can be used separately within the structure of a major and minor workout for not only the delts but for other muscle groups as well.

Continuing on with our discussion of training muscle groups two consecutive days, Tuesday is a minor workout day for blasting the delts. Perform the exact exercise program as listed, but only perform two sets of each exercise (which is approximately one-third the total number of sets required). This two-step or double-blast split training program will work the delts quite efficiently.

During the previous workout session we explained to you the performance of the one and one-half rep system advanced bodybuilding technique. Now that you understand fully how to use this training technique, you can vary the concept and divide the total rep into quarter and third phases. By doing this you will work only that aspect of the muscle that you wish to bring out into vivid prominence.

During this minor workout you will not include the ten-second measured movement isometric stop pause rep. You will turn up the volume of your training intensity on the dumbell lateral raise exercises either separately or collectively by alternating three partial reps (explained in the Training Past the Burn Bodybuilding Technique No. 5 "Power Four-

Shawn Ray shape-training his delts with heavy dumbell laterals.

Russ Testo represents animated posing at its very best.

Rep/Tri-Pump System" in Chapter Ten) to one full range of movement rep, continuing the three-to-one ratio to momentary positive failure.

During one set you might do the beginning or low range third of the movement, yet during another set the partial third rep might well be in the middle range (which will work the muscle belly maximally). A final set might conclude with one third partial reps in the upper peaking range of the exercise.

CHAPTER SIX

Massive Muscle Pumping

There are, of course, numerous other approaches to modifying anabolic high-volume training but one of the most startling and unusual we have ever heard of is the system used by New York bodybuilder Richard Simons to gain **25 pounds of muscle in 21 days!** Richard told this author (Dennis B. Weis) about it one evening while riding on a bus in Miami, Florida.

He began by saying that the system was, to him, a condensed high-volume version of training in that he would perform an average of only four exercises each workout on a rotational schedule, Monday, Wednesday and Friday. He went on to say that the key to his condensed method of training is to work the involved muscle group with a high number of sets at maximum poundages that correspond to the particular multiple-rep set. His workout ethic is to maintain a maximum concentration of mind on his training effort with perfect execution of movement each and every rep of every set. To achieve this he allows for proper physical and mental recovery by resting on Tuesday, Thursday, Saturday and Sunday. This keeps his body and mind from becoming overtrained.

His workout days are not written in stone. If, for example, he comes into Monday's workout negative — perhaps through lack of rest or extreme muscle soreness from lactic acid accumulation — and feels that it will take away from his maximum concentration on a particular exercise (or the total workout as a whole) he will move the exercise or workout ahead to Tuesday. This is known as the **24-hour float method.** If only one exercise is affected the Wednesday and Friday workouts remain the same. However, if the total workout on Monday

An informal pose of the ever-lovely Tonya Knight.

must be moved up to Tuesday, then the Wednesday and Friday workouts should be moved to Thursday and Saturday respectively. After explaining his workout concepts to me, Richard then wrote out his **condensed high-volume training** schedule for me. This is the training schedule he follows:

Monday

1. Supine (flat) bench press — Using a barbell (though sometimes he uses dumbells) he does sets of 15, 10, 8, 4 and 1 reps, then rests for 5 minutes. Next he does 10 hard work sets of 5 to 6 reps each. When these are completed he takes another short rest and finishes up with 3 sets of 10, 15 and 20 maxi-pump reps.

A change in training intensity is always necessary to create a new muscle response (and up his bench press power base), and here two or three one-inch-thick high-density sponge rubber pads and a cambered bar (similar to the Jackson cambered squat bar) are useful. The rubber pads should be cut to a length that will cover the chest from the collar bone (clavicle) to the sternum, and wide enough to add protection to the extreme outer pec region. Richard custom cuts his rubber pads to 1″ x 9″ x 19″. Your measurements may differ.

Now it's just a matter of placing rubber pads in position on the chest and of lowering the cambered bar quickly to the chest with a slight (note, only *slight)* bounce so as to give an initial boost and distribute the weight over a greater area of the chest. Yet another way to use rubber pads as a shock/rebound technique would be to place two pads, one on the top surface of two bench press wooden safety boxes (which have been previously arranged and measured), so that the edges of the barbell plates will touch the rubber surface in a rebound effect just before it is touching high on the chest.

This shock/rebound technique is best used on the 15 and 20 maxi-pump rep sets.

Chris Cormier works his way through a killer quad workout in these two pics.   *Start*

Finish

2. Leg press — Richard selected this leg exercise because of four immediate and obvious advantages it has over other thigh-bombing exercises. First, there is no oppressive weight on the shoulders causing a spine compression. This will allow for maximum freedom of breathing and oxygen saturation which is necessary for increased rib cage circumference and respiratory and cardio-vascular benefits. Second, with no effect of spine compression, there is a corresponding marked decrease in the anatomical strain on the lumbo-sacral region. Third, little concern is needed regarding balance, because the weight is within the center of gravity and this gives the option or freedom to explore the outer limits of physical strength safely. Fourth and finally, the leg press is performed on a machine. It is a mechanically controlled movement that allows for stress where it needs to be. Richard, for example, takes a somewhat wide foot placing on the platform where his feet are 18 to 24 inches apart and angled out at 45 degrees or slightly more. From this extended position he

Sergio Oliva – "The Myth" – in training action, doing triceps pushdowns on the lat machine.

hard work sets of 15 reps each. He finishes off his leg press program with two quick pump-out sets of 20 and 30 reps.

3. Lat machine pulldown — Richard performs this exercise using the conventional straight and angled dorsi bar. The best bars are those which offer a parallel grip.

Pro Tip: Custom fabricate an angled dorsi bar so that the cambered part is up rather than down. This will allow you to position the little fingers higher than the thumbs, which allows for a more complete scapular rotation.

Richard begins this exercise by first taking a wide enough hand spacing on the bar that his forearms are never parallel during the movement. He takes a false grip (thumbs wrapped around the bar) and always makes sure that the bar is positioned high in the palm of his hand (near the base of the meaty part of the thumb). He will then take the path of most resistance by first pulling his shoulders down. Then he begins the actual pulling motion with his elbows (his hands only act as hooks in an extension of himself to the bar), making sure that his arms rotate out to the sides. Just these actions alone will stimulate more lat involvement and minimize biceps and forearms action. As the bar touches the base of his neck he will try desperately to touch his elbows at an imaginary point behind his back. This action must be done without hunching over and, if done correctly, the shoulder blades will rotate inward. Richard imagines himself squeezing a tennis ball between them. This is the feeling he wants to achieve for maximum contraction of his lats. Slowly he extends his arms back to the starting position at which point he leans forward somewhat so that he can get his shoulders into a semidislocated state and s-t-r-e-t-c-h the scapulae attachments outward for maximum back width.

For the sake of variety and due to the number of high-volume sets that he does, he will, at times, do lat pulldowns so that the bar touches the chest below the pec line. On these he will arch his back and lean backward 30 degrees to as much as 70 degrees from vertical as the bar touches. Though generally his hand spacing and grip is as described previously, he will, at times, take a narrow hand spacing of eight to twelve inches, using a supinated

will take in two or three big gulps of air and slowly lower the weight, bringing the knees wide and outward to the sides of the body. This is impacting on the inner thighs to say the least. He begins by doing four sets of 30, 20, 15 and 10 maxi-pump reps. He then goes to 10

(palms up, curl) grip. This variation of the pulldown seems to work well and involves the lats in a different way. It is a favorite of Sergio Oliva and other top bodybuilders. The particular action of this lat pulldown to just below the low pec line requires that the arms pull all the way in to the sides of the body. The aim of these or any other lat exercises is to first pull exclusively with pure lat action alone before involving the biceps by bending the arms. To up the percentage of his lat involvement, Richard will always chalk his hands prior to gripping the bar, and uses power wrist straps to help minimize biceps involvement.

Richard bombs his lats by opening with sets of 25, 20, 15, 12 and 10 maxi-pump reps. These are followed up with a 12-set blitz of 10 reps each. He finishes off with a pump-out set of 15 to 25 reps. This completes a heavy Monday workout session.

Wednesday

1. Barbell press behind neck — I remember well the unique and totally isolationary manner in which Richard said he does this exercise. He sits on the floor with his legs outstretched and his back braced securely against the foot of a stationary flat exercise bench. He readies himself by rotating and pulling his shoulders back as if standing at attention. This subtle move helps to eliminate the shoulder pain usually associated with this exercise. He is now ready for his training partner to position the heavily loaded bar correctly in his hands. The correct hand placement is achieved when his forearms are perpendicular to the upper arms (biceps) when the bar is being pressed off the back of his traps. His elbows are kept directly under his hands (knuckles face ceiling), and

Porter Cottrell doing presses behind the neck to develop his muscle-studded delts and back.

pointing out to the sides and down. From this position he then takes a couple of deep breaths. Holding the second breath, he begins pressing the barbell to an arm-extended position. At two-thirds of the way to lockout he forcefully expels the air from his lungs. At the overhead lockout position he will inhale a deep breath of air and hold it. He then lowers the bar back down to the base of the neck, exhaling air while doing so. Breath in again. This is called ''double oxygen'' saturation. The bar touches in a feather-like fashion and the next rep begins. Occasionally he presses the barbell only four to six inches above his head rather than going to complete lockout. He begins by performing 15, 10 and 8 repetitions and then, after a rest, he gets into the serious muscle growth by attacking his delts with 10 brutally hard sets of 6 full reps each, finishing up with a final blitz set of 25 lightweight reps.

2. Barbell shoulder shrug — On this particular exercise Richard, by the strength of

Aaron Baker and Vince Taylor compete for a big title win.

his trapezius muscles alone, moves mega poundage by raising his shoulders in a very direct up-and-down shrugging motion, trying like mad to touch his traps to his ears while at the same time extending his head backward as far as possible. He then squeezes and tenses his traps for all they are worth.

He is always very conscious not to rotate the shoulder joint, for this would take away from the very direct trapezius stimulation he is achieving with the straight up-and-down motion. He always chalks his hands prior to each set just to make sure that his vice-like grip on the bar never gives out before the traps become fully pumped. Sometimes, when this isn't enough, he will then use training straps for extra holding power.

There are training sessions where he grasps a heavy dumbell in each hand and then positions himself sitting lengthwise on a flat bench with legs outstretched. Seated, holding the dumbells with a neutral hand position (palms facing and parallel to each other) with the arms hanging straight down and in line with the shoulders, he is able to perform the purest shrugging action known. The arms are kept perfectly straight during the movement, and thus biceps action is kept to an absolute minimum. Because the dumbells are hanging as they are the resistance is now in the center of gravity instead of in front of it when using the barbell. The seated shrug eliminates those little knee kicks (especially if the legs are outstretched on the bench) that normally occur during the standing barbell shrugs towards the end of a fatiguing set. A cambered bench press bar (with the cambered portion of the bar facing down) positioned under a flat exercise bench is another option. One set of 20 and one of 15 reps is performed then it is on to 8 sets of 10 to 12 muscle-searing reps, finishing off with a lightweight flush set of 15 to 20 reps.

Pro Tip: Sometimes Richard tips his head towards his chest while going for a maximum squeeze at the top of the shrug movement.)

3. Leg extension — There is honestly nothing unusual about the manner in which this exercise is performed. He begins with a set of 25

Tom Platz – one picture is worth a thousand words when it comes to describing training intensity!

and another 20 reps followed by 6 sets of 15 reps each, then a pump set of 20 and one of 30 reps.

Pro Tip: Jr. Mr. A Robert Harrop grasps high on the back of the seat, while raising his glutes off it 6 inches or so. His legs are facing downward at almost 45 degrees. He terms this as an incline leg extension.

4. Machine leg curl — Richard visualizes that this exercise is to the hamstrings of the legs what the biceps curl is to the upper arms. It is executed in a flowing full contraction-and-extension manner. He curls the legs and tries to touch his heels to his glutes. He flexes the top of his foot towards his shin through all ranges of the contraction and extension of the movement. Yet, at other times, he extends his feet in the opposite direction because he feels this effect in the soleus muscle of the calf strongly. To Richard, this creates dual muscle stimulus in the hamstrings and the calves all

in one exercise. Sets of 30, 20 and 15 reps, then 6 sets of 10 to 12 reps are performed, followed by a final 20-to-30-rep set.

Pro Tip: Richard adducts or turns his feets inward to stress inner hams on some sets and on others abducts or rotates them outward to hit the outer hamstrings.) End of Wednesday's workout.

Friday

1. Neck extension and flexion — The exercises for this muscle group are of the manual resistance type performed with the help of a training partner. Anterior flexion (front of the neck), posterior extension (back of the neck) and lateral contraction (for the sides of the neck) are performed for a combined 10 sets of 20 reps each.

2. Close-grip triceps extension — This exercise is performed in a supine or flat position on an exercise bench, using an EZ-curl bar. The elbows are sometimes positioned so

Francesca Petitjean… Great glutes, babe!   ***Start***

Finish

62

Aaron Baker, Porter Cottrell and Lee Priest. These three fantastic views of abdominals show what development can be accomplished by special work.

that the lower arm could be extended to arms' length and lowered directly in line with the nose. At other times the elbows are positioned back at approximately 45 degrees past horizontal. The lower arm is then lowered to the surface of the flat bench behind the head and then extended to lockout, which was in line with the shoulders. Richard picked up this unique triceps extension variation from Ed Yarick, a trainer of three Mr. Americas years ago. Sets of 20, 15 and 10, 6, 3 and 1 are completed and this is followed up by 11 sets of 5 or 6 power reps and a usual 20-rep pump set.

3. Close-grip standing wall curls — On this exercise, which tests the strength and power in his biceps, Richard begins by grasping a loaded EZ-curl bar with a 4-to-6-inch hand spacing. He then leans back against a wall (a stationary post or door jamb is much better) so that his back is flat against it for support. His legs are straight with his feet slightly forward from his body (approximately 18″) with the barbell held at arms' length, resting against the front of his thighs. He keeps the elbows well behind the plane of his body with the insides of his biceps touching his rib cage. From here he curls the barbell (which is brushing the front of the body all the way up) to just below the low pec line. This action seems to work both the inner and lateral heads on Richard's biceps.

At other times he curls the barbell in to his neck. In doing so his elbows move forward and up which means that some deltoid action is taking place — not enough, however, to detract from the maximum peak squeezing and tensing effect he is able to accomplish on the biceps in this position. He then contracts the biceps muscles a for a full two counts on each and every rep.

He uses the same sets and reps as in the triceps extension exercises just mentioned. (Pro tip: During some workouts, at the conclusion of the final rep of a particular set, Richard steps away from the door jamb and chest curls the weight up in the positive phase and lowers in negative style for 15 or so seconds for an additional 2 or 3 reps.)

4. Stiff-legged deadlift — On this exercise he uses an Olympic barbell so he can grasp the lip edge of the 45-pound plates (called snatch-grip deads). With the knees in a semi-locked position, arms locked straight at the elbow joint, one 45-pound plate in each hand, and using the muscles of his lower back and hamstrings, he raises up to a vertical position where he rotates his shoulders back and thrusts his chest out. Sometimes he does this exercise while standing on the floor and other times while standing on the end of a flat exercise bench which has been securely bolted to the floor. At other times he exchanges the discs for a wide grip on the bar itself, using a

Roger Stewart and Lisa Lorio – Can't think of a reason why Roger wouldn't want to do donkey calf raises.

false grip. Again, he stands on a flat bench but with his toes placed exactly at the end. Then he stands up slowly, but then, when he begins the descent for his next rep, he lowers the bar as far as possible below bench level.

He does sets of 20, 12, 8, 4, 1, 5, 10 and 15 reps.

5. Donkey calf raise — The first thing Richard does is set his Rheo H. Blair calf block into position. (This piece of training equipment was literally light years ahead of its time and still is today.)

The block is six inches in height and allows for noninterference of the stretching at the bottom of the movement. The ultimate in stretching is achieved because the block has a rounded edge and is completely covered with a 1/2″ thick rubber foam and a 1/8″ thick piece of ribbed rubber on top of that. This allows a bodybuilder to really grab hold of the surface with the toes and balls of the feet (without pain) and go into the calf-building super stretch without any fear of slipping off the block.

Richard uses one of two basic foot positions on the block. Position 1 (toes 12 to 16″ apart with the heels 4″ apart) develops the inner calf, but only coming up on the ball of the foot and big toe. In position 2 (toes 8 to 12″ apart with the heels much, much wider, as if assuming a pigeon-toed stance) it is most important to come up on the lateral or outer edge of the foot for maximum outer-calf stress. Richard assumes either one of these two positions without his shoes on. (Personally we feel that it is best to wear shoes which offer a high degree of traction and have a very thin, flexible sole. The best shoes that we have found that serve this purpose are the low-top Otomix: For information call 1-800-444-6620.) He then bends over until his upper torso is perpendicular to the floor and supports himself by placing his elbows on another bench or on a horizontal bar which is about waist height and 30 to 36″ away from the Blair calf block. Now it is just a matter of bending his knees and dropping down (to protect his lower back), allowing his workout partner to mount him in a position directly over his hips. He then locks his knee joints and begins with a set of 30 maxi-pump reps. Richard rests for under a minute between sets then continues his journey into the pain zone by doing sets of 20, 12, 15, 20 and 30 maxi-pump reps.

Sometimes he does what he terms a standing donkey calf raise where a workout partner sits astride his shoulders. He feels that this particular variation allows for a more direct approach to the stretch at the bottom of the movement. Either one of these two exercises becomes especially intense if the workout partner holds a pair of 40-pound (plus) dumbells in his hands.

If a workout partner is not available for the donkey calf raises, he improvises by doing them on a vertical leg press machine, or if things come to the worse, he attaches a very heavy dumbell or some cast iron dumbell plates to a dip belt and goes from there. (Pro

tip: Between sets of the donkey calf raises do alternating one-legged donkey calf raises using just your own bodyweight. This is done while still maintaining good form. Richard's methods of transition from two to one leg is as follows: With both legs absolutely locked at the knee joints he s-l-o-w-l-y lowers both of his heels down to the maximum negative stretch contraction position, actually trying to touch them to the floor. This is his starting point for beginning the set. From here and again with a s-l-o-w deliberate rep speed he raises his heels

Lee Priest doing an informal lat spread.

through the positive muscle contraction phase, going up on the balls of his feet and finally shifting his weight distribution to the first three toes (big toe and next two) of each foot at the top of the peak contraction.

At this point he bends his left knee joint and shifts his weight distribution to the right leg, which is still maintaining a knee-lock position. He then lowers s-l-o-w-l-y on the right leg through the complete negative stretch contraction, pauses for a one-second stretch and

SISSY SQUAT

Experience the ultimate leg pump-up.

then raises back up through the positive muscle contraction phase. He holds this "peak contraction" with the right leg for a count of two and then bends his right knee joint and shifts his weight distribution to his left leg and locks this knee joint. He then proceeds to the

sequence in the manner described for the right leg again.

It is important to remember that, although only one leg at a time is being worked, both feet are gripping the ribbed rubber surface of the calf block, but with one leg bent and the other leg straight. He does this in a smooth and rhythmical motion, rather than rapidly, for 50 maxi-pump reps. Doing this movement in between sets helps to maintain a muscle fatigue tension threshold for maximum gains. Sometimes, if he can't make it into the gym, he does a weightless workout for the legs (using just his own bodyweight), supersetting this exercise with the sissy squat for 10 nonstop supersets. He does 20 to 30 maxi-pump reps on each set of the alternate one-legged donkey calf raises and 12 to 15 maxi-pump reps on the sissy squat. For those of you who are not familiar with the sissy squat, we offer you this brief description.

Stand in an upright vertical posture next to a stationary post, power rack or chair, etc. With a slight absence of knee lock, place your feet approximately 12 to 18 inches apart, with heels inward and toes rotated out laterally, just slightly. Vince Gironda says the feet should be 13" apart and the knees 17" wide.

To maintain a perfect balance in this "fire-bombing" quadriceps exercise, lightly grasp hold of the stationary post, etc. with one hand.

Now, with just your own bodyweight, rise up on your toes or, if you wish, place your heels on a 4" x 4" block of wood. Lean your upper torso backward (approximately 45 degrees from vertical) until you feel a maximum stretch contraction in the quads, especially just above the knees. Your upper torso and thighs will be in alignment with one another if you have done this correctly.

While maintaining this inclined, lying back position (you will basically be at a 45-degree angle to horizontal position), slowly lower your body by bending your knees, allowing them to thrust forward. Allow the upper torso and thighs to descend to where the shoulders are directly over the heels and beyond. Do not relax at this point. Keep continuous tension on the thighs by doing a smooth direction reversal at the bottom of the negative stretch

Vince Taylor – the winner of countless pro bodybuilding titles.

66

(approximately parallel to the floor) phase by straightening your thighs and driving your hips forward till you are once again at the nonlock starting point. Remember, as you come up, to push off on your heels while pulling the front part of your foot up off the floor.

Begin the next rep immediately. With absolutely no pausing, continue until you have completed 12 to 15 maxi-pump reps in nonstop, nonlock style. You can really enhance your precision of technique in the sissy squat by following some of the tips mentioned for the hip belt and hips-off hack squats listed elsewhere.

It is a very good idea to practice the sissy squats with just your own bodyweight until it becomes a natural movement. Remember the saying, " practice makes perfect." We prefer to take it one step further and say, "perfect practice makes perfection." This makes sense because, if you practice the sissy squat or any other exercise for that matter, using sloppy form, you will never develop a precision technique.

Lee Priest understands focused concentration.

Once you have mastered a precision technique with your own bodyweight you can begin to use extra weight in the form of a cast iron plate or a dumbell or dumbells. Of the three options, the loose plate is the easiest to accommodate because all you have to do is hold it securely against your chest with your free hand while maintaining perfect balance with the other. Holding a barbell (as in a front squat position) or holding dumbells extended at your sides does not allow for the degree of leanback you achieved with your bodyweight

alone. The reason is that your balance is compromised because your hands are not free to assist you. This is a very minor obstacle to overcome. You can attach a 4-foot length of 1/2" rope securely around your waist (or tie it to the front of your lifting belt, directly in the center) then tie the other end of the rope at chest level to a stationary post. This will free up your hands so that you can use the barbell or dumbells, and at the same time allow you to maintain the proper inclined layback position — and with perfect balance.

Sometimes Richard not only supersets this bodyweight-only thigh exercise with calves, but from time to time he supersets the sissy squat (using a Roman chair exercise unit) with Duc leg presses on a vertical leg press machine.

Chuck Sipes, on the other hand, would take the supported bodyweight-only sissy squat to the outer limits of muscle stimulation by doing cumulative repetitions, finishing off with 20 maxi-pump reps. We explained in detail the premise behind cumulative repetitions on pages 81 through 84 in our book, *Mass!* (Contemporary Books, Inc., 1986). The bottom line is that if you want the ultimate in granite-hard quads, laced with deep cuts, then do as Richard Simons, Chuck Sipes and many of the west coast bodybuilding champions did and still do to this day — do sissy squats!

Richard is into leg work in a big way — especially using the advanced superset technique just described. Sometimes he supersets sissy squats with leg curls or uses any one of the following combinations: back squats with front squats, leg presses with leg extensions, leg presses with leg curls (nonlock style).

Supporting the huge energy requirements necessary for a condensed high-volume training program of this sort requires a food and supplement intake of 9000 calories per day, with 1560 of that being in the form of complete proteins. For Richard this was a whopping 390 grams of proteinand he did say that most bodybuilders could probably meet most of their energy demands on 5,000 to 6,000 calories per day and 250 grams of a quality dietary protein. Boy, wouldn't Richard's high-cal days make John Parrillo smile!

CHAPTER SEVEN

Training Effects of Anabolic High-Volume Training

There are a number of facts we have learned about the effects of high-volume training where 12 to 15 sets and more are performed per muscle group in a workout. First there is the psychological trauma of exerting so much willpower just to get through the workouts each week. Such sustained effort eventually cuts into the stamina of even the top pros. The Bulgarian Sports Camp strength and power scientists, under the leadership of Angel Spassov, have done some rather extensive research into the methodology of training on athletes in that country. Their research has been brought to the western world through the published writings of such individuals as Leo Costa Jr. and Russ L. Horine, D.C., co-authors of *The Serious Growth Training Strategy.* For more information call 1-800-582-2083.

The Bulgarian research group discovered that healthy athletes between the ages of 22 and 25 have a significantly greater capacity to handle higher volumes of training than those who were 10 or more years older, and that after the age of 35 high-volume training must be decreased somewhat and proper recovery methods followed. This is due to the aging process in which the production of natural testosterone decreases and the metabolic process begins to slow.

Their findings also indicated that resting blood testosterone and glucose levels increase dramatically during the first 20 minutes of a serious training session, and then begin decreasing at about 55 to 75 minutes into the workout, though not quite to the original resting levels prior to the workout for at least two more hours.

Leo Costa Jr., posing his huge-beyond-belief physique at a recent contest.

Armed with this information it seems that there may not be enough testosterone and glucose to create a natural anabolic training effect in the muscles of older athletes, especially during the latter sets of the high-volume training programs we have presented thus far. When a bodybuilder is training two and three muscle groups with a multiple of exercises for each — or even a single one for three different muscle groups — as illustrated in the Richard Simons condensed training, the number of high-volume sets and accumulated work time it takes to perform them (without

Milos Sarcev gives new meaning to the V-taper.

counting rest between sets) exceeds the time grid for optimum blood testosterone and glucose elevations. There are 12 other variables as well which must be given consideration when reviewing the concepts of anabolic high-volume training. The following listing is based on the research findings of Dr. Fred C. Hatfield, Ph.D — "Dr. Squat."

Variables Affecting Recovery Time

1. Larger muscles take longer to recover than smaller muscles.

2. Predominantly white (fast) fiber muscles take longer to recover than do red (slow) fiber muscles. (White fiber muscles are suited to power whereas red fiber muscles are suited to endurance.)

3. High-intensity exercise with weights exceeding the 80 to 85 percent maximum level require greater recuperation time than do high-rep (under 75 percent maximum intensity) exercises.

4. Full-range movements typically cause greater amounts of connective tissue damage and necessitate greater recovery time than do partial-movement exercises.

5. Older lifters (e.g. above 35 to 40 years of age) require more recuperation time than do younger lifters.

6. Recovery rate can be improved as a result of properly conceived aerobic weight-training programs, or retarded with generally little or no aerobic efficiency training.

7. Bigger lifters take longer to recover than do smaller lifters.

8. Nutritionally sound eating and supplementing habits can significantly shorten recuperation time, while poor dietary and supplementation practices can prolong it.

9. Drugs and other substances that are anabolic agents (e.g. anabolic steroids) reduce recovery time, whereas most types of recreational drugs (e.g. alcohol) can markedly increase recovery time requirements.

10. Eccentric (negative) muscle contraction causes increased recovery time requirements.

11. States of overtraining — whether biological or psychological in origin — increase recovery time requirements. So does undertraining.

12. A generally healthy body recovers faster than an unhealthy one (e.g. diseases, infections, etc. impede recovery).

Paul Dillett displays his amazing freaky size to good advantage in this relaxed shot.

CHAPTER EIGHT

Techniques for Instant Growth

One of the most immediate disadvantages of anabolic high-volume training is the super drain of energy it imposes on the body. As a result, the intensity of the workout generally suffers. The main difference in actual training intensity is really a function of volume. When performing a huge number of hard sets such as those listed previously, the bodybuilder will almost unconsciously reduce the amount of effort put into any one given set in order to save their training energy for the remaining multiple sets.

Mentally, a bodybuilder will become de-tuned to the training sets he or she is doing after 90 minutes or so when growth hormone releases have declined. Many bodybuilders who favor the high-volume training style realize that staying mentally focused for each and every training set during a workout is an issue that must be dealt with, and are taking some very necessary steps to up their dynamic muscle and strength equation in this problem area.

Ultra Sets

Many of the top bodybuilders we have observed in training are using ultra sets, which combine two different exercises within a particular set to develop more than one muscle group at a time. Many consider compound exercises to represent general exercise movements such as barbell or dumbell squats, bench presses, deadlifts, behind-the-neck presses, power cleans and curls, etc. While this is an accurate assumption, a bodybuilder will usually do a barbell clean or a press overhead, etc. separately but not generally as one complete exercise.

Porter Cottrell pro bodybuilding's best-built firefighter, without a doubt.

Edgar Fletcher builds awesome mounds of trap muscles by performing dumbell shrugs. ***Start***

Finish

Rather than doing multiple sets of each exercise, separately, many bodybuilders are combining two separate (but complimentary) basic primary exercises which produce a fluid movement. This is ultra set exercise training at its optimum level of efficiency and intensity. Examples of some ultra sets which use basic primary exercises are: dumbell curl and press overhead (This ultra set can be performed either standing or seated, with one or two dumbells, and with the reps performed alternately or simultaneously.), barbell clean and front squat, barbell back squat and standing calf raise (Jesse Hoagland safety squat bar is excellent for this purpose), clean and jerk and clean and press (both of which can be done with dumbells or a barbell), and barbell deadlifts and barbell shrugs (3 shrugs for each consecutive deadlift).

We had the opportunity recently to take a hardcore workout under the guidance of big Jack O'Bleness at his private Monster Maker Gym in Apple Valley, California. For those of you not familiar with Big Jack, suffice it to say he is one of the top private trainers responsible for many "natural" bodybuilding champions in the world today.

Within the structure of Jack's hardcore **Monster Maker Workout** was ultra sets of clean and push press exercises. This ultra set was executed by cleaning the weight to the shoulders from the floor and then modified to combine a jerk press overhead to lockout. The feet remain parallel and in line. There is a three-inch dip of the knees as the weight is thrust overhead. Do not confuse the push press with a jerk overhead. We did from 12 to 20 continuous reps per set while inhaling three to six deep rest-pause breaths between each rep. This ultra set exercise was done with a comfortable poundage which kept our breathing and metabolic rate elevated throughout the workout.

How does one's breathing and metabolic rate stay elevated throughout the entire workout when performing the clean and push press? Well, perhaps if a bodybuilder were only to perform two or three sets of this exercise during the entire workout, this would not be possible. However, this was not the case. A pure Monster Maker workout requires a bodybuilder to do one clean and push press (ultra set) for every two sets of an exercise for a muscle group (with the exception of the arms and delts), and between select muscle groups as well.

This rather unique training concept is a far cry from the conventional rest-pauses we are normally used to taking between sets. Words fail to describe the physiological feeling we experienced when doing this ultra set between the various sets of exercises. One thing is very evident. The lower back, traps, biceps, triceps, forearms and deltoids most definitely benefit in a muscle-building sense in addition to the cardiorespiratory experience.

Dave Dupré, Jack O'Bleness and Karen Reed.

Ron Love

The Monster Maker Workout is among the very best training experiences that we body-builders could experience. Another advantage of training the O'Bleness way is that maximum gains are stimulated in the muscle cell struc-ture, without any apparent trauma to the joints of the shoulders, elbows, wrists or knees. Jack O'Bleness offers private one-on-one telephone

consultations utilizing the Monster Maker training concepts. He can be reached on a non-collect call at 1-619-247-4298.

Continuing on with how bodybuilding champions utilize ultra sets, here are a couple which are worth describing in more detail. They are the one-dumbell (or barbell) press and the squat and the supine lying bent-arm pullover and the three-way diametric French press.

One-dumbell (or barbell) press and squat
Hold a dumbell at the prepress shoulder position and begin pressing it overhead while simultaneously lowering your (upright) torso into a slightly below parallel squatting posi-tion. When the dumbell has reached the lockout overhead position, continue to hold it there while you ascend out of the squat position before lowering the dumbell to shoulder level. This ultra set can be performed one-arm style with a barbell or with two dumbells but one tends to have to fight existing balance problems so these options are not quite as appealing as the first one mentioned.

Lately many bodybuilders have taken to doing ultra sets in the form of the two-hands-behind-the-neck press and full squat. The procedure to follow is the one recommended for the single dumbell press and squat.

Next is one of the all-time favorite ultra set exercises.

Denise Rutkowski looks diamond-hard at a recent pro show.

Supine bent-arm pullover and three-way diametric French press

Lie in a supine position (flat on your back) on an exercise bench with your shoulders positioned at the end of the bench and the back of your head extended over the end and downwards towards the floor. Rest a plate-loaded diametric bar (EZ-curl style) on your lower chest and use a false grip. (Thumbs are on the same side of the bar as the fingers rather than under it as in the normal conventional style used in grasping the bar for reverse curls, power cleans, etc.) Your handspacing should be at the narrowest bends of the cambered bar out from dead center. With your elbows tucked close to your sides, take a deep breath and lift the bar up (and in a combined horizontal

Milos Sarcev deep in thought at a recent show.

direction) over your chest and face until you've lowered it so that the plates make contact with the floor. Depending on the flexibility of your shoulder joints, you may wish to experiment with different barbell plate diameters and bench heights to find a comfortable range of movement.

Immediately pull the bar from the floor, and as the bar reaches the forehead area (with elbow joint flexion and pure triceps power) extend your forearms upward. As you near completion of extending the barbell to arms' length, raise your head slightly to facilitate a powerful follow-through. To achieve the most triceps action out of the exercise, try to keep your elbows stationary and pointed inwards and towards the ceiling. The back of the upper arms should form an approximate right angle to your supine upper torso. Breathe out and lower the bar to the starting position on the chest. This completes one repetition.

This unique ultra set stimulates the latissimus (lats) and pectorals (chest) during the bent-arm pullover phase, and the triceps during the French press phase. The French press (second half of movement) can be initiated not only at forehead height as mentioned, but also from behind your head or from the area at the nose (as the world's master bench presser Ted Arcidi prefers to do it).

The bar should always be pressed up to an arms-extended lockout position along an imaginary vertical line with the area you choose to press from, be it behind the head, forehead or the nose.

Ted Arcidi, "the boss of the bench press" blasts his massive delts with some monster reps in the behind-the-neck press.

Many bodybuilders favor doing this ultra set by performing 18 repetitions per set of all three versions of the French press phase nonstop. The first six reps are done with the triceps extensions started from behind the head — reps seven through 12 follow and are performed with the triceps extensions phase started from the forehead. On the final six reps (12 through 18) the triceps extensions are begun from the nose.

Many bodybuilders will select one or two of the ultra set exercises listed and incorporate them into their normal anabolic high-volume training program for three to five sets of eight to ten reps on average. We remember one champion bodybuilder telling us about an unusual set and rep scheme using the previously mentioned supine bent-arm pullover and three-way diametric French press which he used for developing rugged lat and triceps power. It goes something like this.

Set No. 1 — 5 pullovers/5 presses
 (add 10 pounds to the bar)
Set No. 2 — 4 pullovers/5 presses
 (add 10 pounds to the bar)
Set No. 3 — 3 pullovers/3 presses
 (add 10 pounds to the bar)
Set No. 4 — 2 pullovers/3 presses
 (add 10 pounds to the bar)
Set No. 5 — 1 pullover/1 press
 (add 10 pounds to the bar)
Continue on with the 1 pullover to 1 press ratio adding 5 to 10 pounds each time until your limit is reached.

A variation of the above program is to do 5 pullovers/5 presses, then reduce the barbell by 20 to 30 pounds and finish off with 10 pullovers and 12 presses. This completes one series. Do a total of 2 to 3 series. Sometimes to pump up the intensity of the 10 pullovers and 12 presses "burns" are done to finish off the set. These are done by lowering the bar down

Ron Coleman appears to be chiseled from a block of granite.

to the nipples and let the elbows roll out wide so as to be in line with the shoulder joint. Press the bar up in a close-grip bench press style over the chest to 3/4 lockout. For the sake of variety some bodybuilders will lower the bar down to their throat or face instead of chest. Continue these non-stop partial reps until you sustain a burning pump sensation.

Bodybuilding champions have found ultra set exercises allow them to stay more mentally focused, set after set, which, in turn, significantly stimulates muscle gains in multiple muscle groups.

Another approach to staying mentally focused within the confines of anabolic high-volume training is by training only **one muscle group per day.** We dealt with this method of training in our book *Raw Muscle!* (Contemporary Books, Inc., 1989) as did Don "The Ripper" Ross in his critically acclaimed book *MuscleBlasting!* (Sterling Publishing Co., Inc., 1988).

Generally when a pro bodybuilder trains *only one* muscle group each day he will do so within the structure of the high-volume training plan (HVT) that we mentioned at the beginning of chapter one. He will be doing 20 to 30 mega-sets (which is almost equal to the number of sets a natural anabolic steroid-free body-builder will use in a total-body workout), but when compared to working two to three muscle groups during a training session (where 60 to 90 sets are done) the total of 20 to 30 sets will now almost seem like nothing.

You may immediately question the rationale behind the pros' choice of training one muscle group each day because the selected muscle will be trained at most only once every seven days. We'll go on to explain this, but first we want to illustrate the very basic concept of one muscle group a day training by outlining an awesome biceps-bulging, button-busting, forearm workout.

The biceps — The biceps begin the workout where dumbell preacher curls are supersetted with barbell preacher curls. (When two exercises are performed within the same muscle group, this is often called a compound or "true" superset.) A straight long bar is used the second half of this superset as opposed to the EZ-curl bar because it allows the hands to be in a palms-up position. This position works the biceps maximally. Using an EZ-curl bar would reduce the stress load on the biceps due to a semi-neutral or suitcase grip orientation. Begin the superset with two loaded dumbells that allow you to do eight reps in a semi-loose style. Grab a dumbell in each hand and place the elbows very close together (perhaps 8 inches or so) about 3 inches down from the crown of the padded surface of the 45-degree angle of the bench.

The dumbells should be held so that each hand is at least parallel or higher if possible. This is achieved by trying to lift the little finger up as high as possible and in so doing pronate the hand. If the thumb side of the dumbell is higher than that of the little finger (in many cases this would resemble the hand orientation when using a diametric or EZ-curl bar) then some of the stress load is transferred to the brachio-radialis rather than the low biceps aspect and you do not want this effect to take place.

When raising, try to end each rep with the inner part of each dumbell four inches wider than the lateral deltoid. This means that with your elbows stationary you will consciously rep slightly outward so that the hands are wider apart at the end of each rep than at the beginning. Lower the dumbells all the way down through the negative stretch contraction phase but don't lower them so far as to hyper-extend the elbows.

Berry DeMey blasting through some intense preacher bench curls.

It is generally advised that the shoulders be rounded forward over the crown of the bench throughout each completed rep, but since this exercise is going to be done in a loose training style the shoulders can be pulled back during the positive muscle contraction phase. Upon completion of eight full reps, do either four top or bottom (alternate these from superset to superset) 1/3 "burns." Without any rest whatsoever, place the dumbells aside and take a 15-to-20-inch handspacing, thumbs over the top grip, on a long bar (which has been previously loaded to approximately 70 percent of the total weight of the two dumbells).

Really bury the armpits deep into the crown of the padded preacher bench, with the elbows eight to 11 inches closer than

Chris Cormier eyes the judges.

Start

Steve Brisbois is careful to observe strict form to blast deep muscle fibers.

Finish

handspacing. Now begin curling in an ultra-strict superslow fashion. This time make sure that the shoulders are rounded over the top of the bench and the head is tilted forward during each complete rep cycle. To insure maximum development of the cephalic vein on the outer head of the biceps, adhere to the following pro tips: When doing the preacher curls with dumbells, there is usually one weaker arm which lags behind during the ascent through the positive muscle contraction phase. Keep your eyes on the wrist of the arm that is the weakest. This action often will give you a strength boost and help your weaker arm to keep pace with the stronger arm.

If you want to increase your curling strength capacity (and who doesn't) then reduce the distance from the palm to the elbow of each arm by curling or flexing the hands forward by pure wrist action. Curl the hands up as the dumbell or barbell is lowered down to the fully extended position at the bottom of the movement. Extend or uncurl the hands by

wrist action, but curl the hands forward again as you curl the massive barbell up, again extending the hands back near the top of the movement. Frank Zane would do this often to add another progressive level towards peak contracting the biceps. Curl the hands up to begin each rep. Perform 5 to 6 supersets of up to 8 reps.

Nobody knows how to build huge shapely arms, laced with raw muscularity any better than Larry Scott. He and he alone is responsible for popularizing many of the technical aspects of these two angle-specific biceps exercises. He has done this through his own empirical writing, and in the audio and visual display presented in his exciting and highly informative "Biceps and Triceps Weight Training Hidden Secrets" video.

Forearms — The forearms are trained next by doing the standing barbell reverse curl or, for a change of pace, reverse curls on the preacher bench (using an EZ-curl bar for 8 reps). Next is the seated barbell wrist curl (palms up, using a false grip for 15 reps) and, finally, the seated barbell wrist curl (palms-down style for 15 reps).

The above three exercises are done as a triset series, one after the other without rest. Rest 30 to 45 seconds between each series until five complete trisets have been performed. This done, twenty-five to twenty-seven total sets have been performed for the biceps and forearms. Compared to previous workout programs for this muscle group (where the pro was doing 25 to 27 sets twice and sometimes three times per week), these 25

Larry Scott, the "Dick Clark" of bodybuilding.

Bruce Page was one of the first "big-armed" Canadians. Although by today's standards Bruce's 18-inch guns may appear modest, during the 50s he was a leader in unusual muscular arm size. Page, who later became one of the sport's top writers, was known for his well-shaped, high-peaked bis.

to 27 sets performed only once a week may not seem like enough. With seven long days to wait before the arms are again trained, many bodybuilders fear that they are not doing enough. Let me answer those fears by quoting a man whose arms were truly outstanding.

One of bodybuilding's top writers, the late Bruce Page, was once questioned about the **one-muscle-group-a-day** training system and here is what he had to say: "A great many exercises that you do for other bodyparts will stimulate the biceps. For example, any kind of rowing that you do for the lats, barbell or dumbell, will work the biceps. Chinning behind the neck for lats or upright rowing for shoulders will work the biceps. So, although these movements are not direct biceps exercises, they will stimulate the muscles sufficiently to maintain the size until you work it again.

"The same holds true for other muscle groups. As you work the arms, accessory muscles of the shoulders, lats and pecs come into play in many various ways so that there should be no concern as to the length of time between direct workouts on the various muscle groups."

We have given to you what we believe to be a most workable example of the one-muscle-group-per-day concept. However, this is only the tip of the bodybuilding iceberg, so to speak. There is still a network of factors within this system of training that influences the development of superhuman strength, huge muscle mass and deep cut muscularity.

We'll begin outlining the detailed training strategies the pros use when training only one muscle group per day while blending in these vital factors. The pro will usually begin the program by doing a strength and muscle mass inducing exercise. A key factor to accomplishing this is to incorporate a stress loading one, or two-dimensional "pyramid" system. Within either of these two "pyramid" options there is a slow but progressive increase in the poundages (usually 2-1/2 to 3 percent increase for each rep reduction), and a corresponding decrease in the reps (minus 2), from set to set until one or two maxi-power reps are achieved.

Geir Borgen Paulsen strains the fibers in his XXXL training shirt.

An example of **one-dimensional pyramid** training is the one former IFBB Mr. World Chuck Sipes used to bench 570 pounds at a body-weight of under 220 pounds (without the aid of a bench shirt!). The following example of Chuck's pyramid is part one of his extensive bench press program. Refer to page 206 in our book *Raw Muscle!* for the complete program.

       2 sets x 6 reps
       2 sets x 4 reps
       2 sets x 2 reps
       4 sets x 1 rep

This is a rather unique one-dimensional pyramid in that double sets are done at each stress load increment. The weight jump factor increases every two sets with a corresponding minus 2 in the rep grid. On this particular pyramid the 4 blast singles are considered to be the strength-building sets.

There are a couple of other modifications of the one-dimensional pyramid system that many of the pros will use from time to time. The first modification is the **one-dimensional pyramid/superset.** This pyramid, as the previous one, includes increased stress loads or poundages with a corresponding decrease in the rep demand, but with a difference. Here's an example:

       Set 1 — 70%M x 10 reps
       Set 2 — 80%M x 8 reps
       Set 3 — 85%M x 6 reps
       Set 4 — 90%M x 4 reps
       Set 5 — 95%M x 2 reps
       Set 6 — 95%M x 2 reps

It may appear so far that this particular one-dimensional pyramid is nothing out of the ordinary. However, there is a difference, and here it is. The first three sets are done exactly as they are listed, but, beginning with the fourth and concluding with the sixth set, a key isolation exercise is added to the above pyramid and performed in superset style. That means if you were doing high-bar full squats leg extensions would follow. For the pecs it could be barbell bench presses to the neck or V-bar dips supersetted on the last three sets of the pyramid with incline (30 to 40 degree) dumbell flyes. T-bar rows followed by barbell straight-arm pullovers on a decline bench, and so on. The pros will do between 8 and 12 reps on each and every set of the isolation exercises in an effort to create the utmost in sculptured muscularity.

Paul Dillett, bodybuilding's "Man at Large."

Former Mr. World, Mr. Universe and strength star Chuck Sipes.

Some pros will reverse the superset procedure and do a pre-exhaust technique within the structure of the last three sets of their one-dimensional pyramid supersets. Some strength coaches may argue that supersetting or pre-exhausting a muscle doesn't go with the logic of how strength develops and muscle fatigue works, and there is some truth to this statement. But since superhuman strength is secondary to increasing maximum muscle mass for pure muscle-builders, they will tend to go with the ultimate superset or pre-exhaust pump-out system.

Another one-dimensional pyramid that many of today's top bodybuilders use for developing strength and muscle bulk is the **"5 x 5 modified system."** The major proponent of this system is Bill Starr, strength coach at Johns Hopkins University, and a contributing consultant to *MuscleMag International*.

	Day 1 (Heavy)	Day 2 (Light)
Set 1 —	65%M x 5 reps	65%M x 6-8 reps
Set 2 —	80%M x 5 reps	80%M x 6-8 reps
Set 3 —	88%M x 5 reps	84%M x 6-7 reps
Set 4 —	88%M x 5 reps	84%M x 6-7 reps
Set 5 —	88%M x 5 reps	84%M x 6-7 reps

One-dimensional pyramid systems such as the three we have listed are some of the very best to use in the strength-gain segment of a workout. However, some of the bodybuilders we have talked to on both the amateur and the pro levels favor a two-dimensional pyramid system. The two-dimensional pyramid reaches an apex on the strength and muscle-bulk enhancing sets and then, to complete the pyramid, the stress loads are decreased as the reps are increased. This is achieved by a plus 2-to-4 from set to set in a descending order from the top of the pyramid apex. Sounds complicated? Well, let me try to explain. The basic idea is to stop at each stress load increment when working up to the top of the pyramid. There is a technical point regarding this system that must be addressed.

One of the worst things a bodybuilder can do to the pyramid system is to extend it beyond its strength and muscle-building capacity. Some of the really rugged top bodybuilders use a pyramid system based on twelve sets (six set increments ascending to the apex and descending six sets down to the bottom of the pyramid) for a single select exercise. Overpyramiding in this manner could decrease the effectiveness of the gains for all but the most rugged pro. A much better approach for us normal beings would be six sets to reach the top of the apex then the reversing order on the down side, only done at every other decrement. For example, to modify the one-dimensional pyramid superset into a two-dimensional system, two back-off sets would be done (90%M x 4 reps and 80%M x 8 reps). Most bodybuilders find that a five-to-seven set, two-dimensional pyramid system for a single exercise adequately meets their training demands.

As already mentioned, optimal rest time between each set will average one-and-a-half minutes and never exceeds five minutes, unless otherwise indicated.

There are many other modifications of the one- and two-dimensional pyramid systems of the champions, and we have listed some of these throughout this book.

After the strength and muscle mass pyramid system (or one of its modifications) is completed, the remainder of the one-muscle-group-per-day workout session is dedicated exclusively to the fine-tuning of killer cuts

Andreas Munzer has the judges' undivided attention.

Start

Finish

muscularity. There are many proven training techniques by which to accomplish this task. We showed you two of them (supersets and trisets) within the biceps and forearms workout. Another of the all-time favorite body-blitzing techniques of many veteran pros is the **"down-the-rack dumbell or barbell principle."**

We'll illustrate this pro technique for blow-torching the deltoid complex. Let's hypothetically assume that the barbell press behind the neck was the exercise of choice incorporated into a pyramid system.

Having completed the final set of the pyramid, the **down-the-rack principle** begins. An awareness of kinesiology is most helpful in guaranteeing success here. Why? Because it is useful to know exactly what muscles are "helping muscles" in each exercise. A hard and fast rule is that you can do back-to-back exercises which target the very same aspect of the muscle, but the helping muscles must be different in order to ignite a maximum response in the muscle cells. The synergist, or helping muscle, in the press behind the neck is the triceps. So, to begin down-the-rack, an exercise using a different synergist should be selected. An excellent exercise to illustrate my meaning is the two-dumbell upright rowing motion. The synergist in this exercise is the trapezius. A specific warmup is not necessary

unless you feel the need because the delt complex is already warmed up with oxygen-rich blood from the previous exercise. For the sake of illustration, let's say the two-dumbell upright rowing motion begins with a pair of 60-pound dumbells. Six solid reps are done. Put those back on the rack and then, without resting, do the 55s — for six blazing reps. Go right to the 50s for a muscle-flushing six, etc. Continue until a sixth and final set is completed with the 35-pounders.

These six non-stop sets of 6 reps equals one series. Working down the rack from the heavier to the lighter poundages in five- or ten-pound decrements will take less than five minutes, providing the dumbells are loaded up and in a sequential order prior to starting the series.

A protracted rest-pause of 2-1/2 to 3 minutes is taken and then a second six-set series is done using the same rep grid, but with a totally different exercise. The two-dumbell press overhead could be a logical choice. Granted, the triceps, being the synergist (or helping muscle) in this movement, have been worked already, but they have had sufficient time during the two-dumbell upright rowing series to recover.

After this second series is completed, another 2-1/2 to 3 minute rest-pause is taken. A third series is then begun with perhaps a rather direct isolationary exercise, such as the two-dumbell lateral raise (standing or seated or bent over) for six non-stop sets of 6 reps. Usually three of these series is enough for even the most hardcore pro bodybuilder. Every once in awhile though, depending on their existing energy levels, an occasional fourth series is performed.

There are some key points to getting the maximum benefits out of this training system. Doug Stadele, a former Mr. California, says that muscles respond to two different things — heavy tension (heavy weights) and a lot of tension (reps for shape, etc.).

This can be accomplished by using heavy poundages that you don't have to struggle with and that will allow a precision technique to be maintained. Also, never shut off or relax

◄ Ursula and Milos Sarcev.

Charles Clairmonte

the tension on the muscle during any phase of the rep or between the reps. In other words, keep the weight moving. One of the best ways to stay within the continuous maximum-tension range is to do only the middle 3/5 range of the positive and negative phase of each and every rep, but not on every set.

Much of the success of the down-the-rack principle will be determined by speed. Speed, speed and a bit more speed. Speed is required both in the actual performance of the reps and in the "racing the clock" pace (quality training) used to get through the rest-pause between each series of sets.

As the reps become a little more difficult to do with super speed, especially in the latter sets of a series, do what a pro would do — let your precision technique exercise form fail just a bit, but not in an exaggerated cheating style.

Loosening your exercise style just a little will allow the rep grid within each set of a series to be completed. Speeding the rest-pause between each series of 6 sets is also very

Lee Priest

important in achieving maximum success with the down-the-rack principle. Most bodybuilders eventually decrease their rest-pause between each series by a third, or even by a half. As their body adapts and grows accustomed to the extra stress, the rest-pause phase can be reduced even more, but to probably no more than a quarter of the former rest-pause time. To accomplish this with the utmost expediency, we suggest you work through these five **descending levels of rest-pauses.**

Level V — 2-1/2 to 3 minutes
Level IV — 2 to 2-1/2 minutes
Level III — 1 to 1-1/2 minutes
Level II — 45 to 60 seconds
Level I — 30 seconds

Stay with each level for approximately one to two weeks.

In addition to using tension, superspeed reps, and a "racing the clock" rest-pause between series, the pro bodybuilder uses some additional strategic but logical intensity progressions within the down-the-rack principle. They are as follows:

1. Sometimes, rather than doing a one- or two-dimensional pyramid system for a single strength/muscle mass exercise and then combining it with another exercise utilizing the down-the-rack principle, during each muscle group workout, the pyramid system and down-the-rack principle will be performed on a separate workout day.

An example of this would be a delt workout. Two basic multi-joint exercises will be used while incorporating a stress-loading pyramid system. The two exercises selected can, of course, stimulate the same aspect of the deltoid complex if need be. However, each must use a different set of synergist or helping muscles.

The standing barbell press overhead or the barbell press behind the neck could be used for a one- or two-dimensional pyramid system.

After the completion of this pyramid, and an appropriate rest-pause, do the barbell upright rowing exercise. The same pyramid system could be used in this exercise as the one previously mentioned, but for the sake of variety, it might be better to use a one-dimensional for one exercise and a two-dimensional pyramid for the other.

2. During the next deltoid one-muscle-group workout, use only a killer cuts muscularity, down-the-rack principle. Use a wide variety of isolationary shape-training exercises. Each one should be thoughtfully selected to target a different aspect of shoulder training.

One exercise should target the frontal or anterior aspect of the deltoids, while another is used to pump up the medial or lateral aspect, and finally one or two others are used for the development of the posterior (or rear delt) aspect. One series of six nonstop sets of six reps are performed for each of the three aspects of the delt.

3. Some bodybuiders will modify the down-the-rack principle of one series (six nonstop sets of six reps) of two or three separate exercises into a down- plus up-the-rack 12-set series using just two exercises. This system begins by working down the rack in 5-to-10-pound decrements for six sets. But, rather than stopping, work back up the rack, stopping at each one of the previous downward decrement stages to increase the poundage on the way back up.

The above sequence can be reversed into an individual up-the-rack (working from the lightest to heaviest poundage increments) or a combined down-the-rack modification.

4. While a 6-rep grid was suggested in the detailed example of the down-the-rack principle, it was not a number intended to be carved in stone. Many bodybuilders will use a holistic rep system within the structure of the three-to-four series. Assuming that the down-the-rack system has not been modified to an inverted style, the first series might use 6 to 9 reps, the second series 10 to 14 reps, and a third series 15 to 20-25 reps and so on. We are all individuals with our own stress levels. By experimentation, find out what sets and reps suit you best on any given day.

Lou Ferrigno – the big screen's biggest Hercules.

Danny Hester, Tonya Knight and Lee Priest.

5. Within the listing of the intensity progression, we mentioned that the pyramid system and the down-the-rack principle are each performed separately on alternate workout days for the same muscle group. This seems to work out fine when a select muscle group is only trained once every seven days or so.

However, when a conventional workout pattern is followed where a muscle group is trained at least twice and sometimes three times per week, the training rationale changes slightly. The pyramid system would be done exclusively during one training week, but not with the same progression each workout.

To get a handle on how to vary the progression from workout to workout, refer back a few pages to the 5 x 5 modified system, which is an offshoot of the intensity manipulation methodology we spoke of earlier in the book. On an alternate training week a saturation bombing down-the-rack technique (or one of its modifications) is the preferred technique for developing razor cut muscularity. (You could also use supersets, trisets or giant sets, etc.)

So far we have shared with you a rather extensive commentary on the multiple-exercise approach when training one muscle group per day. Sometimes, however, veteran pro bodybuilders will wave off the multiple-exercise approach to train with just one selected exercise, regardless of whether they are training for strength/muscle mass or deep-cut muscularity. The rep selection will vary so as to meet the training goals of the individual.

Actually, the multiple-exercise approach sets the tone for doing only one exercise, because it was from doing a variety of movements that the pro, through experimentation, found one particular exercise that is uniquely best for his personal training wants and needs. It is not at all unusual for this one selected exercise to stimulate all aspects of a muscle group into more herculean size, plus cut-to-the-bone muscularity.

We remember well Rock Stonewall, a former IFBB Mr. North America physique star, doing only one exercise from time to time to bulk, define and broaden his shoulders. The one exercise he used to accomplish this was the seated alternate dumbell press. We are going to use this exercise as the initial reference source to explain the single exercise methodology. One had to marvel at watching him crank out set after set of this exercise until he had completed a 20-mega-set blitz. He would make sure that he did 6 to 8 reps every set without fail while also guaranteeing that rest-pauses of only 30 to 45 seconds between sets were taken. His selection of reps is interesting because he would do the vast majority of his sets in the 6-rep range. This was long before the National Strength Training Association or the modern-day hercules Ted Arcidi knew that the number 6 was going to be one of the most effective rep schemes for building monstrous muscle size.

We weren't able to monitor Rock's one-exercise 20-set blitz as often as we would like to have done, so we don't know what type of modifications he made to keep the gain factor going.

We've seen other variations of the one exercise only, one muscle group per day concept. As those of you who read our book *Raw Muscle!* (Contemporary Books, Inc. 1989) may remember, we talked in detail about a system called "riot bombing." This was an excellent example of the concept as it applied to the one muscle group per day theory. The riot bombing system illustrated the absolute outer limits of a two-dimensional pyramid principle. We've seen and heard of plenty of bodybuilders who have done 20 mega-sets for a single exercise. Generally not too much preparation goes into the 20-set approach. As a result, we have almost become numb to the commonality of it.

One day information came across our fax line regarding some East Coast bodybuilders who were using what they called the **"division of sets technique"** on one exercise only. As we read the fax transmission we expected to read something about 20 sets and we were not disappointed. It said that, for them, the limit of the technique maxed out at about 20 sets, but that this figure had been exceeded on occasion by a couple of bodybuilders who were experimenting with it. One of them did 33 sets on one exercise only. That got our immediate attention. We desperately wanted to find out more about this training technique, and we did!

Basically the technique uses a 1/4 (25%) to

1/2 (50%) to 1/4 (25%) formula of sets. The first one-fourth of the sets is for warming up and stretching. The next one-half of the total sets is the barometer strength and muscle mass builders. The final one-fourth of the sets is for pumping up or flushing the muscles with oxygen-rich blood.

During the division of sets technique, begin with one warmup set, two barometer sets and one pump-out set. During workout number two the warmup and pump-out sets increase

Darrem Charles

by one each, and the barometer sets increase by two. In the third workout, the formula increases to a 3:6:3 division of sets, and continues on in this progressive manner each successive workout until you reach the maximum number of the ratio of sets formula you can recuperate from overnight.

Here is a look at the program after five workouts.

North American champ Jeff Poulin believes in a no-nonsense approach to training.

Division of Sets Technique

Warmup Sets
1/4
5 sets x 35, 30, 25, 20, 15 reps
Barometer Sets
1/2
10 sets x 10 reps
Pumpout Sets
1/4
5 sets x 15, 20, 25, 30, 35 reps

After we had deciphered the base formula (1:2:1) of the technique and its rather aggressive cumulative sets concept, it was clearly understood how the 20 sets were arrived at after only five workouts. What we needed to know in more detail was how the rep selection was determined for each of the three parts of the formula and what, if any, its limitations would be.

We were told that the repetition schemes for the warmup and pump-out are chosen almost instinctively from the 30% to 60% of a maximum single-effort range. The rep jump factors when moving either down (warmups) or up (pump-out) from one set to the next don't necessarily have to follow the above sequences. You can work from a minimum base of 15 reps up to as many as 50 reps when choosing the reps for warmup or pump-out sets.

As we continued our dialogue with the East Coast bodybuilders they told us that the division of sets technique was especially effective when training a slow-twitch muscle complex such as the forearms, abdominals or calves. They said that the barometer sets are the pulse-point of this technique. For developing both maximum muscle shape and deep penetrating muscularity, a minimum of 8 sets of 8 reps to a maximum of 10 sets of 10 reps in the 70% to 79% range of a maximum single effort should be done. (See above diagram.)

The amount of poundage used in barometer sets is always based on a fixed percentage of maximum. If, for example, 100 pounds was the selected poundage for upper-arm biceps work using a compound curl bar (see photo in Chapter Ten), then that is the poundage you will use for each and every barometer set.

The only time the poundages will increase or decrease is if you are doing more or less than the reps specified. Rest-pauses are minimal on this technique. Inhale and exhale for five to ten very deep breaths between each set. That's it!

Developing awesome power and herculean muscle mass requires a totally different rep selection. There are three barometer set applications that a bodybuilder can go with. The first two are 6 sets of 4 reps and 6 sets of 6 reps. These are done in the 80% to 90% range of a maximum single effort. The third one is most interesting because eight barometer sets are done, but with a rotational two to three reps in the 90% to 99% range of max.

Begin with one warmup set followed by two barometer sets and one pump-out set. On the first barometer set do three big triples, and on the second do a double. Continue on in the manner described for each proceeding workout, taking care to do the first one-half of the barometer sets for triple reps and the final one-half for double reps. By the time you are finished with your fourth workout your barometer sets will appear as follows: 4 sets x 3 reps, and 4 sets x 2 reps. Beginning with workout five do 5 sets x 3 reps, and 3 sets x 2 reps. For workout six do 6 sets x 3 reps, and 2 sets x 2 reps. Continue on until you are doing 8 sets of 3 reps.

The time you spend at the barometer level of 8 sets of 3 reps will depend on the frequency of your workouts.

If you are only training once weekly, you have probably squeezed it for all it's worth. If that is the case, it's time to take a week or so off, then add five to ten pounds to the barometer sets (never exceed 15 pounds) and start over from the base formula again. Rest 3-1/2 to 4 minutes between these sets. Be sure to use only power and muscle mass exercises such as barbell bench presses, bent-over rowing, squatting, curls and overhead presses. Never use isolationary exercises when doing 2 to 3, 4 and 6 rep barometer sets.

Regardless of the frequency of the workouts, the duration of the division of sets technique should last no longer than four to six weeks. There is an exception to this, however. Having been told that one bodybuilder put an inch and a half on each calf in only

Start

Tonya Knight knows how to isolate the lats.

Finish

91

Ron Love in a relaxed pose.

week "crash program," and and could only be done once or twice a year.

On reflection, we could see the division of sets technique as a tremendous training principle — if it's not abused. We couldn't imagine even the most advanced bodybuilder ever needing to do 20 mega-sets on a single exercise, let alone 30-plus sets.

For the natural anabolic steroid-free bodybuilder, a limit formula of three warmup sets, six barometer sets and three pump-out sets for each major muscle group would

Paul Dillett stuns the world.

eight workouts, we investigated further. He started with the base formula of 1:2:1 on the first workout, using 10 reps on the barometer sets, and followed through to an 8:16:8 formula on the eighth and final workout. A quick calculation told us that an unheard of total of 32 sets on "one exercise only" had been completed on the seated calf raise machine!

This most definitely exceeded any of the limitations on the warmup, barometer and pump-out sets to say the least. What surprised us even more was the frequency of these workouts. It wasn't once or twice a week as we might have suspected, but every other day, including weekends during a 15-day time frame! Talk about a super intense crash program. Wow! It's obvious that a program of this magnitude can only be followed as a two-be better. For a minor muscle group, an acceptable exercise limit would be a 2:4:2 ratio.

What we'd like to do now, while we are still on the hot topic of the one muscle group per day training concept, is to share with you some more pro tips for getting the most potential muscle growth out of the deltoid exercises we have mentioned. The first exercise we'll talk about is the dumbell press and its variations.

The methods of pressing will vary from set to set. During one set each rep should take approximately three seconds in the pressing (positive) phase, one second holding the dumbell(s) at the extended arms-over-the-head position, and four seconds in the lowering (negative) phase.

During another set you might press the dumbell(s) up to lockout within one second, hold for one second and lower within two seconds. Accompanying these slow and super-speed rep variations, different tracking pattern

techniques are also to be incorporated. Perhaps on one set the Arnold press (180-degree rotating dumbell press) is chosen, where the movement begins with the dumbells at shoulder level with the palms of the hands facing the frontal deltoids. This position will give the appearance of a rep in the positive peak contraction phase of a dumbell curl. (See illustration.) Keeping your wrists straight, begin pressing the dumbells upward vertically while slowly rotating the hands so that when they reach ear level they will be in a neutral (hands in the position of a hammer curl) or palms facing position. Continue to press and rotate the hands to an overhead lockout position with the palms facing forward. Reverse the procedure when lowering to the starting position and begin another rep. On another set you might wish to give the Larry Scott overhead dumbell press a try. This rather unique style of pressing begins with your elbows in alignment with your shoulders, palms facing forward. Begin pressing the dumbells through the middle 3/5 of the actual

Charles Clairmonte, Dorian Yates, Milos Sarcev.

Lee Priest picks up where Lee Labrada left off.

movement (starting point is 3 to 4 inches above the delts), but not straight up vertically. With the dumbells tilted so that the little finger side is ever so slightly higher than the thumb side (takes stress off biceps somewhat and directs it to delts), swing or pull the elbows behind the ears or head as you press them out in a wide smooth arc till the bells touch 4 to 6 inches above the top of your head in a non-lockout fashion. At this point tilt your head forward for an even better contraction in the delts. Lower and repeat.

Another slight variation to the Scott dumbell press is to begin with the bells at shoulder level, and press them in a partial rep to a position where the elbow angle between the forearm and upper arm reaches only 90 degrees (triceps of upper arm is approximately parallel to the floor in this non-lock press).

We have observed other pro bodybuilders work one muscle per day by bombing their delts in the following way: Taking a 16 to 24-inch handspacing on a barbell then doing wide-grip upright rows by pulling the bar to their lower pec line (elbows are parallel to the floor). This handspacing, combined with pulling the bar to the lower pec, will stimulate growth in the lateral head of the delt like no other exercise.

Pro Tip: Do barbell upright rowing while in a kneeling position.

Do 12 reps, then immediately grasp a pair of dumbells and press them overhead simultaneously to nonlockout. Now slowly lower your slightly bent arms out to the sides (laterally), in a negative rep fashion, slowly, for a count of ten. When the extended arms reach a position parallel to the floor, bring them into a shoulder rest position. Continue your set by performing an additional 14 repetitions. This completes one triset or pre-exhaust series. The pros will do six to seven more series in the manner described, but you will only be asked to do two or three series at most. The intensity on the wide-grip upright rowing can be upped by holding the last three reps (reps 10, 11 and 12) for a slow count of four to five seconds when the bar is at the low pec line. The champions go from one exercise to another in rapid fashion with absolutely no rest within a series. Rest-pauses of 2-1/2 to 3 minutes are then taken before launching into the next series. The two key words to success in this system are *moderation* and *speed.* A moderate poundage in all the exercise sets must be adhered to. It will be impossible to do the pre-exhaust series if you're struggling with heavy or limit poundages.

What we have given you is a brief overview of how amateur and pro bodybuilders use high-volume training to guarantee almost continuous muscle gains. Though many of these bodybuilders make enough money in the sport to accommodate their marathon training sessions, they in fact do cut back on their high-volume training (while upping the intensity of the workouts) to make even greater muscle-building progress and thus avoid some of the injuries and staleness caused by depletion of the body's natural mineral and enzyme stores. To preserve vital energy and minerals by stepping back from all-out training punishment once in awhile can only enhance long-term bodybuilding development. Pro bodybuilders tell us that they monitor their capacity to overtrain by following the three-step checklist that the former Eastern Bloc training coaches used on their strength athletes and bodybuilders. This will require the purchase of a blood pressure cuff, a litmus paper kit, and a microscope.

The first step in determining overtraining is to measure blood pressure as soon as you wake every day of the week (for an accurate resting pressure reading), and again immediately following heavy stress, such as a high-volume workout. If the bodybuilder's diastolic pressure exceeds 100mmHG and/or if the systolic pressure is up 15 percent or more from the previous day, then the intensity and training volume load should be reduced. Sounds technical but the procedure can easily be mastered.

The second step is to measure the pH balance of the arterial blood. This is performed by pricking the finger with a sterile pin so that a blob of blood can be tested on the litmus paper. Normal blood has a pH reading of 7.4. The litmus paper test will show excess levels of lactic acid buildup. Should the pH dip below 7.3, it is a definite sign of overtraining. Follow the same training advice for this test procedure as step one.

The final step is to test your blood for a white blood cell count. Though this is the most difficult of the three steps, it can be accomplished with the use of a microscope and an accompanying glass slide with grid markings for monitoring cell numbers within any given blood spot.

The expense of purchasing the necessary items for the three-step test and learning the procedures may seem burdensome, but, after doing the steps a few times in the privacy of your own home, the convenience and expenses saved from lab tests and costly office appointments with a sports medicine expert will seem well worth the effort.

A further test for overtraining that the Eastern Bloc coaches use is called "**adrenal suppression testing.**" Although extremely accurate, it is out of the reach of any average gym member. Nevertheless, it is worth a mention. A catabolic hormone which breaks down protein into amino acids and transports them to the liver for conversion into glucose for energy, this drug will suppress cortisol secretion from the adrenal gland if the bodybuilder is not overtrained. But, if the bodybuilder is in a state of being overtrained from prolonged high-intensity workouts, then the cortisol secretions will remain highly elevated, even after the administration of the DM drug. The anti-inflammatory cortisol hormone is not only released during the high-intensity exercise, but also during periods of emotional stress.

When overtraining has been determined, progressive steps in proper nutrition, rest, mental attitude and proper training procedures must be initiated to recreate an anabolic muscle growth state within the body.

It is interesting to note that the adrenal suppression test is being used in the United States to diagnose excessive activity and inflammation of the adrenal glands when a positive test reading is indicated.

Laura Creavalle has it all!

CHAPTER NINE

The Total-Body Workout Concept

To prevent the onset of overtraining the pro bodybuilder will, through very careful and thoughtful planning, gradually reduce his training intensity and load volume. This can be achieved by planning a worthwhile cyclic program of primary and secondary workouts which take no more than 75 to 90 minutes to complete.

All of the major muscle groups – quadriceps, back (including traps, lats and spinae erectors) and chest – and minor muscle groups – hamstrings, delts, triceps, biceps, forearms, calves, neck and abs – are to be trained three alternate days per week. Each workout will have a maximum accumulated time of 90 minutes and perhaps less. Four days per week are reserved for total rest and relaxation.

Each workout begins with the super position primary phase where two anti-stress muscle groups are trained with a variety of compound and isolationary exercises consisting of multiple sets and reps of varying intensities. When this is completed the secondary phase is entered into, and all the remaining major and minor muscle groups are trained with one compound or isolationary exercise (your choice), but for only one **four-component set** of eight hard, full reps to positive failure, followed by two to four forced reps, two to three negatives and four partial-burn reps. Sounds complicated, I know, but I will explain more further on.

The second workout day will begin again with the primary phase of the workout but this time with two different muscle groups. The two muscle groups worked in this phase from the previous workout are rotated into the structure of the secondary phase (short maintenance) of the total-body workout.

Charles Clairmonte

On the third and final workout day that is to be performed in a seven-day period, choose yet another two different muscle groups for your primary phase. All the previous muscle groups which have already served in this capacity from workouts one and two are now put into the rotational sequence of the secondary phase. Here are some structured **three-day rotation total-body workouts** which best illustrate the concept of primary first and secondary phase training.

Primary Phase

Workout No. 1

Upper Back

Wide-grip front pullups: To do this exercise properly, the hands should be placed 32 to 34 inches apart, or as far apart as comfort will allow. To keep this exercise (and other lat movements) from involving the biceps to any great degree, it is important that you secure the bar high in the palm of the hand with a thumbless (false) overhand grip. When the body is suspended by only the fingers in this exercise, it becomes more of a biceps exercise than lat-building. The same holds true for other lat exercises such as barbell and dumbell rowing, various pulldowns, and seated cable rowing, etc., where both straight and angled bars are used. Therefore, regardless of which lat exercise you are doing, **always** secure the bar high on the palm of your hands.

A fail-safe way of doing this is to always apply a heavy coat of magnesium carbonate chalk to your hands each and every set (or use power straps, or both) to secure a vice-like grip.

Grasping the overhead pullup bar, with your arms as straight as possible, raise your pecs towards the bar while arching your back, while at the same time making yourself narrow by doing a scapular retraction (drawing the scapulae or shoulder blades close together). If you're not sure of how to do this, then imagine yourself squeezing a tennis ball between the shoulder blades. This is the movement you are after. If you've executed this starting position correctly, you will be leaning slightly forward ahead of the bar. Your elbows will be behind the plane of your upper body throughout the positive phase of each rep.

The scapular retraction technique (tennis ball squeeze) will not only help muscle up your lats, but will help you maintain proper hip and shoulder (lock) relationship necessary for an efficient pull of power in your deadlift movements, especially during the initial thrust off the floor.

Shawn Ray and Lee Labrada beam with confidence.

Now tilt your head back (looking up towards the ceiling) and, with an arched back (scapular retraction) and chest high, pull upward quickly and touch your chest below the low pec line (sternum) to the bar. If you have done the movement correctly up to this point your upper arms should be touching the outer aspect of the lats, and the elbows are pulled down and back beyond the plane of your upper body.

The entire movement should be accomplished without any excessive body movement or knee kicking (in fact, relax hips and legs). Now slowly begin to lower your body through the negative stretch phase of the exercise. As you do so, semi-dislocate (by relaxing) your scapulars from their retracted position by rotating them outward. This is accomplished by pushing backward from the bar (this subtle action could best be described as doing an ultra-high incline bench press movement) as you lower your body down to the starting point. Really make a concentrated effort both mentally and physically to s-t-r-e-t-c-h the scapulae attachments ultra-wide. One of the biggest problems in explaining exercises (or movements of any kind) in print is translating the kinesthetic sense (the enhancement of total-body coordination) in a holistic manner. This is the body's instinctive response during training.

The description of the scapular retraction and rotation system is a classical example of this. Larry Scott has also explained this system in his best-selling book *Loaded Guns*, but he took his description of it one step further by including a visual and audio commentary of it in a VHS *Hidden Secrets, Back and Abdominal Weight Training*, video. Should you wish to explore this further, we highly recommend that

Mike Ashley

Debbie Muggli, Kim Chizevsky and Laura Creavalle.

Chris Cormier and Kevin Levrone bring back memories of Sergio and Arnold.

you call 800-225-9752 for more information on this and other selected weight-training video presentations from Larry Scott and Associates.

One of the most appreciable ways to force the lats into doing more of the work (and hence spread wider) is by leaving the fingers and palms as much out of the exercise when doing wide-grip front pullups. This can be done by padding the overhead bar with some armoflex.

Rather than gripping the bar, flex your wrists over the top of the bar and hang supported in this manner while you perform the pullups. This is a pro technique that many champion bodybuilders have used from time to time to help them develop a flaring V-shaped back laced with granite-hard muscle.

Most of the time the champs will use a vice-like false grip on the bar while keeping the wrist straight (neutral). This action alone (whether doing pullups, pulldowns or variations of barbell and cable rowing) will allow for maximum contraction of the scapula. This is not the case, however, when the wrists are extended or flexed over a padded bar. The middle third of the wide-grip front pulldown works the infra spinatus, while the final third of the positive contraction phase stimulates the rhomboids.

John Sherman

Middle Back

Seated horizontal long-pull cable rowing or barbell bent-over rowing: On the seated cable rows be sure that your elbows are turned in or downward and not flared out. This action will work the lats maximally while involving very little biceps assistance.

When bracing your feet, make sure that there is a slight bend in the knees. This action will relax the hamstrings and create less tension on the lower back. As with all back exercises, use an arched posture. Do not allow the shoulders to round forward because the pecs will become involved in the movement and you do not want this to take place.

The final third of the positive contraction phase of this movement develops the teres.

On the barbell bent-over rowing (space index fingers 28 to 34 inches apart when grasping the bar), pull your elbows out away from the sides of the body to develop mid-back thickness. Always pull the elbows higher than the level of the flat-back arched position. Another way to build lat width and thickness is to hold every third rep in the peak contraction positive phase for a count of six seconds.

Lower Back

Stiff-legged deadlift standing on bench: Tracking patterns for this exercise are discussed elsewhere in this book. However, there is one aspect of the **tracking pattern procedure** that deserves some additional commentary. Generally, a bodybuilder is advised to use a pronated or palms-down grip when doing this exercise. Even when the hands are heavily coated with chalk, the grip can become the weak link in the exercise and will begin to fail during the latter reps of a maximum repetition set (the one set with the most poundage involved).

The best method for bypassing this problem is to use a hook grip. To secure a hook grip, first wrap the thumb of the right hand under and around the bar – pushing down hard so that it wraps around the bar as far as possible. Then wrap the index and middle fingers of the right hand in a counter direction over the top of the bar. Finally, wrap the remaining fingers of the right hand over the top and around the

Tonya Knight *Start*

Finish

101

Start

Lee Priest

Finish

bar. Do the same for the left hand (knuckles-forward style) to secure the best grip possible. This hook grip is guaranteed to give you that extra holding power needed for the successful completion of a maximum-repetition set of off-bench stiff-legged deadlifts. Hook grips can also be used for many other exercises when it is determined that a conventional grip is the weak link which stops your successful comple-

tion of an exercise set. The hook grip may be somewhat painful at first, but it will soon pass. You can protect your thumbs from the potential ravages of the hook grip by using Johnson & Johnson "Coach" athletic tape.

Prone hyperextensions: This is probably the very best exercise for working the erector muscles of the lower back. It was a firm favorite with Vasili Alexeyev, an eight-time world champion Olympic lifter and one of the strongest men in the world. Within the structure of his workouts it was not uncommon for him to use 200 pounds plus for sets of five reps in the hyperextension exercise. One has to wonder that, if Vasili hadn't included this exercise in his training program, would he still have toppled more than 80 world records (seven of which were smashed in one evening of lifting), during his Olympic lifting career?

The immediate advantage of performing the hyperextension exercise is (when done properly and with discretion) the almost non-existent compression on the spinal column. This is an advantage that the previous deadlift exercise couldn't offer. We are, therefore, going to suggest that you alternate this exercise with any other erector movement you might wish to perform. For example, if you do the stiff-legged deadlift standing on the bench during a workout, be sure to do hyperextensions during your next lower back workout.

Performed as suggested, this exercise will develop cobra-like thickness in your erectors and a tensile contraction strength beyond compare. It will also allow you to use herculean poundages in such exercises as deadlifts and squats, but, due to your added new erector strength, you will experience less compression on the spinal column.

The hyperextension is performed on a special bench built for this purpose. If you don't own a hyperextension bench you can use a flat exercise bench, but be sure to place your body at a right angle to it (upper frontal thighs only on the bench) so that your kneecaps don't rub around under your own weight while doing the hyperextensions. If you're ever on vacation or away from home and desperate, you can also use the resilient surface of a padded table or arm of a sofa if the other two options are not open to you. Of the four options, three of them unfortunately will require a training partner to hold your feet steady.

The Russians have been known to use a padded buck horse (commonly used in gymnastics) and a padded curved block for each ankle which was attached to wall bars. Using

Kevin Levrone and Dorian Yates – It doesn't get any better than this!

the ankle pads would circumvent the necessity of a training partner to hold the ankles. Additionally, two large, high-density foam pads were strapped to the buck horse with a three-inch separation between each pad. This was done in preparation for a second exercise on the buck horse known to most bodybuilders as the Roman chair situp. When the Russians perform this exercise, the coccyx (or tail bone) fits between the pads, allowing the lifter freedom of movement without rubbing the tail bone raw. If you have access to a buck horse then the information we have just shared with you will be helpful should you decide to use one for hyperextensions.

Assuming that you have access to a hyperextension bench (BFS Glute-Ham Developer is the very best model sold for this), here is the most effective way to use it: Stand within the confines of the bench unit, facing the padded platform. Leaning forward, lower your hip area onto it (prone face-down position) while securing the achilles tendon area of your heels under the roller pads at the rear of the unit. Double check that the top edge of your pelvic girdle is in contact with the front edge of the padded platform. Never position yourself forward beyond this point because your hip-joint extensor (butt or gluteus maximus and hamstrings) end up doing more work than the erectors. Your upper torso (from the lumbar vertebrae to the top of your head) should be hanging over or beyond the edge of the platform at a 60-degree angle. Lightly rest your

V-BAR DIP

For the sake of clarity this graphic illustration depicts the bodybuilder facing away from the "V."

hands behind your head or lower back if you wish. Now flex your hips while at the same time arching your back in a swan dive position. Never hump your back.

Inhale deeply, and without expelling, raise your head up to try looking at the ceiling while you slowly contract your thoracic (lumbar) spine until your upper torso (shoulders) is level with (or above) your pelvic girdle. This will be an imaginary line which is parallel to the floor. You can extend your spine upwards a further 10 to 20 degrees beyond parallel to the floor if you find it comfortable and safe to do so.

Additional flexion up to 30 to 45 degrees beyond poses a potential danger in some people due to the force compressing the vertebrae. So, be warned, the exercise is safe as long as you're sensible enough to work within your own physical limits. Above all, *never snap your upper body into position,* but rather use a controlled rep speed of three to five seconds in the positive muscle-contraction phase.

Sometimes it is a good idea to hold the terminal point of spinal muscle contraction statically for 5 to 30 seconds (perhaps on the final rep of a set).

Pointers: Performing the negative phase of the hyperextension, begin expelling the air from your lungs and slowly lower your torso at the rate of 3 to 5 seconds (on occasion 5 to 30 seconds) down to the starting point, which is a 60-degree angle from a horizontal position to the floor. Work up to 15 to 20 reps for regular workouts, though at times when you're feeling particularly energetic you may try to do 50 or more reps. Never underestimate the value of ab work. The abs can help absorb 30 to 50 percent of the stress you place on your lower spine, especially when bending forward during workouts or daily chores.

Pectorals (Upper pec, minor)
Incline (30 to 40 degrees) dumbell press.

Pectorals (Lower pec, minor)
Kneeling cable crossovers: When doing this exercise, it is important to use a false grip on the overhead pulley stirrup handles, on a cable crossover machine. From the kneeling position, tuck your chin down firmly into your chest. With your arms outstretched laterally (while slightly bent) in a raised crucifix or V

Charles Clairmonte reminds us that it must be "wash day."

position above your upper torso, bring the stirrup handles downward in equal semi-circular arc movement until they touch just in front of and six inches away from your lower body.

Many of the champions will rotate the stirrup handles so that their palms are facing forward or supinated so that the little finger side of the handles touch at this peak contraction phase of the movement. They will squeeze and contract their inner pecs for a count of two seconds, before returning the handles to the starting point. Remember to always inhale air into your lungs during the negative stretch and expel during the positive contraction phase throughout the exercise.

Pro Tip: A nice variation to the above exercise is to position an adjustable flat bench midway between the floor pulleys on a cable crossover machine and use them for decline, flat or incline cable crossovers.

Other exercise variations on the cable crossover machine: The most common method of doing cable crossovers with the overhead pulleys is by standing. If you decide to do them in this manner, remember to step forward about two to three feet from the pulley alignment and stagger your feet by placing one foot forward about two feet. Now lean forward slightly and pull the handles together.

When Boyer Coe uses cable crossovers with the pulleys in the overhead position, he does them one arm at a time. Clarence Bass (prolific writer for *Muscle & Fitness* and author of the "Ripped" books) uses the bottom pulley position to do the movement in a standing jackknife position.

Pectorals (Lateral aspect, thorax)

V-shaped parallel-bar dips: Place a small mounting box midway between the widest opening of the upright support posts of the V-bar (only on the models that don't have crossbars at the base of the uprights). Now, while facing the inner V of the bars, stand on the pedestal or crossbar and assume the exact position which you would be in at the beginning or starting point of the dip.

Grasp the V-bars with a thumbless or false grip (palms and heels of hands facing outward instead of inward as with a suitcase or neutral grip) and the thumbs to the rear. The distance between the thumbs should be approximately 32 inches. Not only is this the most comfortable grip to assume (especially if the bar is fabricated from a round steel tubing), but also it places minimum stress on the biceps. With your arms straight and your elbows locked, tuck your chin into your chest. Next, round or bow your back and shoulders forward. Slide your feet off the crossbar and position them parallel or under your face slightly in front of the abs. Your posture will appear like a scimitar, or curved, single-edge Arabian sword.

Sue Price surely spends more time in the gym than at the Rocky Cola Cafe.

Relax your abdominals and inhale a deep breath of air. Slowly begin to lower your body through space while flaring your elbows out laterally in alignment with your shoulder joints. With pinpoint concentration, never allow the elbows to drift rearward beyond the plane of the upper body.

Continue to bend your arms at the elbow joints, lowering your body until the outer aspect of your pecs are two or three inches away from your hands. It is important to mention that Larry Scott uses this exercise almost exclusively in his pec-pumping routine. When doing so, he will go for an extra stretch (contraction) in his lower pecs, stopping the rep when his elbows are midway between shoulder height and straight overhead. Then he will do what he calls "double bounces," or measured movements, where he only pulls himself up 10 to 12 inches from the bottom of the negative stretch contraction and back down again (controlled half-reps). He repeats this sequence more than once.

Larry will also inhale short breaths during the stretching phase of his double-bounce

Milos Sarcev, John Sherman and Andreas Munzer wind down after a hard day's work.

technique (quickly exhaling the air from his lungs during the measured movements) which allows his rib cage to expand fully. But this is only possible because his abdominals and serratus are relaxed as much as possible. Should you try this, then after your double bounces are completed, concentrate on pulling with the power of your pecs to raise your body by straightening the arms by small degrees (while continuing to keep your elbows rotated and wide to the front) until you assume the "top" starting point of the pec dip.

The feel you are looking for (and bear with me in this) will be very similar to the one you could imagine feeling during the positive phase if you could perform a decline press and a cable crossover simultaneously. It may sound obscure, but when achieved, that's the purest form of pec contraction you will ever hope to experience.

If you don't have the strength or flexibility to do full range of motion V-bar dips in the manner described, then do them to within your own limited range of movement. From the "top" starting point you might begin by lowering just an inch or so, then pull right back up to the starting point. Then, each proceeding workout try to lower yourself a couple of inches further than in the previous workout.

Pro Tip: One of Larry Scott's favorite pec-bombing techniques is to superset, or alternate the V-bar dips with another good pulling exercise that uses the same basic movement. In this case it would be 15-degree decline dumbell flyes. This is done for a three to four series. At the bottom of the negative stretch contraction, on the decline dumbell flyes, he will flex his neck and raise his head a few inches off the bench. This little action assists him in creating an even deeper stretch in his pecs.

Until a few years ago, Vince Gironda had one of the only gyms in the nation to feature the "V" dipping bar. That has since changed. Larry Scott and his associates now manufacture an excellent V dipping bar. Call Larry and his associates at 1-800-225-9752 for more information on this unique piece of training equipment.

Vince "The Finger" Gironda, a.k.a. the Iron Guru.

Econo-Time Secondary Phase

Thighs
(Vastus medialis and lateralis, quads, hips and hamstrings)

Hip belt squats: This unique exercise first caught our attention through two published articles by John McCallum in the March and April 1970 issues of *Strength & Health* magazine. The articles, which were titled "Hip Belt Squat" and "The Hip Belt Squat Routine" (from the "Keys to Progress" series) praised this exercise as "...the absolute best for adding muscle bulk to the lower thighs." At that time we, and many other bodybuilders, didn't realize the impact that this exercise could have as a natural anabolic muscle stimulator. Our focus and just about everyone else's in the Iron Game was on Arthur Jones and his exercise system using special Nautilus machines.

In particular, our attention was riveted on Casey Viator and the fantastic gains in fresh new muscle growth he was experiencing while using the Nautilus in his preparing for some very major physique title wins. To return to the hip belt squat... decades have passed without much being heard of in regards to hip belt squats, but there have been six pieces published (from 1983 onward) and at least one television segment (ESPN's *American Muscle*, 1988) on this exercise.

Casey Viator returns from a long retirement.

HIP-BELT SQUAT

The "anabolic" equalizer.

Chris Cormier

For those of you who are not familiar with the hip belt squat, we suggest that you consider purchasing the VHS squat video from the Westside Barbell Club, 1469 Demorest Rd., Columbus, Ohio 43228. This video features a powerful live-action demonstration of the hip belt squat. Watch and discover how this potent anabolic blasting exercise can ignite the ultimate in thigh supergrowth – naturally. The cost of the video is $29.95 plus $3.00 shipping/handling. You might also consider buying a hip belt from the Westside Barbell Club as well. The cost is $79.00 plus $5.00 postage ($10.00 outside the continental US). We are now going to include some very necessary **tracking pattern** procedures for the hip belt squat.

Place two flat exercise benches (or very sturdy nontipping wooden platforms of the same height) to form a V-shaped configuration. When seen from above, the benches should be spaced far enough apart at the opened end of the "V" to accommodate the width of your selected squatting stance. Place a sturdy chair or box midway between these benches. This will serve as your loading platform for the weight you will be using. Place a heavy dumbell (the weight you intend to use) on it. The combined height of the loading platform and the dumbell should approximate knee height when you are standing on the benches.

Though your center of gravity in the hip belt squat will be extremely low when compared to other squatting movements (such as the Olympic high-bar squat), don't expect to use herculean poundages. Rickey Dale Crain, who is acknowledged as one of the greatest squatters of all time, discovered that doing just 3 sets of 10 to 12 maxi-pump reps with 275 to 300 pounds in the hip belt squat was brutally rough on his bionic quads, hips and hamstrings. He was capable of a "power-style" squat with well over 700 pounds at a bodyweight of around 175 pounds at the time!

Next, step up and take a moderately wide stance of 18 to 24 inches astride the flat exercise benches and directly over the loading platform. The exact width between your foot placement is your decision. You must feel comfortable and safe. Position the hip belt (or a leather dip belt, modified if you prefer) around

Vince Taylor skillfully displays his world-class symmetry.

the top of your hips and glutes. Attach the dumbell to the hip belt, positioning it so that the bar fits snugly but comfortably near your crotch. Now come to an upright position, lifting the dumbell off the loading platform. Have a spotter remove the loading platform.

Laterally rotate your feet out 45 degrees from parallel. This subtle action of rotating the feet out when combined with an 18 to 24 inch heel-to-heel stance will place stress on the outer edge of the foot where the power is, rather than on the weaker inner side of the foot.

Your body should be in an upright position where the shoulders and hip joints are in alignment. Never bow or hump your back so as to collapse your chest. If you do, your balance and weight will shift to your heels and put more tension on the spinae erector muscles; which is a problem associated with many thigh and back exercises but not with the hip belt squat. So why mention it? Because we want you to get into the habit of always assuming a flat back position with a slight inward arch in your lumbar region. It is a good idea to always hold your chest high by inhaling a deep breath and filling your lungs just prior to beginning any exercise, whenever possible.

Keeping your chin high and parallel to the floor will help your center of balance. One of the ways to acquire the correct feeling of a flat

back with a slight arch is to sit upright on a stool or bench. Inhale deeply and try to elevate your chest as high as possible in an effort to touch your chin. When done correctly it will automatically contract the muscles in the back so your spine and back feel locked into one solid piece. This technique was perfected by Tommy T. Kono, an eight-time Olympia weight-lifting champion. Not only would he use this technique, which he coined the "pouting pigeon," in the manner described, but he recommended it be used prior to beginning the pull-in exercises such as snatches, cleans and deadlifts.

Tommy was not only an experienced Olympic lifter of world caliber, but he also won the F.H.I.C. version of the Mr. World and Mr. Universe physique titles. A bodybuilder would do well to heed his words of training wisdom.

Now prepare to begin your squat descent by inhaling as Tommy suggests. With your bodyweight evenly distributed, **slowly** de-

Sharon Bruneau knows how to peak on contest day.

111

scend with control down to about three inches above parallel, till you become comfortable with the hip belt squat. Later, as your strength and flexibility increase, you can break parallel by allowing the hip joint to descend below the level of the knee joint by approximately two to four inches. But **never** at the expense of knee joint integrity. During this negative phase you might consider doing each rep at a slow, controlled speed. For more information on rep speed, refer to Primordial Muscle Shock Strategies "The 50-Rep Blitz" in Chapter Eleven.

During the squat descent, your knees and shins should remain in line, while your hip joint moves slightly forward. (Bring the hip joint as close as possible to the knee joint so that at the lowest point your hips are over the instep or middle of the foot.) The knees should never abduct (turn out) or adduct (turn in).

One of the ways you can stabilize the knees is to wrap them. Wear the knee wraps snugly but not too tightly as they can pinch the patella tendon against the bottom end of the femur, causing a grinding action.

Fred C. Hatfield, "Dr. Squat," does advise against wearing knee wraps for every workout. He says that doing so can cause a disruption or disfigurement (ultimately a quad tear) in the muscle tissue against which the fabric presses. He adds that this will usually occur right at the line where the wrap ends. Most quad tears, he says, are associated with a lack of flexibility as well. So, in this respect, it would be wise to include plenty of Parrillo leg (quad) fascial stretching within your leg workouts.

Upon completion of the negative phase of the hip belt squat, **without hesitation,** begin the ascent. Remember that even a .5 to 1 second delay can cause you to lose the valuable elastic muscle energy so necessary for the initial drive out of the power pocket.

On this the positive muscle contraction phase, a faster contraction speed should be used. Again, refer to Primordial Muscle Shock Strategies "The 50-Rep Blitz" for additional information.

With a flat back and your chest held high, ascend by raising your head then your chest and finally shoulders first. If you push with your legs first, it will cause the hips to raise

faster than your shoulders. This will cause your upper body to lean forward, thereby shifting your balance towards the heels. Approximately one-third of the way up you may hit a sticking point. This can be caused by either using too much weight or a leverage disadvantage (you have rounded your back). There are two actions you can take if this happens. One is to drive the hips forward. And, if this is not enough, use your hands to push off from your thighs to help bypass the sticking point. Spotting can also be done by having a helper on each side of the body. Each spotter places one hand under a hamstring and a hand under the chest to assist if necessary.

Sometimes balance other than a "round back" can be a problem, especially when the hips raise faster than the shoulders. This can be yet another cause of a sticking point. If you don't have a spotter, it would be a good idea to position your exercise benches within reach of a stationary object such as a post, power rack or parallel bars, etc. In this way you can reach out and grasp the object to help you through a sticking point. An added bonus here is that you can, by using an upright fixed object, maintain a very upright squatting position. This will create maximum muscle tension on the thighs and minimize stress on the lower back.

Begin expelling air from your lungs as you finish the upward positive contraction phase of the rep. Do not lock your knees out, rather keep continuous tension on the thighs by maintaining a 15-degree bend in the knee joint. Perform between 10 and 20 maxi-pump reps.

When you feel your balance is perfected, a wooden broom handle may be placed on the shoulders to simulate a squat bar. I mention this only because many hip belt squatters seem to prefer this method, once they have mastered the movement. Hip belt squats performed on a flat surface such as we have described tend to emphasize the quads, hips and hamstrings equally.

Pro Tip: Performing on an incline maxes out hips and hamstrings, while decline hip belt squats really terrorize the lower quad development maximally.

Dorian Yates – four-time winner of Mr. Olympia.

Calves (Gastrocnemius)
One-legged heel raise.

Deltoids (Anterior, front)
Parrillo delt rows with a wrist strap attachment: Refer to *High Performance Bodybuilding* by John Parrillo.

Triceps (Long and inner medial head)
Reverse-grip barbell bench press.

Biceps (Lower brachialis)
Barbell or dumbell Scott curls (preacher bench).

Forearms (Extensors)
Barbell or dumbell (palms-down) wrist curls.

Abdominals (Upper retus abdominus)
Butterfly crunch (quarter crunches).

Shawn Ray Knows how to bomb the deep fibers of the delts. **Start**

Primary Phase

Workout No. 2

Delts (Anterior/medial front and side)
Seated barbell press behind neck

Delts (Medial side)
Barbell upright rows: Take a conventional shoulder-width grip and, while keeping the bar close to the body, pull it from a hanging mid-thigh position to within one inch of your chin. While at this position, tense and shrug the traps upward.

Vince Gironda recommends that the bar be 12 inches in front of the body during the movement rather than close. One problem that generally arises with Vince's method, however, is that the elbows do not remain above the bar and thus the exercise tends to stimulate frontal delts rather than the medial head. Vince also says the shoulders should be rounded and down and not hunched back. This action will eliminate trap involvement.

Finish

ATOMIC TRICEPS-BLASTER
PUSHUP

This bodyweight-only exercise is sure to develop the ultimate in trip hammer triceps.

Delts (Posterior, rear)
90-degree bent-over dumbell lateral raise

Delts (Medial, side)
Three-way dynamic delt lateral raise: Raise the dumbells from mid-thigh to shoulder level for six consecutive reps. Without pausing do six reps from shoulder level to overhead. Finally, do six reps from mid-thigh to overhead in one complete movement.

Biceps (Belly)
Dumbell incline curls (45 to 50 degree). Use a thumbless grip and supinate at top of curl.

Biceps (High/outer peak)
Single-dumbell concentration curls.

Triceps (Long and inner medial head)
Reverse triceps bench dips: Place two flat exercise benches parallel to each other and approximately three feet apart (further if you're very tall). Place your heels on one bench and your hands (behind your back) in a palms-down position on the other. With the tips of your index fingers touching one another or six inches apart, and your upper torso, which is in an upright seated position, forming a right angle with your legs (which, in turn, are slightly bent), slowly bend your arms as fully as possible while rotating your elbows outward. Keep your back as close to the bench as possible.

Try to lower yourself down until the upper arms are at right angles with the forearms. Press back up by straightening the arms fully to the starting point. (Repeat the movement for a predetermined number of reps.)

Practice this exercise with just your own bodyweight to begin with. As the exercise becomes easier, with the help of a spotter, add resistance in the form of barbell plates by laying them on your upper thighs.
Pro Tip: Elevate the foot placement 6 to 12 inches higher than the hands.

Triceps (Long head)
Atomic triceps blaster pushup: Begin this exercise with your body at the starting point shown in the line drawing. Commence from an "elbow stand" in which the entire forearms as well as the hands (palms flat and spread approximately 4 inches apart) are resting on the floor directly under your face. With your torso in rigid and sloping position and your feet on a raised surface of a flat exercise bench or wooden box, inhale deeply and hold.

Slowly straighten your arms, as in a regular pushup, until the elbows are completely locked out and straight. Expel the air from your lungs prior to locking out the elbows. Lower yourself again to the elbow stand position, inhaling air while doing so. When you utilize

Harry Dodich

this unusual pushup movement, you will be lifting only about 80 percent the bodyweight that you would do in a regular floor-dipping style. No matter though, the stress load in the atomic triceps blaster is much greater on the triceps than on the pecs, and it is much more conducive to the development of huge horseshoe triceps.

Forearms (Flexor, belly)
Barbell wrist curls (palms up): Begin by sitting on the declined end of a propped up flat exercise bench. Adjust yourself so that your forearms only (not triceps) rest on the padded surface and the back of your hands are hanging over the padding at its lowest point. The slope of the inclined surface before you need not be too acute, 20 or 30 degrees is ample. Slightly press inwards on your upper arms with the inside of your knees to hold them in place. Now you're ready to begin.

Take a four to six inch thumbless false grip (palms upwards) on your barbell. Lean forward with your upper torso until the angle between the biceps and forearm flexors is less than 90 degrees. Maintain this position as you do full-movement wrist curls. This exercise can be done in a double-drop sequence where 20 full-movement wrist curls are done as heavy as possible.

Immediately reduce the poundage by 50 percent and, without hesitation, do 10 reps more letting the bar roll down to the end of the fingertips each time. Then do 10 more contin-uous reps of the full-movement wrist curl while keeping the barbell firmly in the palm of the hand (without unrolling to the fingertips).
Pro Tip: Be sure that you have plenty of chalk on your hands, and use some Armoflex for added thickness to the gripping area of the bar. This is sure to help you develop mighty forearms and a killer crunch grip.

Forearms (Extensors)
Reverse-grip EZ-bar curls: This exercise can be done while standing or on a preacher bench. If you go with the preacher bench, the top edge should be stationed three inches below your pec line.
Pro Tip: Lean back from the bench as you lower the weight. This will cause a tremendous stretch on the brachialis and forearms.

Larry Scott says that, to add impressive size to this area of the forearm, the exercise should be performed on a curling machine with only the middle 3/5 of the movement used. His procedure for training the forearms using the two listed exercises would be to do the barbell wrist curl in a single-weight drop fashion (as described), and upon completion immediately do the reverse-grip EZ-bar curl (in the middle 3/5 range of the movement) in a double-weight drop technique – by doing 10 reps, drop the poundage 10 pounds, do 10 more reps, drop 10 more pounds, then do 10 final reps. This is a combined five sets of two exercises – one series. Larry will do three to five series.

No matter how good the above exercises and techniques seem to be working for you, it is always a good idea to include plenty of variety in your forearm training (or any other muscle group for that matter). By doing so you will eliminate the onset of accumulated residual injury and overtraining of the central nervous system. Within the forearm program, for example, a simple change of an exercise – such as substituting the wooden dowel wrist-roller exercise in place of the barbell wrist curl – can add to your forearm gain factor. It's just a matter of supersetting reverse-grip EZ-bar curls and the wrist roller (palms upward). The wooden dowel should be 8 to 10 inches in length and 1-1/2 to 1-3/4 inches in diameter. Attach 30 to 40 inches of 1/4-inch rope and enough weight to allow you to wind it all the way up and down three times per set.

No physique is quite complete without rippling forearms, as displayed here by Lee Priest.

Econo-Time Secondary Phase

Back (Trapezius)
Kelso barbell shrugs

Thighs (Adductors, inner)
45-degree leg press (wide foot placement)

Calves (Tibialis, shin)
Standing toe pullbacks: A variation to this exercise would be to sit lengthwise on a flat bench, heels extending off the end slightly, while using a DARD (now renamed the "Dorsi-Flex") device for developing the tibialis dorsiflexor shin muscles. Dards are available from J.A. Fitness/DARD, Box 576, Itasca, IL 60143 (800) 223-5503. The price is approximately $39.95 plus $4.95 P&H.

Chest (Upper pec minor)
Barbell bench press to neck. Use a Smith machine if possible.

Abdominals (Lower rectus)
Hanging vertical crunches or lying incline leg raises.

Primary Phase

Workout No. 3
**Thighs (Quads, vastus medialis
or inner teardrop muscle over knee)**
Machine hack slide squats (hips-off style): The ideal foot position in this exercise is to have the heels touching and the rest of the foot rotated out laterally at 45 degrees (V-shape).

There are two ways of doing this movement on the hack machine. You can either descend in the negative phase with your hips off the sliding platform and on it during the positive contraction phase, or you can keep the hips in contact with the padding during the negative stretch contraction and driving you hips forward (hips off) during the positive contraction phase.

Pro Tip: When doing the hacks on a machine, place your feet low on the foot plate, well back under the body, supporting yourself on the balls of your feet (heels touching, toes-out position). Keep your back flat against the sliding platform and your shoulders and head forward looking downward.

A guideline to knowing if your stance is correct is to bottom out on the movement. If you can press your heels into your glutes, and the distance between your knees is approximately 20 inches, your tracking pattern is technically correct. Remember that this is only a guideline. The reps are to be performed in non-lockout style. Never bottom or top out fully. This way the thighs are under constant tension. Above all, support yourself on the balls of your feet throughout each and every phase of the rep.

We have even observed some of the pros doing a form of sissy hack squat by keeping their hips off the sliding platform during both the descent and ascent phases while on the balls of their feet in non-lockout style.

Pro Tip: Use a weight which is just one-fourth of

Bruce Patterson enjoys the fruit of his labors.

Start

Shawn Ray

Finish

a max single effort in the barbell back squat. Do sissy hacks with this weight to positive (+) and negative (–) failure. Do just one all-out blowtorch set till you can't even budge the weight an inch!

Thighs (Quads)

Roman chair squats or barbell front squats.

Thighs (Hamstrings, leg biceps)

Hanging dumbell leg curls: This exercise is discussed in Chapter Twelve.

Calves (Gastrocnemius)

Standing calf machine heel raises: If you have a movable calf block, position it 16 inches back from the machine so that your body is angled forward at 80 degrees or so. You will experience a tremendous negative stretch and positive phase contraction when doing them at this angle. For gastro peak you may do donkey calf raises.

119

Calves (Soleus)

Seated heel raises: Be sure that your lower leg and thigh form a 90-degree angle. This will essentially immobilize the gastrocnemius, thereby leaving all the flexion of the ankle to the soleus. There is a rationale in doing exercises for the soleus last in the calf program.

The gastro muscles fatigue more quickly than the soleus. Therefore, it is usually best to do gastro exercises prior to soleus movements.

Abdominals (Lower)
Hanging knee-ups.

Abdominals (Upper)
Gironda concemetric double-up crunches.

GIRONDA PRONE-DUMBELL ROWING

Utilizing the special elbow "tracking pattern" as described in text.

120

Econo-Time Secondary Phase

Back (Outer lat aspect)

T-bar rowing or Prone barbell rowing on a high bench. For the latter, place two sturdy benches or wooden boxes which measure 18 to 24 inches in height parallel to each other, 26 inches apart. Position a barbell on the floor (horizontally) midway between the two boxes. Then put a flat exercise bench atop the two boxes. Make sure that the combined structure is both level and safe. Lay lengthwise in a facedown position on the padded bench surface. Reach down and grasp the bar with either an overhand or, if you wish, an underhand grip.

You have a choice of handspacings which consists of narrow (16 inches), medium (26 inches) or ultra-wide (36 inches). When using the medium handspacing your arms should be hanging down directly in alignment with your shoulders (or at right angles to your body, and the forearms vertically above the bar). The barbell should be clear of the floor during your rep cycle. This will be dictated by the height of the box and bench combination and, of course, the diameter plate size used on the long bar. Therefore, you must adjust until it is the right height for you.

Keeping your wrists straight, pull the barbell up to the underside of the bench and to midpoint of the abs. Keep your elbows close to your sides at the top of the peak contraction. This elbow technique really works well with the underhand (curl) grip. As the barbell touches the underside of the bench, hold for a short count of three, then **slowly** lower the bar to the starting point and repeat. The upper torso and legs should not assist the complete range of movement in any way. The performance of this exercise must be confined to lat and arm motion only and will prove useless otherwise.

Vince Gironda has his own unique version of this exercise. He holds a pair of heavy dumbells, not a barbell, in his hands with his arms hanging straight down and his knuckles forward. From this position he pulls the dumbells up high while flaring his elbows out at 90 degrees, right angle, to his body. As the upper arms and elbows align with the shoulder joints (forearms form right angles to the upper arms), Vince lifts his head and legs to a crescent position off the bench surface (only

Ron Love, a former Detroit police officer.

his stomach remains in contact with the bench) and arches his back. His shoulder blades are squeezed back together and down.

He holds this position for a slow count of two. Then, while still holding the dumbells at the top of the peak contraction of the movement, he moves his upper arms back alongside his body and holds this second position for another count of two. He then returns the dumbells to the starting point and repeats. Sometimes he will lay the dumbells on the floor after each rep momentarily, just to relax the hands.

Pro Tip: Use a cambered bench press bar (cambered bend to be angled towards the floor) for a greater range of movement. Don't forget to apply a heavy coat of chalk on your hands prior to doing this and other rowing variations.

Chest (Upper pec, minor)

Incline (30 to 40 degrees) dumbell flyes: The generally accepted tracking pattern on this exercise is to start with the dumbells held at arms' length above the chest. With wrists locked in a palms-facing (neutral) position, neither extended backward or flexed forward, the dumbells are lowered and raised in an arc. Rather than bringing the dumbells in an arc to a point arms' length above the chest with the wrists locked in a neutral position (the usual style), it would be much better to bring the dumbells together **over the forehead** at the completion of the positive contraction phase. At the same time as you do this, extend the wrists backward and touch all four plates of the dumbells together while mentally – as well as physically – squeezing and contracting your pecs for all they are worth.

The two-part action of bringing the dumbells together over the forehead and extending the wrists backward will give you an unbelievable peak contraction, especially on the inner aspect of the pecs. From here the wrists can be locked in a neutral position as the next rep is begun. Now, rather than keeping the wrists locked straight – especially as you near completion of the negative contraction phase – at the bottom of the movement, again extend the wrists backward. This will really ensure an extra stretch in the lateral aspect of the pecs. Generally, the wrists should be locked in the neutral position during the middle 3/5 of the incline dumbell flyes.

Pro Tip: This exercise can also be done at a 10-degree angled incline. The forearms can be rotated (don't confuse this with the wrist extension and flexion technique just discussed) from the conventional heels of the hand facing downwards to a pronation or palms facing downward at the bottom of the stretch contraction phase. Lee Labrada does them in this manner from time to time. Not only does it stimulate the lateral aspect of the pecs, but it serves as a means to lessen rotator cuff trauma.

There is one other pro tip that we want to share with you regarding the tracking patterns of the flye variations when using either dumbells or pulley cables. Never "press" the

Lee Labrada – the Frank Zane of the '90s.

dumbells or cables upwards. Pull them together by thinking intra-muscular tension into the pecs. One of the best ways to describe this movement is as follows: While using a steel spring or rubber strand expanders (often called chest expanders), begin by lying lengthwise on your back on a flat exercise bench. Grasp the handles of the expanders at arms' length directly above your chest. Unlock the elbow joints just slightly. Pull the arms out horizontally till they are in alignment with the shoulder joints (hands about 24 inches apart). From this position, **slowly,** while resisting the pull of the strand expanders, allow the arms to return to their original starting point over the chest.

If you can grasp the concept of how this exercise is done then you will have no problem understanding our previous instruction to **pull** the dumbells or pulley cables together, and not press them when doing the flye or any of its variations.

Delts (Lateral)

Single-dumbell leaning incline lateral raise: Lay on your left side on a standing 45-degree incline bench or sit leaning on the seat back of an adjustable dual exercise bench. With a dumbell in your right hand (remembering to keep the little finger side of the hand firmly against the inner face plate of the dumbell) raise it slowly outwards from your side to approximately an eye-level (outstretched) position. Lower and repeat the entire sequence for a predetermined number of reps. Reversing your body position, switch the dumbell to your other hand and work your left lateral aspect of the deltoid in the same manner.

Standing barbell press overhead: This exercise is begun in one of two ways. The first way is to clean the barbell from the floor before the pressing movement is begun. Suffice it to say we do not have the scope and space necessary to list in detail all the intricate tracking patterns necessary for pulling or cleaning a barbell to the shoulders. We can, however, direct those of you purists who would like to master this outdated yet classical movement to an article which appeared in 18 installments in Bob Hoffman's *Strength & Health* magazine. The series was titled "The ABCs of Weightlifting" by Tommy T. Kono and was published from February of 1969 to December 1972.

FLICK-STYLE GRIP

Wrist is extended back prior to pressing thrust (illustration A).

As pressing thrust begins, wrist is straightened (shaded arm – B).

At sticking point wrist is once again extended back (per illustration A), and to the arms-locked position.

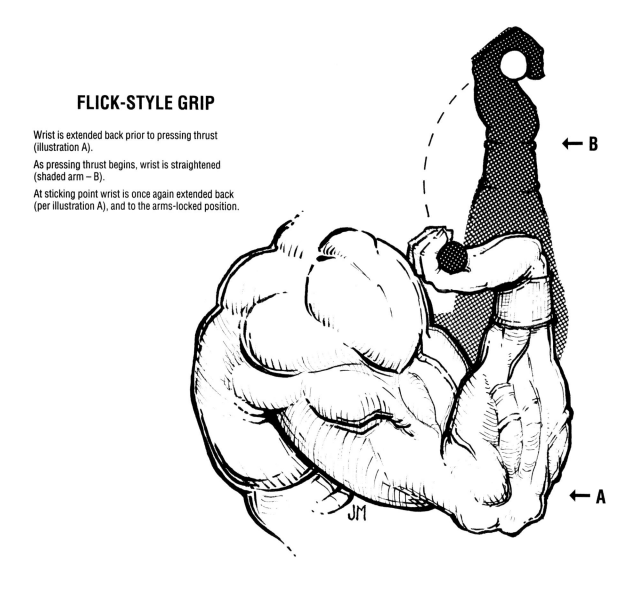

← B

← A

The second and more conventional way to begin the exercise is to take the barbell off a set of adjustable squat racks before pressing it. The racks should be positioned at approximately two inches below shoulder height. *We remember former IFBB Mr. World Chuck Sipes mentioning that by doing the press off a squat rack he could devote more effort to the actual press movement itself, instead of having to clean or pull the barbell from the floor.*

To initiate this process, begin by standing in front of a barbell that is positioned at the correct weight for you on the squat rack. Your feet should be spaced about 16 inches or so apart (shoulder width), and parallel to each other. This stance will give a greater degree of

fore and aft balance. Think of the center of your bodyweight as being between the middle of the heel bone and between the ball of the foot and the first joint of the big toe. This is the area you want the bar to be directly above when it is being pressed vertically overhead. *Pro Tip:* Center your balance on the balls of your feet and, in effect, grip the floor with your toes as you press.

Take an approximate shoulder-width hand-spacing on the bar, with a false or thumbless grip. Dip slightly under the bar and let it come to rest solidly on your frontal deltoids, clavicle and sternum junction. Come to an upright position. Take one step back from the squat rack if necessary so that you will have an unobstructed area for overhead pressing. Lock your knees.

Commence pressing with a downward, and inward angle or inclination to the forearms and elbows. If this position has been assumed correctly, the back of the upper arms (triceps) and elbows will be supported on the outer aspect of the lats. The wrists should be extended backward as far as your flexibility will allow. Hold the bar away from the palm of the hands more into the fingers. Without any hip or leg momentum begin the pressing thrust with all the might and power you can channel from your triceps and deltoids. As you do, bend or flex your wrists forward so that the hands (clenched-fist position) are now almost vertical (in line with the forearms) as the bar is being pressed vertically in front of your face. Remember to keep your elbows out to the sides but not to an exaggerated degree, your back flat but with a distinct curve to the lower spine, and your shoulders and hips lined up with your back when viewed from the side.

Don't allow the body to lean backward away from the bar. This will not only move the delts away from the gravitational line of the bar, but can cause the upper back to hyperextend. Extending the neck and head back to a point where you are looking up at the bar can cause this to happen also.

Keep the body balance on the balls of your feet and not centered over the heels. While doing this you must also keep your feet flat on the floor. Do not raise your heels or toes. Balance can also be disturbed by bending the head forward too much and looking down. You should be looking straight ahead with your chin parallel to the floor. A sticking point or dead space generally occurs during the press, especially on the latter reps of a heavy set.

As the bar arrives at this sticking point you must do two things. First, extend the hand back by wrist action and allow the bar to roll from the palm of the hands back again into the finger position you started your initial rep with. This backward momentum of the bar will help keep the weight moving.

The second action is to thrust your hips forward while raising your chest. Be sure to strongly tense your midsection while thrusting the hips and raising the chest. It helps to stabilize the spine. Wedging or bowing into the

Lee Priest in the thick of it.

weight when it is beginning to slow down will effectively shorten or lower you physically so that the bar can bypass the sticking point. As the bar bypasses this area, bend or flex your wrists forward once again so that your hands are in line with the forearms for the rest of the rep.

As you probably know, the press overhead is primarily a deltoid developer from its starting point on the clavicle/sternum junction to where the upper arms align with the shoulder joints. From then onward the triceps, part of the trapezius, and the serratus magnus take the weight to arms' length overhead. With this firmly in mind, powerfully extend your arms to a full vertical locked-out position overhead.
Pro Tip: Hold the lockout position for a slow count of six while you isometrically contract those coconut delts for all they are worth. Now slowly lower the bar back down to the starting point.

125

Triceps (Long head)
Twin-pedestal triceps pulley extension ("V" handle): This is a Larry Scott favorite and is discussed in vivid detail in his *Hidden Secrets* video.

Triceps (Lateral, outer head)
One-dumbell seated triceps extension.

Forearms (Wrist flexors)
Barbell behind-the-neck wrist curls

Forearms (Finger flexors)
Thick bar one-handed deadlifts or super grip machine.

This concludes three-day rotational total-body workout.

As you may have noticed within the three Primary First Phase workouts, there is no mention of the number of sets and reps required for each exercise. This was not an oversight on our part. In fact, we are now going to talk about the science of sets and reps as it relates to both the pro and the natural anabolic steroid-free bodybuilder when using the three-day rotational total-body workout.

Society demands that most bodybuilders pay rent, buy food, etc. Meeting these demands requires you earn a living, perhaps while raising a family and going to college part-time. The time factor has, therefore, become master rather than servant. Lack of time seems to be the one problem all of us share these days. We say we don't have enough time for anything, let alone a regular workout program. Lack of time has become one of the favorite excuses for procrastination, for missing workouts, or for finally dropping bodybuilding completely. Many of those who do have some free leisure time can't see themselves devoting two or three hours of their lives to the type of high-volume workouts that we have talked about in this book. To them, it's a splurging of too much time on a single activity.

While it's true that a few fortunate pro bodybuilders earn their living from the sport, and have ample training time, there are others who have to hold down full-time jobs outside the sport. Like the rest of us, these body-

"Peerless Paul" Dillett struts his stuff.

Milos Sarcev

and 30 sets per muscle group could not be accommodated in the 75 to 90-minute time frame set forth in the total-body workout concept of training. The pro, therefore, reduces the number of sets that he or she was previously doing. They will now train each major muscle group with only 12 to 15 sets at most, and a mere 8 to 10 sets on the minor ones. He or she will generally use one main strength-building exercise for a minor muscle group, or two for a major one, doing 4 to 5 sets each using **"power reps."** The muscle group will then be finished off with one or two isolationary, shaping exercises for two or three sets (depending on if it is a minor or major muscle group) of "maxi-pump reps." With regard to further mentioning the power and maxi-pump reps, there is an approximate correlation between the load factor of the barbell or dumbells and the number of reps performed within a given set. The following chart of percentage of maximum repetition will be most helpful for determining what constitutes a power rep and/or maxi-pump rep set in the structured training programs throughout this research manual. This chart is one of the most definite ways to answer the question regarding proper intensity levels of what is considered to be heavy, medium and light training poundages. It lists a particular range of "reps to percentage of max factors" that takes into account differences of one's fast to slow-twitch muscle fiber ratios.

PERCENTAGE OF MAX REP CHART

NUMBER OF REPS	PERCENTAGE OF MAXIMUM
POWER REPS (HEAVY)	
1	100
2 - 3	99 - 90
4 - 6	89 - 80
MAXI-PUMP REPS (MEDIUM)	
7 - 10	79 - 70
11 - 15	69 - 60
16 - 20	59 - 50
(LIGHT)	
21 - 30	49 - 40
31 PLUS	39 - 30

builders feel cramped for gym time and always yearn wistfully for more of it. Yet there is a rather simple solution to all these complaints. When we mentioned to you that the pro bodybuilder reduced his anabolic volume of training drastically from the previous workouts of 20 to 30 sets per muscle group, we were not exaggerating one bit. It is very obvious that 20

Achim Albrecht, Paul Dillett and Chris Cormier trying to appear relaxed before the judges.

NOTE: *There is nothing magical about the transition points of power and maxi-pump rep ranges. These are general guidelines only! Some bodybuilders may find their best strength and muscle-mass gains occur by performing sets in a three to six rep range, while other bodybuilders must do four to eight reps before there is a transition from power to maxi-pump effect. Unique individual variances account for this.*

When doing power reps be sure to do them **explosively** *to develop the fast-twitch muscle fibers maximally. When training in the maxi-pump rep range perform your reps* **slowly** *as the preferred method to induce a high level of optimum tension. This will develop the slow-twitch fibers to their maximum potential.*

Those who read our book **Raw Muscle!** *may have noticed that the percentage of maximum repetitions table on page 199 in that publication varies somewhat from the chart listed above. There is a good reason for this. The repetition ranges, and corresponding percentages of "max" listed above, more accurately reflect an expanded ratio of training reps to percentage of "max" when doing multiple sets of an exercise, when a muscle is reaching higher fatigue levels.*

While the genetic-superior pro bodybuilder has greatly reduced his high-volume training sets for the various muscle groups, we would not suggest that the natural anabolic steroid-free bodybuilder attempt even this modified reduction of high-volume training sets. To do so would invite a burn-off or lowering of blood sugar energy reserve in the body during the workout in progress.

Milos Sarcev in a pensive mood.

When this happens the body reacts by shutting down vital insulin production, which is the primary source for spiking amino acids into the muscle cell. Also, after a few high-volume workouts of this nature, you will start working out on nerve energy, which is not what you want to be doing if you are in any way serious about strength and muscle growth gains. The natural bodybuider who wants to develop a three-point combination of size, power and muscularity (while producing that much sought after "muscle pump") we are going to suggest that you train each major muscle group with 8 to 10 sets and 5 to 7 sets for the major muscle groups. It is important to structure the appropriate training technique(s) to the corresponding sets, as it relates to a particular muscle group.

When training a major muscle group within the confines of the primary first phase of a total bodyblast workout, consider employing the following two-part surefire **Muscle Bulk and Cuts (= Muscle Density) Training System:**

Part One
Choose two general muscle mass and power-producing exercises and perform four sets of six power reps of each one. After completing the two exercises for a subtotal of 8 sets, finish off the major muscle group by doing one shape-training exercise for two sets of ten maxi-pump reps. On a major muscle group like the back, for example, you might opt to go with the wide grip (collar to collar) barbell bent-over rowing – this movement will also target the rear delts – and behind-the-neck pulldowns, using a rather narrow (25 inches apart) hand placement on a pro lat bar, one which is designed to provide a parallel grip. These are two of the best muscle mass producers for sure. The shape-training exercise selected could very well be the barbell stiff-arm pullover performed on an incline situp bench (head lower than feet). Two minute rest-pauses are taken between each of the ten sets performed. *Pro Tip:* The program described can also be modified to accommodate a minor muscle group. Simply use only one general muscle mass and power exercise (rather than two) and

Just another day in the life of Serge Nubret, who always manages to look good.

do four sets of six power reps. Finish bombing the muscle as described in the major muscle group example above.

Part Two

Another peak-efficiency training strategy is to use the "two-and-one" system which was developed and popularized by former Jr. Mr. America Harry Smith many years ago. We'll use the pecs as an example of how this system works for a major muscle group.

Choose a power pressing movement such as the 30 to 40-degree incline dumbell press. The dumbells are selected not only for the muscle density they will create in the upper clavicular pec region, but also for the bilateral function they offer, meaning that each dumbell offers an independent source of resistance. Perform two sets of four to six power reps in this heavy mass-producing exercise. Rest one minute between each of these sets. Immediately following the second set (no rest whatsoever) do one set of ten maxi-pump reps in a shape-training exercise such as the Vince Gironda V-bar dips. This completes one cycle. Do a second cycle. Continue the two-and-one system by doing a third and final cycle, only on this cycle substitute the wide-grip barbell bench press to the neck (on a flat bench) in place of the incline dumbell press. Stay with the V-bar dips for the finishing off movement. *Pro Tip:* A minor muscle group such as the biceps requires only two cycles of the two-and-one system. On this muscle group you could go with the two-hands strict barbell curl and the standing one-arm barbell concentration curl. Another pro tip is to use the dual-tempo, explosive rhythmic principle. Be e-x-p-l-o-s-i-v-e on the maxi-pump reps. The two-and-one system of training (be it for a major or a minor muscle group) produces the following effects:

Use varying grips to attack different heads of the biceps, as demonstrated by Mike Francois.

Start

Finish

Start

1. Strength, as it permits heavy poundages to be used.
2. Faster training.
3. A massive blood-choked pump. Once you start, you will likely discover many variations of the two-and-one system for yourself.

Another way that a bodybuilder could go to pursue muscle, bulk and cuts would be to use a combination of sets and reps on the first exercise for a major muscle group which will work both the fast and slow-twitch muscle fibers equally well. Warm up with a light poundage of perhaps 60 percent of your un-fatigued current one-rep max for six to eight reps. After a rest-pause, begin your initial sets with fast muscle explosive power reps (strict, noncheating) gradually tapering off to some super slow sets using maxi-pump reps. The following **inverted pyramid** illustrates this:

Set No. 1 – 2 reps (plus one or two forced reps)
Set 2 – 4 reps
Set 3 – 5 reps
Set 4 – 6 reps
(Sets one to four are done explosively and develop fast-twitch muscle fibers.)
Set 5 – 7 reps
Set 6 – 8 reps
Set 7 – 10 reps
Set 8 – 12 reps
Set 9 – 15 reps
(Sets five to nine are to be performed super slow and will develop the slow-twitch muscle fibers.

Decrease the poundage on each proceeding set just enough to meet the new rep(s) demand. You are at nine sets here for a major muscle group. There are two or three considerations you might now think about.

You can decrease the poundage for a final 10th set, which will allow you to do a burning pump set of 20 to 30 reps, or you could conclude your workout at 9 sets and go on to another muscle group. A second consideration would be to finish up the 9th set and go to a totally different exercise (perhaps a muscle-specific or isolationary one) and do one set of 20 to 30 reps.

Lee Priest goes for the ultimate peaked biceps.   *Finish*

Alq Gurley performs hammer curls.
Start

Finish

Another way to create a dual effect of training the fast and slow-twitch muscle fibers equally for major muscle group development is as follows:

Set 1 – 6 power reps
Set 2 – 6 power reps
Set 3 – 6 power reps
Set 4 – 6 power reps
Set 5 – 7 maxi-pump reps
Set 6 – 8 maxi-pump reps
Set 7 – 10 maxi-pump reps
Set 8 – 12 maxi-pump reps

Within the structure of the first four explosive, fast-twitch sets, be sure that the poundages remain within the recommended 80 to 90 percent of your current unfatigued one-rep maximum. (Another method is to use Ted Arcidi's graduated six-rep scheme mentioned in Chapter Thirteen.)

Decrease the poundage on each of the proceeding five, six, seven and eight super-slow sets again, as mentioned before, just enough to meet the new rep demand.

Regarding minor muscle groups, you can do a muscle mass building movement and a

power rep selection on the first exercise, and on a second and third assigned exercise you can use a shape-training movement where a muscle-specific or isolationary movement (accompanied with a maxi-pump rep selection) is performed.

For the first exercise you could utilize the four sets from either of the previously listed charts and finish off with a muscle-specific exercise for one or two sets of say 20 maxi-pump reps.

The information we have provided so far is the basis for training a muscle group within the primary first phase structure of the workout. To really turn up the intensity of your training you can incorporate many of the forthcoming **11 Training Past the Burn** bodybuilding techniques and **Primordial Muscle Shock Strategies,** for a nice blend of muscle mass building and shape training for either a major or a minor muscle group.

It is always a good idea to be sure that the bodybuilding techniques and strategies you decide to use stay within the generally recommended guidelines of eight or ten sets for the major muscle groups and five or seven for the

Christa Bauch showing fine form.

Start

Finish

minor ones. Instinctive training knowledge and common sense must be your companion here. Always try to achieve the minimum number of sets required but, on the other hand, if you perform one or at the most two sets beyond the maximum number suggested (ten for a major and seven for a minor muscle group) when structuring your mix of training techniques and strategies for a selected muscle group, it is just not that critical if it means *not* doing the program as opposed to doing it.

A couple of detailed examples of what we are talking about here are illustrated as follows: Let's assume that you have chosen to work a minor muscle group, such as the biceps. The exercises and repetition selections are the standing barbell curl (six reps), dumbell hammer curl (eight reps) and the one-dumbell concentration curl (ten reps).

Perform one set after the other of each exercise in the order listed, in rapid succession. When you have done each of them once – this will be considered one group set – take a

minimum rest and repeat for two more group set sequences. A quick calculation indicates that you have done a total of nine sets for the minor biceps muscle group rather than the recommended seven. This is quite all right, as you have gone beyond your maximum by only two sets. On the other hand, going beyond the suggested 9 sets for a minor muscle group (or beyond 12 for a major one) can be wrongly abused and here's how: Doing so literally deprives the muscles from ultimate growth potential. A good example of this is the implementation (if not modified) of the **Series Training Principle** which was developed by Steve Davis, a former superstar IFBB Mr. World and inventor of the "new breed" bodybuilding concept. Series training represents separate elements of a bodybuilding training protocol. These elements are: the exercises, number of sets, number of reps, limited rest-pauses (between each set) and frequency of workouts. Here is an encapsulated commentary on how Steve Davis suggests using series training.

• Select two exercises for each muscle group. The first exercise is usually a strength-and-power-type exercise, with a second one geared more toward shape training.

• After performing one light warmup set of an exercise, increase the poundage to a level of progressive overload which will allow you to complete six sets of the exercise for the prescribed number of reps.

• Steve Davis suggests a repetition scheme of eight reps for the arms, delts, chest and back, and reps of 15 per set for the calves, spinae erectors, quadriceps and hamstrings.

• Limited rest-pauses between each and every set should be between 30 and 45 seconds for maximum muscle mass increase, and 15 seconds for increasing muscularity.

• Each and every muscle group is trained twice per week in the manner described. To summarize: When series training, a bodybuilder is to do six sets of each of the two exercises for a particular muscle group with the same weight. Reps used are those unique unto each of the selected exercises. Use the same limited rest-pauses between sets, which will be determined by whether you are training for **muscle mass** increase or for **muscularity.**

Upon completion of the six-set series for a select muscle group, rest three minutes before beginning the six-set series for the second and final exercise. Since the number of exercises, sets, reps and rest intervals between sets remains constant, you should vary the poundages used by adding weight to a given exercise each week to accommodate your ever-increasing strength levels. It may only be two-and-a-half-pound paired plates on certain power-type exercises, or as little as one-and-a-quarter-pound plates on the shape-training exercises. In fact, you will notice that it will vary a bit from week to week. In any case, it should never exceed five to ten pounds, because doing so will almost always invite a case of severe overtraining.

The **series training principle** can be implemented into the total body workout concept, primary phase of training, but with

Alq Gurley performs concentration curls.

Start

Finish

135

the following modifications as it applies to the natural bodybuilder. To begin with, series training does not make any distinction between major and minor muscle groupings. To perform two exercises for six sets each for a minor muscle group would be extending maximum muscle gain theory beyond its limits of seven and, to the most, nine sets. Therefore, to use series training effectively in the primary phase of a workout for a minor muscle group do a six-set series of eight reps each with one strength and power exercise, resting 30 to 45 seconds between sets for maximum muscle mass. When the rotation for primary phase workout comes up again for a minor muscle group (which has already been worked in the manner just described) go with a **six-set series** of 15 reps each with a shape-training exercise, resting only 15 seconds between sets for increased muscularity.

Series training adapts very well to the training structure of the major muscle groups in that a selection of two exercises can be utilized for one **six-set series** of each and is within the limits of the maximum muscle gain theory of eight to ten and, at the most, 12 sets.

There are three dynamite ways in which a bodybuilder can utilize the six-set series training.

One – Select two strength-and-power exercises for a major muscle group. Perform one six-set series of eight reps each, resting 30 to 45 seconds between sets and three minutes between series for maximum muscle mass gains.

Two – Choose two shape-training exercises and perform one six-set series of 15 maxi-pump reps each. Rest 15 seconds between each of the six sets in a series and three minutes between each series for increasing muscularity.

Dave Fisher isolating the frontal thighs the old-fashioned way. *Finish*

Start

Three – A favorite of many top bodybuilders is a one-to-one six-set series where the first exercise for a major muscle group is of the strength and power type. (Follow the instruction given in number one above with regard to reps and limited rest pauses.)

The second exercise should accent shape training and follow the reps and limited rest pauses set forth in number two above. The rep schemes suggested by Steve Davis, as applied to the series training principle, are not "holy" numbers. One of the most impacting rep combinations is the **6/12** where six power reps are used in a six-set series power-type exercise, and 12 maxi-pump reps in a six-set series for a shape training or muscle specific exercise. The percentage of max rep chart in Chapter Nine of this book will be most helpful when choosing a particular fixed rep mode.

There is some important information that you should be aware of regarding the time factor variables as applied to the successful completion of series training.

The rest pauses between sets are to be accurately controlled. If, for example, you choose to rest 30 seconds between sets when training for maximum muscle mass, don't rest 30 then 35 and 45 seconds on consecutive sets. Doing so will reduce the demands on your muscles. Some bodybuilders who use series training will employ a decreasing time factor variable. When training for maximum muscle mass increase, they will rest exactly 45 seconds between each of the six sets.

The rest pauses will be reduced by an additional five seconds only after each workout of six sets of the suggested reps with fixed poundage has been completed. When the rest-pauses are down to 30 seconds between sets, a poundage increase of up to five pounds for most upper-body exercises and from five to ten pounds for the back and legs is required. The time factor is then increased to 45 seconds and the sequence, as described, begins once again.

For increasing muscularity the rest pauses begin at 30 seconds and decrease by five-second time intervals down to a minimum of 15 seconds for each and every set – but only if the six sets of required reps can be completed successfully.

Depending upon your immediate muscle

Serge Nubret, the ageless French champion, has built one of the most proportionate physiques of the century. Such physical beauty is timeless.

size and strength requirements, there are other training strategy considerations that you must take into account. It is a good idea to rotate the emphasis of your exercises and ratio of sets and reps for a muscle group every few work-outs. For example: In the primary phase of

Kelso shrug. You might well perform this exercise for four to six sets, and then finish off with one exercise each for the lats and erectors for one or two sets each. For those bodybuilders who are not familiar with the Kelso shrug, here is a brief description of how it should be performed. Paul Kelso, the inventor of this exercise, advises the bodybuilder to first assume a position for the barbell bent-over rowing motion. Using a barbell poundage which will allow you to perform eight to ten reps per set – in a full range of movement – for maximum muscle contraction of the trapezius. Reach down and grasp the bar with a pronated or overhand grip. Space the hands approximately eight to ten inches apart. Extend the arms so that there is absolutely no bend in the elbows. Using the contractile strength of the traps, shrug the weight up toward the chest, aiming the direction toward the middle traps. The idea here is to concentrate on the middle of the back where the lower traps insert, by pulling the shoulder blades (or scapula) together in a downward muscle-squeezing

Rich Gaspari in a national weather service satellite photo.

Ron Love

workout number one the emphasis we put on the back training was for the lats – teres major/minor and the spinal erectors. There was no attention given to the traps during this workout, so the next time you bomb and blitz the back in a primary phase of a total-body workout, your first exercise of choice might well be an exercise for the traps, such as the

Sonny Schmidt, Shawn Ray and Lee Labrada. This is no police lineup...unless they are looking for Mr. Olympia.

motion, not forward toward the ear. Slowly lower the bar back to the starting position and begin your next rep.

This highly muscle-stimulating trap exercise is just one of the variations in the Kelso shrug system. Designed expressly for traps, lats and pecs, this system has the capability of adding as much as 55 pounds onto a bodybuilder's deadlift and 20 pounds onto the bench press in less than 90 days. The book *The Kelso Shrug System* (ISBN-0934-523-38-X) can be purchased by sending $9.95 plus $2.00 S&H to: Middle Coast Publishing, DEPT. K-W, P.O. Box 2522, Iowa City, Iowa 52244.

So far we have explained to you the general way in which champion bodybuilders may reduce their number of previous high-volume sets (20 to 30 per muscle group, etc.) and we have shown how to basically modify the training concept of reduced-volume training to help in your quest for bodybuilding superiority.

We could leave it at that and let you try to figure out how to continue down the road to bodybuilding success; however, we have never done this in any of our previous bodybuiding instructional books and we have no intention of starting now. A champion bodybuilder is always looking for new and exciting ways to challenge his muscles on to maximum gains in mega-muscle mass, and awesome bone-crushing strength.

What we want to do now is show you eleven **training-past-the-burn techniques** (called requisite intensity) that many pros use to supercharge the naturally occurring growth hormone levels in their bodies that will increase the muscle-gain factor. These advanced bodybuilding techniques are to be used in the total-body workout during the primary phase of training.

Few men in their 20s ever look as good as Serge Nubret does in his 50s.

Overview of The Three-Day Rotational Total-Body Workout

Primary Phase – Workout No. 1
Back:
Wide-grip front pullups
Seated horizontal long-pull cable rows or
Barbell bent-over rows
Stiff-legged deadlifts on a bench or
Prone hyperextensions.
Pectorals:
Incline (30 to 40-degree) dumbell presses
Kneeling cable crossovers
V-shaped parallel-bar dips

Econo-Time Secondary Phase
Thighs:
Leg extensions on machine or
Hip-belt squats
Calves: One-legged heel raises
Deltoids: Parrillo delt rows
Triceps:
Reverse-grip barbell bench presses
Biceps:
Barbell or
Dumbell Scott curls
Forearms:
Barbell or dumbell palms-down wrist curls
Abdominals:
Butterfly crunches (one-quarter crunches)

Primary Phase – Workout No. 2
Delts:
Seated barbell presses behind neck
Barbell upright rows
90-degree bent-over dumbell lateral raises or
Three-way dynamic delt lateral raises
Biceps:
Supinated dumbell incline
45 to 50-degree curls
One-dumbell concentration curls
Triceps:
Three-way diametric French presses or
Reverse triceps bench dips
Triceps blaster pushups
Forearms:
Barbell wrist curls (palms up)
Reverse-grip EZ-bar curls

Econo-Time Secondary Phase
Back:
Kelso barbell shrugs
Thighs:
45-degree leg presses
(wide foot placement of 18 to 24 inches)
Calves:
Standing toe pullbacks
Chest:
Barbell bench presses to neck (using Smith
machine if possible)
Abdominals:
Hanging vertical crunches or
Lying incline leg raises

Primary Phase – Workout No. 3
Thighs:
"Hips-off-machine" hack squats
Roman chair squats or
Barbell front squats
Hamstrings:
Hanging dumbell leg curls
Calves:
Standing calf machine heel raises or
Donkey calf raises
Seated heel raises
Abdominals:
Hanging knee-ups
Gironda double-up crunches
Econo-Time Secondary Phase
Back:
T-bar rows or
Prone barbell rows on a high bench
Chest:
Incline (30 to 40-degree) dumbell flyes
Delts:
Single-dumbell (leaning) incline lateral raises
or Standing barbell presses overhead
Triceps:
Twin-pedestal triceps pulley extensions with
V-handle (see text)
Single-dumbell seated triceps extensions
Forearms:
Barbell (behind-the-neck) wrist curls
Thick-bar one-handed deadlifts or
Supergrip machine

CHAPTER TEN

11 Training-Past-The-Burn Techniques

Primary Phase

No. 1 – Power Programs

At the beginning of this book we detailed five muscle density techniques that many of the champion bodybuilders use in their anabolic high-volume training strategies. We now mention them again briefly because we feel that, individually, they can be adapted in the volume of sets you will be using for a selected major or minor muscle group.

To recap, they were: six-week rapid muscle mass technique, big-six and ten-set magic, the Davis set, Eastern Bloc training system, and the "wave" program. Other extremely effective systems of training that we also mentioned are as follows: one- and two-dimensional pyramid principle, down-the-rack, division of sets, etc.

If, for some reason, these muscle mass and power oriented programs are not a part of your training at this particular time, then by all means feel free to structure your primary phase of the total-body workout around shape-training, where you would use eclectic super flushing techniques, double antagonistic supersets, or staggered-volume training.

Please remember that all these techniques should not be employed at the same time. Only one should be used per muscle group and only one or two, or at most three, within the weekly training program. Do not perform any other exercises for a selected muscle group unless it is an elementary part of one of the above power techniques.

No. 2 – Cyclic Strength Gain Workout

Many of the giants of power and muscle cycle their training poundages to gradually build up their muscles to superhuman strength and

Rich Gaspari watches 'em grow!

size. The following 11-week program is one of the best methods for this purpose.

Week No.	Percentage of Max (%)	Sets	Reps
1	70	3	5
2	80	3	5
3	75	3	5
4	85	4	3
5	80	3	5
6	90	4	3
7	85	4	3
8	95	4	2
9	90	4	3
10	100	4	2
11	95	1	1

Within the structure of this particular program, a bodybuilder can choose one power-type exercise and perform it in solo straight-set fashion – resting three to four minutes between

Tom Platz has such intensity that even his face is well-developed!

INCLINE TRICEPS "POWER CHEAT"

To experience the ultimate in trip-hammer triceps power and size try these two pro tips:

1. Hold the upper arms (biceps/triceps) in the same vertical plane of motion as the bar travels (directly from forehead level) to an arms-extended power lockout.

2. On occasion use the following "5-Set Principle." First set is a warmup of 30 to 50 reps. Next do 3 hard work sets of 15 reps each.

All 15 reps of each set are continuous in cadence but are done in three parts. Reps 1 to 5 are strict, 6 to 10 are controlled "power cheating," and reps 11 to 15 are partial or measured movement burns. Finish off with a flush set of 25+ reps.

sets. When and if you get your rest periods down to only one minute or less, then you might try performing the exercises in double-drop fashion by reducing the poundage by 20%, then doing more reps, then dropping the weight yet again (but this time 30%) and going on to positive failure. **Note: Double-drop on your final set only**

Quite a few of the bodybuilders we are acquainted with especially enjoy using this cyclic strength workout, and triple-drop combination, on the incline barbell triceps extension cheat exercise. This exercise is performed by lying back on a 60-degree incline bench, gripping the bar with a six-inch handspacing, **but** with this unusual "economy of motion" difference. There is a subtle shift of the hands, turning them somewhat diagonally, so that the bar rests across the palms and directly over the wrists and it is the forearms then that do the supporting. From here it's just a matter of doing short power-stroke reps from the forehead to an arms-locked-out position for fast gains. As care must be taken to secure the

Dorian Yates

performed while standing, seated, kneeling, or on a flat, incline or decline bench.

3. Hands neutral, as in a suitcase grip where the palms are parallel to the body. Vertical dips, various dumbell extension movements are examples of this, as are some variations of pressing movements.

Using these grip variations will just about guarantee maximum stimulation and growth in all aspects of the muscle fibers in the triceps.

It is a good idea to change the volume and progression intensity of the 11-week cyclic strength gain workout every so often. One of the best ways we know of to accomplish this is by alternating it with the **Austin Gym 15-week strength cycle.**

The following table of sets, reps and intensity levels best represents this 15-week training progam as it applies to all major exercises.

Shawn Ray

weight safely at all times, it is best to use a Smith machine when doing this unusual movement.

After you have completed the assigned number of sets and reps for this exercise, follow up with one or two isolationary shape-training exercises for the triceps; doing two to four sets of eight to ten reps of each.

Hand position in triceps exercises can be basically divided into three types. At each workout session try to use at least one exercise that accommodates each of these positions. The three reference positions are:

1. Hands pronated, where the palms are facing away from the body as in the exercise mentioned above, or other triceps French press variants. (Triceps pushdowns on the lat bar are included in this classification as well.) A pro secret that former IFBB Mr. World Steve Davis taught us when doing this exercise is to keep the heels of the hands lower on the bar throughout the entire range of movement. This is accomplished by bending the hands back at the wrists toward the forearm.

2. Hands supinated, in which the palms are facing upward, as in a reverse-grip triceps curl, or kickbacks when using close, medium or wide handspacing. These exercises can be

145

A photographer needs to grab a wide angle lens to get all of Paul Dillett in the frame.

Week No.	Sets	Reps	% Max
1	2	15	66
2	3	12	69
3	3	10	72
4	2	10	50
5	3	8	80
6	3	6	85
7	3	4	90
8	2	10	50
9	4	5	90
10	5	5	92
11	5	3	96
12	2	10	50
13	3	5	94
14	3	2	98
15	3	1	102

The above training cycle will increase your strength gains as well as your muscle tissue density. We credit Bryan Wadie for introducing the highly efficient and effective **Austin Gym Way** training program through a series of published articles in *Powerlifting USA* magazine during 1990 and 1991.

Michael Francois blasts his upper pecs.

No. 3 – Interval Intensity Training

The original idea behind **Interval Intensity Training** was developed by former world powerlifting champion Walter Thomas as a means to upgrade his power for setting world records. The idea behind this system is to utilize the concept of periodization where the program is divided into training cycles and workouts.

To begin this program, start by training with a poundage that is 80% of your current one-rep maximum single effort for six primary work sets of four consecutive reps. (Example: 80% of 300 pounds = 240 pounds) The first training cycle is what Mr. Thomas terms the **experimental version,** and lasts ten weeks in duration. With regards to the training frequency, the advice is to work out on three alternate days per week (Monday, Wednesday, Friday). A very important key to this program is to add five pounds of weight every two weeks to the primary work sets (six sets of four reps).

Using the example above, a bodybuilder will train weeks one and two with 240 pounds, weeks three and four with 245 pounds, weeks five and six with 250 pounds, weeks seven and eight with 255 pounds, and weeks nine and ten with 260 pounds. At the completion of the ten-week cycle, rest for three-and-a-half days, and then test for a new one-rep max single. This particular ten-week cycle is a one-time deal. From here on each experimental version cycle is followed for only five weeks, while the rest period will go up to one week. Continue with the experimental version for as long as gains are forthcoming. If overtraining becomes noticeable, change over to the **modified version,** which is basically the same thing except for the training frequency, which is reduced from three to two per week (Monday, Friday).

A bodybuilder who is training within the structure of a total-body workout which includes the primary phase (where each muscle group gets only one major workout a week) should modify his interval intensity training system once again to accommodate only one training session per week.

This program can be used for a major or minor muscle group, but it is especially effective for the chest and particularly when applied to the bench press. Not only will the strength and power equation be upgraded tremendously using this system, but more herculean size, diamond definition and rugged muscularity in the pecs and delts will become startlingly evident. When using this system on the bench press it is very important to do a **four-second full pause** at the chest on the fourth rep of each of the primary work sets.

If a bodybuilder is using this program for a

RING FLYES – DRAWING A

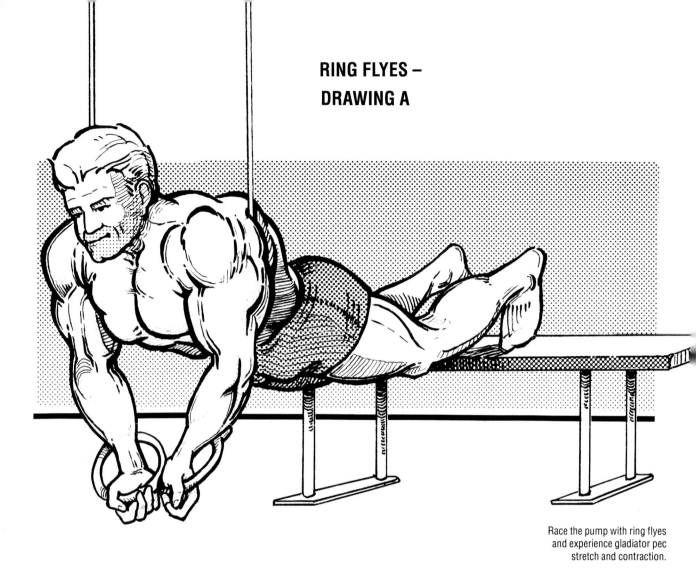

Race the pump with ring flyes and experience gladiator pec stretch and contraction.

major muscle exercise such as the bench press, one or two isolationary muscle-shaping exercises can be done for two to four sets of 11 to 15 reps. There are many exercises that we could suggest for this purpose, but one of the most unusual is one that former IFBB Mr. Olympia Larry Scott used for a fast pec pump when he trained at Vince's Gym in North Hollywood (when preparing for his Mr. Olympia wins). The exercise is called ring flyes. The rings themselves are of the type used in gymnastics competition, covered in leather. They are each secured to a rope or heavy nylon strap which is mounted into a ceiling beam or joist as support. The rings are suspended shoulder-width apart at about the same height off the floor as the height of a typical exercise bench (18 inches).

Now position a flat exercise bench approxi-mately three-quarters of the length of your body from the hanging rings but in line with them. You are now ready to get into starting position.

a) Kneeling on the floor with the end of the bench behind you and the rings in front of you, grasp the inside of each ring with a palms-forward position. Bring them close to the front of the upper torso, down near the low sternal pec and upper to mid ab region as depicted in the illustration. If you have taken the correct position, the rings will be in contact with the back of your lower arms. Keep your arms almost locked out but with a very slight elbow bend.

b) Walking backwards while holding onto the rings, place your toes securely on the top of the flat bench – feet wide enough apart (6 to 12 inches apart) for good balance.

RING FLYES – DRAWING B

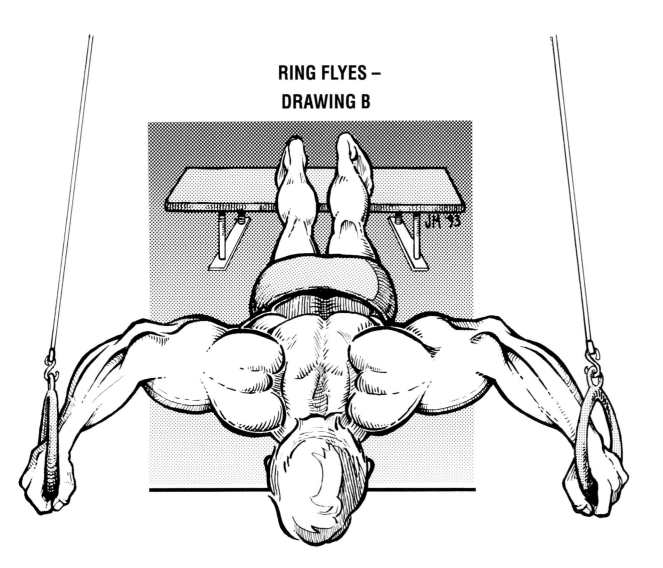

c) While bending your knees slightly, keep your upper torso rigid. Slowly begin to initiate an inverted or prone flying motion (just the opposite of supine bent-arm dumbell flyes) by lowering your body, face downward, in a sloping or decline motion. Keeping the arms as instructed (slightly bent at the elbow, see above), rotate your wrists simultaneously until you are literally spread-eagled with your chest six inches off the floor.

d) In the bottom, max spread-eagle stretch position, the upper arms and elbows are almost in direct alignment with the shoulder joint but, because of the slight bend at the elbows, the palms of the hands are slightly in front of the shoulders.

e) During the actual descent, breathe deeply.

f) Now slowly, with pure pectoral tension contraction, pull the arms back into the starting position. (This should not imitate a pressing movement but should be a drawing in or pulling together movement.) At the top of the movement lock the arms out and pull the hands together as close as possible, squeezing those inner pecs for a long, lasting pump. From time to time it would be a good idea to do half-plus quarter-rep burnouts in the lower spread-eagle, middle and top positions as you finish off the last reps of the final set or two. This maximum-contraction ring flyes exercise will produce the ultimate shape you desire in the pecs.

Pro Tip: Elevating the feet on a higher bench plane than described will allow more upper pec stimulation. Placing the feet on the floor rather than on a bench places the stress line on the low sternal pec region.

Ring flyes are not an easy exercise to

Charles Clairmonte, Porter Cottrell and John Sherman.

master by themselves. There is a special prep-aratory exercise that is especially designed to shock your system and prepare it for this super pec-pumper. We call it the **dumbell rollout** and this is how it is performed: Place two loaded dumbells on the floor, about shoulder-width apart. Position them so that you can grasp them with a neutral (palms-facing) hand position.

Upon grasping them, extend your legs behind you just as if you were going to assume the starting position for the conventional pushup or floor dip. Roll the dumbells out to the sides by spreading your arms wide apart till you are spread-eagled, as in the ring flyes. Now bring them back to the starting position, following a similar execution of movement to that used in the ring flyes. This precision-training technique will really prepare you for the ring flyes.

Larry Scott sells the hanging rings as part of his state-of-the-art Signature Equipment line. For price information on the rings give Larry a call at 1-800-225-9752.

Interval intensity training, and other sys-tems which suggest the use of power reps, will create the maximum amount of stress within the given muscles you are attacking, but only if you do not use cheating movements (where you distribute most of the stress on muscles other than the ones you are trying to work), or increase the T.E.R. (training efficiency rate), or speed up the pace of your workout. There are, of course, exceptions to the rule (as in the Eastern Bloc Training System, etc.). Pace your workout by taking long rest pauses of three to four minutes between sets, and sometimes even extra long ones of five minutes and more.

There is no need for oxygen debt fatigue to become the enemy of strength building.

Perhaps the six primary work sets of four solid reps each is too impacting on your body to begin with. If this is a volume-loading training problem to you, we suggest that you use the **five pounds per week gain** modified version of the original interval-intensity training system. With this program, the originator, Steven Dewitt, suggests doing a warmup set for 10 to 15 reps. Take a brief rest and, while doing so, add only enough poundage to the bar that will allow you eight easy reps for the second set. Take another rest and this time add enough weight to let you grind out eight tough reps, going to positive failure on the third set.

The fourth and final set is the heart of this system. Use a weight which will allow you to do a maximum four-rep set to positive failure.

This completes the first training day cycle. On the following second and third workouts use the same poundage progression as the previous one, but with this important difference – add one additional rep on the fourth set during each of these workouts. To clarify this further, you will be doing five reps on the fourth set of the second workout and six reps on the fourth set of the third workout. Beginning with workout number four, add five pounds to the poundage used in the fourth set. Back-cycle the reps in this set down to a base of four, and begin a new training sequence. Gradually you can add a fifth and sixth set of four reps each. This will put you into a new dimension of the interval-intensity training system.

Jim Quinn shows great muscularity.

No. 4 – Tightrope Training

A main priority to most bodybuilders is the building of strength, not only in the muscles, but also in the tendons and ligaments. Most are familiar with what muscles are made of but some of you may not be aware that tendons and ligaments are two distinctly different bodily tissues, though some bodybuilders unsuspectingly make these two words interchangeable when talking about hardcore power.

Lee Labrada

Tendons are best described as being a somewhat elastic connective tissue which join each end of a particular muscle to bones (often to form a joint). Tendons have the capacity for developing a deep-rooted superhuman strength when trained correctly.

Ligaments, on the other hand, are rather tough and flexible fibrous sheaths which are attached around each and every joint in the body. Their function is to stabilize or keep the bones fully in place, while allowing the necessary movement around the joint hinge for muscle contraction purposes, but never at the expense of separation, dislocation or bending of the joint hinge the wrong way.

Many bodybuilders will develop super tendon and ligament strength by doing half and quarter squats and deadlifts, lockout presses, and by lowering heavy weights from the barbell curl top position. One former pro IFBB superstar bodybuilder, Chuck Sipes, developed his superhuman strength with a method of training which he called "support training." He did this by supporting huge weights across his shoulders in the squatting movements and over his chest in the supine lockout bench press positions. He found that this method stimulated his muscles and, in particular, the tendons and ligaments, forcing growth to a much greater extent than anything else.

There are only two exercises used in support training and, as mentioned, they will be in the bench press and squat. Be sure to structure them within the appropriate antistress muscle group selection in the primary phase of training in your total-body workout. (Don't overtax arms or legs by incorporating them after heavy squats or chest work.) The following information will describe the performance of each exercise and volume of training load.

It is important that you always use a lifting belt for not only these heavy-duty training sessions, but others as well. The lifting belt will prove especially valuable when used for the heavy squat supports, because when it is cinched up fairly tight, it creates an increase in inner abdominal pressure for an added training effect of stability and reduction in spine compression. Be careful not to cinch it up too tightly, though, because doing so can – in some individuals – interfere with veneal blood flow back to the heart and this, in turn, can create an oxygen debt. We suggest that you loosen the belt up between sets to bypass this training problem. There are many belts to choose from, but one of the best we and many of the pro bodybuilders (like IFBB Mr. Olympia competitor Lee Labrada) prefer is the training belt from Valeo (1-800-634-2704 for information).

Heavy supports – bench press position:

Begin the exercise with a poundage which is approximately 20 to 30 percent over your current maximum single effort (MSE). With the barbell loaded and in position on the upright bench support rack, and with two capable spotters to assist you, assume a supine or flat position on the bench. Reach up and grip the bar with the handspacing that you normally use in the bench press exercise. Inhale deeply (an oxygen saturation technique many of the champions use) rather than breathing the air in **after** the bar is in position over the chest. The rib cage has the greatest capacity for expansion prior to lifting the bar. Filling the lungs to capacity also lifts the chest higher, thus reducing the distance the bar must travel when you do complete a full range of motion during a single-rep attempt. With very short movement of perhaps one-eighth to one-quarter bend in your elbows, lift the bar off the upright bench support rack. With the help of a spotter's guidance, move the bar horizontally six inches – by locking your arms out – until it is directly over your chest. Support this massive poundage from five to ten seconds (longer, if possible) and then, with the help of

Start

your spotter, guide the bar back into the support rack. Take a few minutes' rest between sets. When you can hold the weight for four sets of 20 seconds, then by all means, add more weight.

Mike O'Hearn pulling a heavy dead "sumo-style" and looking good.

Finish

Heavy supports – squat position:

Adjust your squat rack so that it is approximately six inches lower than your shoulders when standing. Load a barbell in position on the rack. With your spotter in position, approach the bar. Taking a thumbless grip (relieving pressure on the elbows) space your hands approximately three to six inches wider than your shoulder width. (Make sure you chalk your hands prior to this.) Dip under the bar and center it across your posterior (rear) deltoids and the middle of the traps (your normal squatting position). If you are in the correct position, the bar placement will be slightly below the top of the anterior delts. It is always a good idea to chalk the area where the bar will be positioned on your shoulders just as an added measure to help keep the bar securely in place. Inhale deeply and, with your back straight and somewhat arched, apply maximum contractual pressure of the thighs, unrack the barbell and straighten up to lock out your legs. While in the vertical or upright position, hold this monstrous poundage for four sets of 20 seconds each. It is of the utmost importance to always have capable spotters ready to assist you. In addition to this, it would be an excellent idea to use a power rack for your support training procedures. We do realize, however, that many of you reading this information may be saying silently that you train alone, without spotter assistance, and don't have the luxury of owning a power rack. If this is your training situation, we would strongly suggest that you don't attempt support training as we have described it. That would be our firm advice **if** we didn't have another training option open to you, which we do, and here it is…

The Harvey Maxime bar:

One of the greatest advances ever made in weight training equipment as far as we are concerned was the invention of the Harvey Maxime bar back around 1948. For one reason or another, the popularity of it never caught on with the bodybuilders of that decade or any other, for that matter. Perhaps it was years

"I'd have given anything for legs like he's got." – Arnold speaking about Tom Platz.

DEADLIFT USING THE HARVEY MAXIME BAR

Nothing improves a bodybuilders lock-out power, pulling power and tendon and ligament strength better than some training sessions with a modified Harvey Maxime Bar.

BAR, CHAIN AND SHACKLE
FOR HARVEY MAXIME BAR

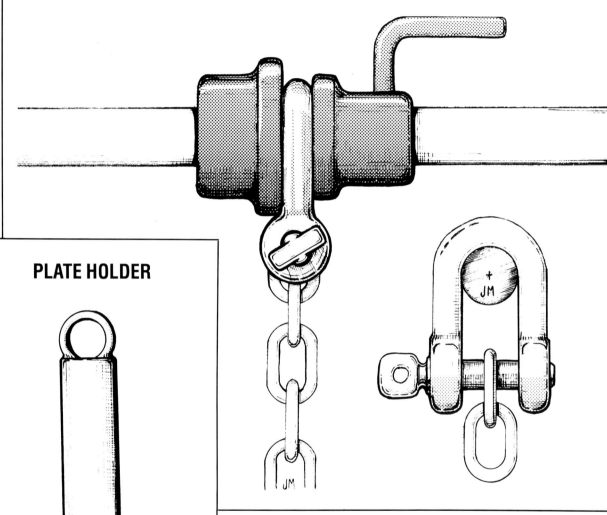

PLATE HOLDER

ahead of its time, much like Vince Gironda's concepts on abdominal training (frog situps or crunches, etc.) or that of Rheo H. Blair, one of the nation's leading teachers of "super nutrition" back in the 1960s. Use of his special daily Blair diet, consisted of three cups of his unique milk and egg protein powder mixed into a quart of dairy cream, followed by an effective protein digestant such as Peptain HCL. Although a radical approach to muscle cell regeneration, it would seem, with its high dietary fat content, it worked well for bodybuilders like Larry Scott (the first IFBB Mr.

Olympia), Don Richard Howorth, and Gable Paul Boudreaux, just to name a few of Blair's followers.

Gironda, like Blair, is a colorful, mysterious and controversial pioneer in the physical culture scene. Like Rheo before him, Vince is often openly ridiculed for his radical departures (from the norm) on exercise techniques and nutritional research; yet, today his unorthodox ideas have been honored by the subtle compliment of imitation. You will find many who have rediscovered Blair and Gironda principles of training and nutrition and called them their own.

Much to our surprise and disappointment, the subtle compliment of imitation has never materialized with the Harvey Maxime bar and we are not sure why. With its use you virtually eliminate the need for spotters, and you can progress to such a point that a fraction of inches separates the floor from the weight. The graphic art illustrations will make this very clear to you.

All that is required to make up a modified Harvey Maxime bar is two lengths of chain (something similar to three-quarter ton, come-along chain) each equal in length to your height when standing upright with your arms completely outstretched overhead. You will also need a 1″ or 1-1/2″ by 72″ stressproofed steel bar, two inside and two outside heavy-duty barbell collars, and four heavy-duty chain shackles. The shackles will have to be small enough to pass through the link of the chain while allowing the bar to be passed through the shackle itself. The shackles are then put on the bar and held in place by the collars.

The two remaining shackles are secured to the other end of the chain links (after the chain has been threaded through the center holes in the barbell plates you are going to use). The height of the bar is simply adjusted by unscrewing the shackles and increasing or decreasing the links of chain for the starting position of the particular exercise you are doing. If you don't want the hassle of having to thread the chain through the holes of the barbell plates, then use plate holders and attach the shackles to them. The plate holders' convenience is that they allow you to use a larger diameter, heavier gauge chain than would normally fit through the holes in the barbell plates. If you have the capability yourself (or can find a good journeyman machinist/welder), then fabricate a steel threadless coupling sleeve (with the base of a heavy-duty eye bolt welded on) to slide over each end of the exercise bar and attach your remaining two shackles to them. Once you have built this simple training tool, its use will be practically limitless. You can, of course, use it for your heavy supports in the bench press and squat positions, and also on pressouts or for supporting heavy poundages overhead at arms' length. There will also be a few other options that you will undoubtedly think of. With regard to the squat supports and other squatting variations, you might wish to use the Harvey Maxime bar from time to time, but be sure to use a piece of armoflex material for your bar padding. Most plumbing and hardware stores sell this item.

Using the Harvey Maxime bar will expel all former fears and inhibitions from your mind when using heavy poundages because now you are mentally armed with the knowledge that only a fraction of an inch separates the floor from the weight. Because you are not afraid of the barbell anymore, you can develop a respectful contempt for limit poundages as long as you remain careful not to jerk or cheat in the performance of the reps when using this special bar. The rep performance should be smooth and constant tension kept in rhythm with the pull of gravity and momentum created. Because of its impact on muscle stimulation and recovery time, support or tightrope training should only be done every four or five days and only three exercises at the very most should be done on a maximum 10-week training cycle. After training your tendons and ligaments in this manner for 10 brutal weeks, don't be at all surprised to experience **"surge training,"** where many of the poundages you had previously been using in full range of movement exercises now feel extremely light. Just to give you an example – if you were doing Olympic high-bar squats with 250 pounds for 10 reps prior to support training, it is very possible that you may be able to add 10 or even 20 more pounds to the bar and grind out not only the usual 10 reps, but an amazing 18

Start

Dave Fisher with spotter.   *Finish*

instead! This is surge training at its best, and when combined with a total mental Alpha state (where you can disassociate the rep and poundage factor totally from your workouts), then you can exceed all prior self-imposed training limitations for even more dramatic and magnificent bodybuilding gains in muscle size and strength.

No. 5 – Power Four-Rep/Tri-Pump System

This particular bodybuilding training technique combines multiple sets of a four-rep power system with the famous Muscle Beach 21-rep movement (also called the double half and full rep method, or stage reps). This program is a very high-volume oriented workout that has proven to be a real muscle size and strength builder for the serious contest-winning bodybuilder. The initial poundage for 21s is reduced 50 percent to 60 percent from a current unfatigued 10-rep max with full range of motion. Here is how the intensity progression of this program works:

The barbell French press (use an EZ-curl bar) is done either lying or seated for 15 sets of four consecutive power reps. It is then followed by doing the 21-rep movement for five sets, but with this unique difference. Rather than doing all of the 15 sets of the four power reps and then doing the five sets of the 21-rep movement, many of the bodybuilders will alternate one set of the barbell French press 21-rep movement to each three consecutive four power-rep sets.

While this is a very result-producing concept of high-volume training for the genetically superior bodybuilder (who also has a genetic superior recovery ability), it would most definitely cause the average bodybuilder to overtrain – not to mention the fact that it does not fit into the structure of training sets we suggest for major and minor muscle groups. As you may recall, we mentioned that the pros will do 12 to 15 sets for their quads, back and chest, and 8 to 10 sets for all the remaining muscle groups. We then suggested that you, the natural anabolic steroid-free bodybuilder, do 8 to 10 and 5 to 7 sets per major and minor muscle groups respectively. This being the case, it would appear that this particular program would have been best structured in as an **optional** training technique, as part of the high-volume training concepts mentioned at the beginning of this book. So why then do we mention it? We feel that this particular training technique has potent muscle-gain factors that can blend into the primary first phase of training **if** certain modifications are made.

To begin with, rather than doing a ratio of three sets of four power reps to one set of 21s, you will probably want to go with a ratio of two four power-rep sets to one set of 21s. Other modifications will include doing each of your four power-rep sets in superslow style. By this we mean that each and every rep should take ten full seconds in the positive phase (concentric contraction) and five seconds in the negative phase (eccentric contraction) of the movement. This will allow you to do your reps with precision, while creating an ideal anaerobic effect within the muscle with 60-second sets. Robert Harrop, the 1991 AAU Jr. Mr. America, used superslow techniques on his bench work for his chest development and he found that it worked very well for adding fresh new muscle growth.

There are a couple of training tips we would like to share with you now regarding the 21-rep movement. Rather than using the exact same exercise for 21s (where the poundage is reduced 50 to 60 percent) as you did for the sets of four power reps, choose a different exercise for the 21s application. You might find it advantageous to do 21s with seated or kneeling triceps pushdowns on the lat machine, or perhaps the lying barbell kickback. For those of you who are not familiar with this exercise we provide a very brief description: Lying in a supine position on a flat exercise bench, and holding a barbell on the chest with an eight-to-ten-inch handspacing, extend the weight to the rear, on a plane parallel to the floor until the arms are locked at the elbow joint. Bring the bar back to the starting position which is in line with your forehead and begin your next rep. Generally the concept of the 21s is to divide the movement into three parts (two half-reps followed by one full rep). In the case of lying barbell kickbacks you will extend the arms out from the forehead level to mid-range or half of lockout. It should take you

about 30 seconds to complete seven reps of this half movement.

Now, without any pauses whatsoever, extend your arms from mid-range to an arms-locked-out position for seven more half reps. Finally, without hesitation, do seven full-range reps from the starting point to completion. This is one of the most common procedures for doing the 21 system. It can, however, be taken

Geir Borgen Paulsen explores the outer limits of mind-boggling mass.

a step further by dividing the movement into thirds rather than one-half movements. We'll use the kneeling triceps pushdown on the lat machine to explain this modification: Begin in the kneeling position with the triceps bar level with the collar bone. Slowly press the bar from

WRIST-STRAP PULLUPS
(Looped-Wrist Overview)

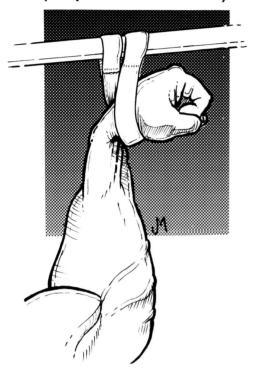

Wrist-strap pullups are a very unique and revealing exercise that can be substituted for the towel chin or any other lat exercise mentioned throughout this book. Preparatory to performing wrist-strap pullups, a pair of heavy-duty canvas wrist straps (2" loop-stitched at the tail end of each canvas strap) must be slid onto a fixed position overhead pullup bar.

The actual exercise protocol is to step up on a sturdy flat bench, stool, etc., and loop your (chalked) wrists through the straps as shown here. Now carefully step off the bench and, while doing so, slowly lower your body to an arms'-length dead-hang position. Relax your shoulder girdle so that it can be drawn or elevated upward and s-t-r-e-t-c-h the lats completely. Be sure to spread the wrist straps fairly wide apart. Upon stretching for a few seconds shrug or crunch the shoulders down and back as you pull your body as high as possible upward toward the bar. Then reverse the procedure for lowering back down to the full stretch position. To get maximum benefits out of this exercise incorporate the appropriate tracking pattern tips mentioned for wide-grip front pullup mentioned the Primary First Phase Workout No. 1, mentioned at the beginning of chapter nine. Work up to 3 sets of 9 reps. When this becomes easy with your bodyweight only, up your ladder of intensity by either adding weight or by doing the 21 principle, etc.

When the body is supported exclusively by the unique wrist hang from the straps it de-emphasizes the use of fingers, palms and biceps. This tends to involve the lats more fully during the pulling motion. This innovative lat exercise was taught to us in some descriptive letter correspondence by the late former IFBB bodybuilding superstar Chuck Sipes back in 1966.

Sometimes a bodybuilder's own weight can become the number one enemy in accomplishing such an exercise as the wrist-strap pullup. If so, this is for you.

Pro Tip: Rather than sliding the canvas wrist straps over the pullup bar, slide them instead over an overhead lat-machine dorsi bar. Now it's only a matter of looping the wrists through the straps and performing the motion to the chest (upper torso is inclined back approximately 30 degrees from vertical), with a poundage which will allow you to do the set and rep scheme mentioned. As your lat pulling strength increases dramatically in this movement, you may wish to attempt the much harder pullup-bar version.

this starting point through one-third of the movement. Return the bar to the starting point through one-third of the movement. Return the bar to the starting point and perform six more one-third reps. Now quickly begin pressing the bar through the middle one-third range of the

movement for seven more reps. Upon completion finish off with seven full reps. On another set of 21s you might finish off the cycle with seven one-third reps in the upper peak range, while skipping the seven full-rep sequence. There are, of course, many other muscle groups to which the training techniques of the four power-rep/tri-pump system can be applied, but of all the ones that come to mind none are more brutal and as severe as doing two sets of four consecutive power-reps of barbell bent-over rowing with a curl grip to one set of the 21-rep movement in the towel chins for three complete cycles.

The barbell bent-over rowing with the curl grip is basically done by grasping the bar with a palms-up close grip and by pulling the bar

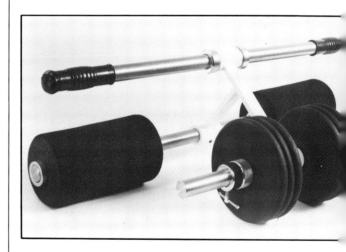

Compound curl bar for "high-peak muscularity."

into the belt line of the waist. You can allow the elbows to travel back, behind the plane of the upper body. This movement will hit the rear delts as well as the lower lats.

Towel chins are done by draping two strong cloth towels over a chin or pullup bar. To begin this exercise (depending upon your strength after the rowing!), grip each of the towels about four to five inches below the bar, and from a full hang begin the first of the three-part 21-rep movement. Whenever you get to the point that all three parts of the 21-rep movement become fairly easy, then lower your hand position on the towels to where, eventually, you are gripping the towel twelve inches below the bar. When this too becomes easy, then add additional poundage in the form of a barbell plate, or dumbell to this bodyweight-only exercise. Take care to tie the added weight around your waist snugly so that it doesn't dangle loosely.

TOWEL CHINS

Densify the lats with towel chins.

No. 6 – Three Sets of Ten Reps Plus

This particular training system, known as the DeLorme-Watkins program of original progression, involves just three sets of ten reps per exercise. With this method you use a poundage which is 50 percent of your current best ten maximum reps, and do your first set with it for ten reps. Take a short rest-pause and do your second set with a poundage that is 75 percent of your current best ten-rep maximum and do another ten reps. Take another rest-pause and do your third and final set of ten reps with a poundage which is 100 percent of your best calculated ten-rep maximum. Much to your surprise the third and final set of ten reps

will require brutally hard muscular effort to complete.

You will notice that we used such terms as **current best 10-rep maximum** and **best calculated maximum reps.** Each term has a slightly different meaning in terms of training intensity. Generally, if you do only three sets of ten reps for one exercise in the same muscle group at the beginning of the workout, then more than likely you could base all three sets against current best ten-rep maximums at the listed percentages. This would be ideal, but you may wish to do a second exercise for the same muscle group, or you may structure two anti-stress pulling muscle groups, such as the lats and biceps, or a pushing grouping consisting of perhaps chest and delts, or chest and triceps on the same workout day. The exercises that you will choose for the lats may involve heavy or low biceps involvement. On the pushing muscle groups of the chest and delts the muscles involved act interchangeably with one another, like members of a family. The bottom line in all of these situations is going to be some type of inroad in the fresh starting strength levels within the muscle. If you elect to do a second exercise for the same muscle group, such as decline dumbell rows for the lats, the pulling strength in this exercise and especially during the critical third and final set will not be near its maximum strength level as it would be for the first exercise performed. Because this pulling action from the lats requires some biceps involvement, be it heavy or light, it is not uncommon to experience a drop in biceps strength when training them immediately after the back. Where previously you could do a current best ten reps with 130 pounds in a biceps exercise (using the compound curl bar), you may now find it almost impossible to do. You will then have to calculate a ten-rep maximum which can range from a hypothetical five to ten percent less, for your third and final set. The DeLorme-Watkins program of original progression for an exercise as mentioned looks like this:

1st set – 50% RM x 10
2nd set – 75% RM x 10
3rd set – 100% RM x 10

Some truly hardcore bodybuilders, upon completing the third and final set, will immediately reduce the poundage back down to 50 percent of their current best ten-rep maximum **first set** and perform rep-outs to failure to where they can't even raise the weight two inches. Each and every rep-out is done in a rhythm of performance where there are no pauses whatsoever during any part of pump then a lactic acid burn. The muscle will then begin to cramp somewhat. As you near the completion of your final rep-outs you will experience the beginning of total exhaustion and you will have to resort to extreme mental tenacity to make the muscles contract. Instead of giving up when it seems hopeless, **do more!**

Dorian Yates and Lee Haney

each rep or between consecutive reps. Each and every rep is deliberately executed so that the muscle re-engages itself at every sector of the movement. Visualizing the muscle you are working as one big muscular contraction in operation, with no assistance from any other muscles of the body, will help you execute this procedure correctly. During various stages of the rep-outs you will feel an incredible muscle

This trains your muscles to obey your will. Use the rep-out method only on the final set of a particular exercise. Never work more than one or two muscles once a week, and only then for a period of four to six weeks. This is one of the pro bodybuilding secrets for acquiring muscle contractile force.

Actually if we could make a slight modification in the original training progression of the DeLorme-Watkins program, it would be to use the heaviest amount of weight, and corresponding reps, on the very first set when you are your strongest. From this point you could decrease the weight on each succeeding second and third set by five pounds on training poundages under 100 pounds, and by five-pound weight reductions for each additional 50 pounds being used over 100 pounds (150 to 200 pounds = decrease second and third sets by 15 pounds each).

No. 7 – Golden Pyramid Strength System

Six-week peaking plan:

WORKOUT ONE	WORKOUT TWO
Week 1:	
45%/8-10, 55%/6-8	45%/8-10, 55%/6-8, 65%/5
65%/6, 65-70%/6 + 6 + 6	75%/5, 80%/5 + 5 + 5, 75%/5
	65%/6-8, 50-55%/8-12 (burnout)
Week 2:	
45%/8-10, 55%/6-8	45%/8-10, 55%/6-8, 65%/5
65%/6, 70%/5	75%/4, 80%/4, 85%/4 + 4 + 4
70-75%/5 + 5	80%/5, 70%/6-8
Week 3:	
45%/8-10, 55%/6-8	45%/8-10, 55%/6-8, 65%/5
65%/5, 70%/4, 75%/3	75%/4, 85%/3, 90%/3 + 3
75-80%/3 + 3	80%/5, 55%/8-12 (burnout)
Week 4:	
45%/8-10, 55%/6-8	45%/8-10, 55%/6-8, 65%/5
65%/5, 75%/4	75%/4, 85%/2, 90%/2, 95%/2
80-85%/3 + 3	75%/8-12 (burnout)
Week 5:	
45%/8-10, 55%/6-8	45%/8-10, 55%/6-8, 65%/5
65%/5, 75%/5 + 5	75%/3, 80%/3, 85%/2
Week 6:	
45%/8-10, 55%/6-8	45%/8-10, 55%/6-8, 65%/5
65%/5, 75%/3, 80%/2 + 2	75%/3, 85%/2, 90%/1, 95%/1
	100%/max out
	(attempt three single reps)

The **Golden Pyramid Strength System** is a systematic bodybuilding strategy to optimize muscle growth and strength. This six-week peaking plan is performed on two nonconsecutive days per week, and works best when using most any of the major and minor exercises mentioned in the Davis Set which was discussed at the beginning of this book. This particular training modality was researched by John Abdo, producer and host of *TN 2000*, nationally syndicated sports/fitness TV series.

Making the system work:

1. The Golden Pyramid System is designed with a blend of alternating percentages, based on your current unfatigued max single effort. If you know what your max single is (without over or underestimating it) then you're ready to start the program. If not, test for a new max single as described in Chapter Two, Muscle Density Secrets – Eastern Bloc Training Percentage System.
2. Use the system only on compound strength-building exercises and never on isolationary exercises (laterals, etc.).
3. Select one and, at the most three, exercises to train within the parameters of the six-week cycle.

Ron Coleman

Mike Matarazzo enjoys shocking lesser mortals with his brutal mass.

4. If you elect to train two or three strength-building exercises, consider using a staggered workout strategy. Begin one or two exercises on the first week and the third exercise on the second week. Your training plan will last slightly longer than six weeks overall. It will eliminate maxing out procedures on all three strength-building exercises during a final peaking week. Another option is to follow that listed on page 113 of *Mass!*.

5. Workout one is of light to medium training intensity, while the second workout of the week is considered medium to heavy (all of which is dependent upon which week you are in the cycle).

6. If your training effort is strong, and you are mentally focused, stay with the top percentage "hard work" set or sets as the case may be. If intensity fails and you can't do the required sets, decrease the top percentage by five to ten percent, but only on that particular workout.

No. 8 - Building Bionic Leg Power!

The Bionic Leg Power System will follow basically the same training methodology as the previous program, but with a slight change in the workout percentage of maximums and, of course, the exercise selection. For this particular program we will use a base of 400 pounds as the example of a current maximum single effort (MSE) in the power-style squat.

Workout program "A":
Percentage of maximum (POM) = 95%
Set 1 - 135 pounds (34%) x 5 reps
Set 2 - 225 pounds (56%) x 5 reps
Set 3 - 295 pounds (74%) x 3 reps
Set 4 - 345 pounds (86%) x 3 reps
Set 5 - 380 pounds (95%) x 3 reps
Set 6 - 380 pounds (95%) x 3 reps
Set 7 - 380 pounds (95%) x 3 reps
Use the high bar Olympic squat during this program.

Workout program "B":
POM = 75%
Set 1 - 135 pounds (34%) x 5 reps
Set 2 - 225 pounds (56%) x 5 reps
Set 3 - 275 pounds (69%) x 3 reps
Set 4 - 300 pounds (75%) x 5 reps
Set 5 - 300 pounds (75%) x 5 reps
Set 6 - 300 pounds (75%) x 5 reps
Again use the high bar Olympic squat during this program, but do the exercise in stop-squat style (pausing completely at the bottom of each and every rep).

Workout program "C":
POM = 85%
Set 1 - 135 pounds (34%) x 5 reps
Set 2 - 225 pounds (56%) x 5 reps
Set 3 - 295 pounds (74%) x 3 reps
Set 4 - 340 pounds (85%) x 5 reps
Set 5 - 340 pounds (85%) x 5 reps
Set 6 - 340 pounds (85%) x 5 reps

During this particular program, rather than using the Olympic high bar squat, go instead with the power-style squat. For those of you who are not familiar with the differences between high-bar and power-style squatting, an encapsulated commentary of each is mentioned in Chapter Thirteen.

The cycling rotation for the above three workout programs A, B and C, and appropriate poundage increases on the "barometer" top building strength sets in each will follow the same instruction given for Bench-Press Explosion in Six Weeks!

A quick scan of the percentage-based sets in each of the three workout programs will give an idea that this might be a walk in the park, so to speak. We can testify to the fact that it isn't! The percentages of maximum are based against a max single effort in the power-style squat, but the bodybuilder is asked to use the Olympic style in programs A and B. This version is much stricter and more isolationary in nature compared to the movement done in power style. In retrospect, you'll find that the intensity levels were much higher than they appeared on paper in their percentage form. However, there always seems to be one bodybuilder around who can defy the odds. So for that individual, whoever that lucky person may be, there is an even more intense method by which to build bionic leg power.

Use high bar Olympic style squats within the structure of program A, but with program B use the barbell front squat, while in program C, use the high-bar Olympic style squat again, but in stop-squat style.

From workout to workout place your feet at various angles so that certain more aesthetic aspects of the frontal quads can be shape-trained.

No. 9 – Bench Press Explosion In Six Weeks

The following **six-week power bench press program** was developed by top bodybuilding trainer John Robbins as a means to developing record-shattering bench press power, quickly.

The intensity threshold of this powerful program requires only two workouts per week, and uses a three-sequence percentage of maximum training approach. The workouts are generally done on Monday and Thursday of each week.

The first training day of week one begins with workout A. Assuming that you are a natural nonanabolic steroid-free bodybuilder who has a current maximum single effort of a 300-pound bench press, your workout poundages and corresponding percentages of maximums for each set are as follows: 135 pounds (45%) x 10 reps, 185 pounds (62%) x 5 reps, 225 pounds (75%) x 3 reps, 255 (85%) x 2 reps. You now finish off this particular program by doing barometer (one-rep) sets with 95 percent of your maximum single effort, 285 pounds (95%) x 1 + 1 + 1 + 1 (four nonconsecutive blast single reps).

Hank Hill

Horseshoes anyone? Lee Priest always brings his own.

The second training day of week one consists of workout B where the top poundage used will be with 85 percent of your current maximum single effort of 300 pounds for three triple-rep barometer strength-building sets. This workout appears as follows: 135 pounds (45%) x 10 reps, 185 pounds (62%) x 5 reps, 225 pounds (75%) x 3 reps, and 255 pounds (85%) x 3 + 3 + 3 **power reps.**

Workout C is the third training sequence (and first workout of week two) and requires you to use 75% of your **(MSE)** 300-pound bench press as your top training poundage for multiple sets of five power reps.

The workout poundages and corresponding percentage of maximum for each set are as follows: 135 pounds (45%) x 10 reps, 185 pounds (62%) x 5 reps, and 225 pounds (75%) x 5 + 5 + 5 **power reps.**

A brief overview of the above program indicates that on the first week you are doing workout A on Monday, workout B on Thursday, and workout C on Monday at the beginning of the second week. Workout A follows on Thursday of the second week, workout B begins on the following Monday of training week number three, and concludes with workout C on Thursday. Workout A begins on a Monday once again in week number four. Continue the cycling rotation for the three sequence workouts (A,B and C) as explained. You will end the program on the sixth and final week with workout C.

To maintain an increasing level of strength in this total program it is necessary that you strive to add five pounds to the top barometer sets each proceeding workout. For example, on Monday of week one, workout A in the program used 285 pounds for four nonconsecutive blast singles. During workout A on Thursday of week two you will use 290 pounds for your top poundage while doing blast singles.

Obviously when you add five pounds to the top barometer percentage of maximum strength-building sets to each proceeding workout of A, B and C, the top percentages of maximum (95%, 85% and 75%) will change slightly. Don't worry about adjusting these percentages, but rather continue to be happy with the five-pound increases. Because there are no poundage increases required in the sets prior to the top poundages in any of the three listed workouts, it is important to stay with those percentages of maximum exactly as they are presented. Assistance exercises can be added into this program. The barbell bench press to the neck – using a collar-to-collar handspacing – for one or two sets of 12 to 15 reps with 62 to 65 percent of your current one-rep maximum will really flush the pectorals.

Marjo Selin and Tonya Knight.

Another beneficial exercise is the vertical dip on the parallel bars, used as a finishing-off movement for the triceps. Do two sets of eight reps.

There are plenty of other adequate assistance exercises to choose from. Some bodybuilders do reverse-grip bench presses for developing lockout power. They will take a poundage they can do five power reps with, and immediately upon completion they'll strip 30 to 40 percent off the bar and go to absolute failure! This is considered one series. They will also perform two or three more series. The secret to getting maximum benefit out of this exercise, both from the standpoint of achieving maximum lockout power in the bench press, and in the development of the long head of the triceps, is to lower the bar down to the abdominals (not the chest), and press up from there along an imaginary vertical line. Do not let the bar travel in an arc toward the bench upright supports as in the conventional bench press.

An assistance exercise for developing blast-off power from the chest in the bench press is the use of 50 to 100 pounds under your current one-rep maximum, and do one set of ten complete reps and a second and final set of 20 half reps. The weight is literally exploded off the chest no more than six to 10 inches.

For the sake of training safety, it is always an excellent idea to have a training partner serve as your spotter when doing bench press and squatting-type movements. Remember that assistance exercises should never dominate a workout structure such as the one listed for the bench press, and that, should you experience the symptons of overtraining, de-emphasize or eliminate them immediately!

At the conclusion of the six-week power bench press program, you will accomplish approximately a 6 to 8 percent gain in bench press performance on the barometer top strength-building sets. From here you could go on to test for a new maximum single effort (MSE) in the bench press and, after taking a one-week layoff, begin a new six-week cycle. Or, perhaps you might wish to test for a max single effort in a totally different exercise, say the 30 to 40 degree low incline dumbell press, and go from there.

Pete Samra, natural bodybuilding champion and owner of Samra Nutrition International, also invented the popular R.E.S.T system for bodybuilders.

Note: Percentages of maximums that are assigned to the corresponding sets and reps in this program, and others throughout this book, are generally accurate and easy to calculate. The programs designed on the percentage system make them applicable to all bodybuilders. All you must do is to multiply the **assigned percentage** for a particular set by your current **maximum single effort.**

No. 10 – The Jaska Parviainen Finnish Deadlift Program

This is a commando tough program designed to increase your rugged muscle back development and strength from five to ten percent. The program is very adaptable, in that the combination of sets, reps and corresponding percentages of max used within the structure of three back-to-back deadlift cycles can be used on both the conventional bench press and the squat. The following three-phase program includes the one-on-two-off/one-on-three-off training frequency, and the workouts which use the light and heavy system (two important training principles which we will be discussing in more detail later on).

This total-package deadlift program consists of three training cycles, each lasting a minimum of six but most generally seven weeks in duration. Traditional assistance or supplemental exercises include one training session a week after the deadlifts, so as not to interfere with vital mental focus needed for that exercise. Only two or three exercises are selected for this purpose. Each will be performed for no more than three sets, using slightly higher reps than those used in a particular deadlift cycle. Keeping the exercise and sets to a minimum will keep you from cutting into valuable total-recovery time, and the slightly higher rep scheme will keep you fresh and mentally focused on the deadlift itself. Certain assistance exercises will be suggested with each cycle, but they are not to be considered absolutes. Muscular strengths and weaknesses may change and so might the proper selection and usage of the traditional supplemental exercises. The heart of this program is to base all your poundages against a current best maximum single effort (MSE) conventional deadlift, prior to undertaking the program. We will list the percentages of that

maximum that you will need to use to find your correct poundage for each set. Let's begin.

Deadlift Dominated

Cycle 1 – Seven Weeks: All of the sets in each two weekly workouts are done for 10 consecutive reps. The deadlift is performed in stiff-legged style while standing on a wooden platform that is 3 feet long by 2 feet wide by 6 inches high. Depending on the diameter of the barbell plates used, the bar should be touching the instep of your feet, but no lower. After pulling the first rep of a set, lower the barbell to within 1 inch of the floor. From that point onward, during a particular set **do not touch the floor with the barbell** until the completion of the set.

Note: % means percentage of your best single effort. For example: 70% of a best maximum single effort of 400 pounds would be 280 pounds, etc.

Week 1
Workout 1: 1 x 27%, 1 x 31%, 2 x 27%
Workout 2: 1 x 27%, 1 x 33%, 1 x 40%, 2 x 27%

Week 2
Workout 1: 1 x 27%, 4 x 33%
Workout 2: 1 x 27%, 1 x 37%, 1 x 44%, 2 x 35%

Week 3
Workout 1: 1 x 27%, 4 x 33%
Workout 2: 1 x 33%, 1 x 40%, 1 x 47%, 2 x 35%

Week 4
Workout 1: 5 x 33%
Workout 2: 1 x 33%, 1 x 44%, 1 x 49%, 2 x 35%

Week 5
Workout 1: 5 x 33%
Workout 2: 1 x 33%, 1 x 44%, 1 x 51%, 2 x 37%

Week 6
Workout 1: 1 x 33%, 4 x 37%
Workout 2: 1 x 35%, 1 x 49%, 1 x 53%, 2 x 40%

Week 7
Workout 1: 1 x 33%, 4 x 40%
Workout 2: 1 x 35%, 1 x 49%, 1 x 55%, 2 x 40%

Assistance exercises during this seven-week cycle could include power cleans, weighted pullups and incline barbell rowing. This concludes cycle number one.

Deadlift Dominated

Cycle 2 – Seven Weeks: All the sets in each of the two weekly workouts are done for five consecutive reps. The deadlift procedure is exactly the same as in the previous number one cycle. There is one variant, however. The deadlift is to be performed in the conventional bent-knee style, as opposed to the stiff-legged variety.

Week 1
Workout 1: 1 x 44%, 1 x 50%, 3 x 55%
Workout 2: 1 x 44%, 1 x 52%, 1 x 60%, 1 x 44%

Week 2
Workout 1: 1 x 44%, 1 x 50%, 3 x 55%
Workout 2: 1 x 44%, 1 x 55%, 1 x 64%
    1 x 70%, 1 x 44%

Week 3
Workout 1: 1 x 44%, 4 x 55%
Workout 2: 1 x 44%, 1 x 55%, 1 x 64%
    1 x 70%, 1 x 44%

Week 4
Workout 1: 1 x 44%, 4 x 55%
Workout 2: 1 x 49%, 1 x 66%, 1 x 75%, 2 x 49%

Week 5
Workout 1: 1 x 49%, 3 x 57%, 1 x 49%
Workout 2: 1 x 49%, 1 x 66%, 1 x 77%
    1 x 71%, 1 x 49%

Week 6
Workout 1: 1 x 49%, 3 x 57%, 1 x 49%
Workout 2: 1 x 49%, 1 x 68%, 1 x 79%
    1 x 55%, 1 x 49%

Week 7
Workout 1: 1 x 49%, 4 x 57%
Workout 2: 1 x 49%, 1 x 68%, 1 x 80%
    1 x 55%, 1 x 49%

The supplemental or assistance exercises in this cycle include power cleans, lat machine pulldowns (using a dorsi-bar) and barbell shrugs. Your set-and-rep scheme for these exercises could follow the guidelines of the DeLorme-Watkins **three sets of ten** (mentioned in this chapter).

Deadlift Dominated

Cycle 3 – Six Weeks: Within the bi-weekly workouts in this third and final cycle of six weeks, **fives, triples, doubles** and **single** reps will be utilized with varying numbers of set progressions. The training technique for the deadlift will change somewhat, in that you will not be using the raised wooden platform

Start

Ericca Kern

Finish

from which to pull the bar, nor will you be doing them stiff-legged. During this cycle do them in your normal conventional style, touching the barbell to the floor ever so lightly each and every rep of the set.

Week 1
Workout 1: 1 x 5/44%, 1 x 3/60%, 3 x 3/70%
Workout 2: 1 x 5/44%, 1 x 3/60%, 1 x 2/70%
    1 x 1/80%, 1 x 1/90%, 1 x 3/82%

Week 2
Workout 1: 1 x 5/44%, 1 x 3/60%, 3 x 3/70%
Workout 2: 1 x 5/44%, 1 x 3/60%, 1 x 2/70%
    1 x 1/84%, 1 x 1/94%, 1 x 3/86%

Week 3
Workout 1: 1 x 5/44%, 1 x 3/60%, 3 x 3/74%
Workout 2: 1 x 5/44%, 1 x 3/60%, 1 x 2/74%
    1 x 1/90%, 1 x 1/94%, 1 x 3/90%

Week 4
Workout 1: 1 x 5/44%, 1 x 3/60%, 3 x 3/74%
Workout 2: 1 x 5/44%, 1 x 3/64%, 1 x 2/80%
    1 x 1/92%, 1 x 1/101%, 1 x 3/93%

Week 5
Workout 1: 1 x 5/44%, 4 x 3/76%
Workout 2: 1 x 5/44%, 1 x 3/70%, 1 x 2/84%
    1 x 1/94%, 1 x 1/103%, 1 x 3/96%

Week 6
Workout 1: 1 x 5/44%, 4 x 3/80%
Workout 2: 1 x 5/44%, 1 x 3/70%, 1 x 2/84%
    1 x 1/96%, 1 x 1/105%

Recommended auxiliary exercises include wide-grip pullups (with no weight attached), or towel chins (explained earlier), heavy one-arm dumbell rows (the starting position of this exercise begins with the arm extended toward the floor, and the hand holding the dumbell at a 45-degree angle to the lower torso, in front of the opposite foot), and prone extensions for the lower back.

With regard to the set-and-rep pattern for these exercises, you might wish to go by your basic training instincts on the wide-grip pullups and prone extensions, doing two or three sets of each for just the right amount of reps to stimulate and stress the muscle to its maximum, but not to overwork it. The heavy one-arm dumbell row is different. You might want to do three sets with all the maximum poundage that you can handle for six consecutive power reps per set. Ted Arcidi, the first

Dave Fisher packs on the plates.

man to officially bench press 700 pounds in competition, feels that **sixes** strike the perfect balance between superhuman strength and massive muscle development. Ted knows what he is talking about. He is, without a doubt, one of the strongest and most massively muscled humans the world has ever known.

No. 11 – The Jaska Parviainen Finnish deadlift program number two:

This Finnish deadlift routine is an updated version of the one previously outlined. It is a sixteen-week program consisting of two training cycles which last five and eleven weeks in duration. The uniqueness of this particular deadlift routine is that it develops a blend of explosive pulling power off the floor, and gravity-defying lockout power.

Deadlift Dominated

Cycle 1 – Weeks 1 to 5: To initiate this cycle, simply follow the exact sets, reps, and percentages of maximum listed for the conventional (bent-knee) deadlift in weeks two, three, four, six and seven listed in cycle 2 of the original Finnish Deadlift Program.

Cycle 2 – Weeks 6 to 16: This particular cycle requires you to use the one-on-two-off/one-on-three-off dynamic training frequency. During weeks 6 through 14 on workout day number one you will be required to perform 3 sets of 10 reps (a light set, a medium heavy set and one very heavy set) in the stiff-legged deadlift while standing on the raised wooden platform described in the original Finnish Deadlift Program.

The percentages of maximum poundages correctly used for each of the three sets in the stiff-legged deadlift are based against your current one-rep capability in the conventional (bent-knee) deadlift when entering into the 16-week program. Traditional assistance or supplemental exercises can be included if need be after the deadlift session, but on workout day number one of each of the 11 weeks. Simply follow the instructions given in the original program regarding assistance exercises.

On the nonconsecutive workout day number two, you will be asked to do only graduated measured movement, or partial lockout conventional deadlifts, with a poundage which is five pounds beyond your current one-rep maximum – full range of movement capability – coming into the 16-week program. This poundage will remain exactly the same throughout the 11-week **cycle number two.**

Starting with week six you will do your measured movement conventional deadlifts – where there is an 11-inch distance between the floor and the bottom edge of the barbell plates – pulling the barbell approximately from the kneecaps to the lockout position each and every rep of the set. The secret to overloading maximally on this exercise is to increase your range of movement very gradually each

The incredible Nasser El Sonbaty, took third place at the 1995 Mr. Olympia.

workout by lowering the barbell one-and-a-half inches during weeks 7, 8 and 9 and one-and-a-

171

Mike Matarazzo and Milos Sarcev strive for points at a recent show.

quarter inches during week 10, by only one inch on weeks 11 and 12, and by three-quarters of an inch during weeks 13, 14 and 15. By week 16 you will be doing full range of movement deadlifts from the floor.

There are two ways of accomplishing the graduated measured movement deadlift. The first way is by using a power rack, where you lower the starting pins (steel rods which support the barbell) and/or build up the platform where you stand during the exercise with pieces of one-by-twelve-inch planks (each two feet in length) during each proceeding workout.

If you don't have access to a power rack, then your next option is to cut two dozen or more of these planks plus a few which are only half an inch thick. Once you have done this it is then just a matter of placing enough of them under the bottom edge of the barbell plates to accommodate the 11-inch starting position.

Once you are set, all you have to do is remove one or two planks from each side to achieve the correct distancing. The following chart indicates the distances:

WEEK NUMBER	INCHES OFF FLOOR
6	11
7	9.5
8	8
9	6.5
10	5.25
11	4
12	3
13	2.25
14	1.5
15	.75
16	0 (on floor)

This graduated measured movement concept is very similar to the one that Ernest F. Cottrell (a bodybuilder/powerlifter we spoke of of in detail in our book *Raw Muscle!*, Contemporary Books, Inc., 1989) used for boosting his deadlift into orbit.

Cottrell's program used the wooden planks concept in the manner we have described, but his poundage overload and rep scheme was slightly more aggressive in nature than the Jaska Parviainen suggestion of using five pounds more than a current one-rep capability. Cottrell would advise a bodybuilder to use ten

DEADLIFT
(Wooden-Plank Concept)

This drawing depicts the deadlift/wooden-plank concept that Jaska Parviainen and Ernest F. Cotrell recommend. Notice the top plank of each stack with the built-in safety feature to keep the bar from rolling off between sets.

Pro Tip: The wooden-plank concept can be applied to the barbell squat and supine barbell bench press as well. It only takes a little ingenuity in arranging one stack of wooden planks (box squat concept – where the power bodybuilder squats until his glutes momentarily touch the stack of planks behind him) for the squat and two stacks for the bench press. If you don't have enough wooden planks for this exercise then perhaps place them on top of some concrete bond beam blocks. The initial heights of the wooden stack(s) during the first two weeks of a program should allow a 1" to 3" power-stroke lockout for the squat

(bend at the knees, etc.) or bench press (bend at the elbows, etc.) movement.

Begin each workout for either of these two exercises by doing two specific warmup sets of 15 and 10 reps, each in full range of motion style with a poundage which is 45% and 60% of a current unfatigued maximum single effort. The remaining instructions are modifications of some of Paul Anderson's ultimate power-training secrets. Rest assured that this training instruction works very efficiently for the power bodybuilder. Load up an exercise bar with a poundage which exceeds a maximum single effort by 10%. With the assistance of a competent spotter or two, perform two sets of 20 to 25 consecutive reps in the 1" to 3" power-stroke lockout movement. Rest 2 to 3 minutes between all sets. Follow this workout for two non-consecutive workout days. One of the best

workout strategies here from the standpoint of localized muscle recovery and systemic recovery of the central nervous system is to train one day and then rest three total days. Your training workout week will be structured around an eight-day cycle as opposed to the common seven-day cycle, but that is of no concern.

Each proceeding eight-day cycle increase your power stroke by 1" simply by removing one more additional wooden plank from the stack(s), while decreasing the consecutive reps by 3. Your ultimate goal is to increase your power-stroke lockout in the squat to 1" to 2" above parallel, and in the bench press by 9". The rep factor will have decreased between 2 and 7. Six to eight weeks is about all the body can endure on this program and then you should consider taking a three-week rest from power lockout training.

percent more than a current one-rep maximum coming into his program. In other words, if you have a one-rep max of 500 pounds in a full-range deadlift, you would then up the poundage to 550 pounds. From here it was just a matter of doing seven to ten nonconsecutive single-blast reps, in a slow, deliberate manner, resting for three to five minutes between each completed rep.

Cycle two of the Finnish Deadlift Program, number two, is as follows:

Gary Strydom

Week 6
Workout 1: 1 x 10/27%, 1 x 10/36%
    1 x 10/42%
Workout 2: 1 x 10/27%, 1 x 5/35%, 1 x 3/50%
    1 x 2/66%, 1 x 1/82%, 1 x 1/94%
    1 x 1/100% + 5 pounds, 1 x 3/82%

Week 7
Workout 1: 1 x 10/27%, 1 x 10/41%
    1 x 10/50%
Workout 2: Same as week 6

Week 8
Workout 1: 1 x 10/27%, 1 x 10/42%
    1 x 10/54%
Workout 2: Same as week 6

Week 9
Workout 1: 1 x 10/27%, 1 x 10/46%
    1 x 10/58%
Workout 2: Same as week 6

Week 10
Workout 1: 1 x 10/31%, 1 x 10/50%
    1 x 10/62%
Workout 2: Same as week 6

Week 11
Workout 1: Same as week 9
Workout 2: Same as week 6

Week 12
Workout 1: Same as week 10
Workout 2: Same as week 6

Week 13
Workout 1: 1 x 10/33%, 1 x 10/52%
    1 x 10/64%
Workout 2: Same as week 6

Week 14
Workout 1: 1 x 10/35%, 1 x 10/54%
    1 x 10/66%
Workout 2: Same as week 6

Week 15
Workout 1: Drop stiff-legged deadlifts off wooden platform and do only assistance or supplemental exercises.
Workout 2: Same as week 6

Week 16
Workout 1: Same as week 15.
Workout 2: Same as week 6

Whenever you are computing poundages by a percentage system and you have an odd poundage, **always** take your answer to the nearest five-pound interval. Example: 342.1

pounds would be moved to 340 pounds, whereas a poundage like 343.6 would be taken to 345.

Note: Workout programs with specific names such as **Building Bionic Leg Power!, Bench Press Explosion in Six Weeks,** and **The Parviainen Finnish Deadlift Programs,** not only work very well for their highly selected muscle groups, they can also be interchangeable, one with the other, and can also be used within the training structure of many other muscle groups.

Remember not to use these, or some of the other systems we have mentioned, on isolationary exercises. An example would be dumbell lateral raises when the barometer sets begin to exceed 80 percent of an unfatigued maximum single effort. Why? Because, as we have said before, the stress loads are much too high and a debilitating injury could occur.

Without a doubt the above-mentioned workout programs will stimulate a very strong adaptive response in muscle mass growth and strength, especially when an impasse in other training systems is being experienced.

Well, there you have it, eleven advanced **training-past-the-burn techniques** that will create the ultimate in strength, mass growth, shape and quality of your muscles.

Please make a mental note that all training techniques should not be employed at the same time. Only one per muscle group, and only two at most should be used within the weekly training programs.

Within the primary first phase of each total-body workout, the two muscle groups selected should utilize the multi-angle training philosophy. By this we mean that two to four exercises should be carefully chosen that will work the insertion, the belly, the length and the width of the muscles at their greatest tension point. Intense exercises are also thoughtfully planned out to create a balanced development of strength and growth within the aspects of the muscles individually and each muscle group pair. For example: within the back there should be a one-third balance between the upper, mid and lower muscles. Abs, on the other hand, need a balance of 50/50 between the uppers and lowers. This is an overview of balances within the individual muscles. With

regard to muscle group pairs, there should be a 60/40 balance between the quads and the hamstrings, or leg biceps. We have only touched briefly on the percentage emphasis of balanced muscle development.

Previously we showed you, through three total-body workouts, how to "hit each angle" of the muscle groups in the primary phase. Continue to train these muscle groups with the exercises selected. Change to different ones only when you hit a training plateau and need to derail it, and not before. Changing exercises during a training plateau is just one of several steps a bodybuilder can use to utilize a substantial new muscle-gain factor.

One final point regarding where the muscle groups of the neck, forearms, abdominals and calves fit into the anti-stress muscle grouping in the primary phase of the total-body workouts. They are considered neutral, and can be included in any of the muscle group pairs. It is now time to give some scope and space commentary to what we call Primordial Muscle Shock.

Laura Creavalle

CHAPTER ELEVEN

Primordial Muscle-Shock Strategies

Econo-Time Secondary Phase

During this secondary intra phase workout we are going to ask you to train the remaining muscle groups. You will be performing only one **four-component exercise set,** doing eight hard, full reps to positive failure. Then

Tom Platz enjoys his time under the lights.

you will continue on with two to four forced, two to three negative, and four partial-burn reps, which could be one-quarter, one-third or half-reps done in the low, medium or high range of the movement. Which you choose will depend on what aspect of the muscle you are trying to bring to prominence.

The pros in the sport of bodybuilding call this econo-time training because each muscle group is carried along, so to speak, with one basic power, or one shape-training exercise and does not require a vast expenditure of training time.

At the very least, this method of muscle building will prevent your muscles from losing size (atrophy) and tone. More than likely it will push them to a new peak. Actually, the one set per muscle group method, as we have just des-

Guru of Heavy Duty – Mike Mentzer.

cribed, is just one of the many superintense training set strategies a bodybuilder can use to provide optimal muscle stimulation. What we would like to do now is to instruct you in the use of a number of proven hardcore **Primordial Muscle-Shock Strategies** (the meaning of which is to work a muscle against progressive resistance, but with a different approach) using the one-set-per-muscle-group concept of training.

One of the keys to bodybuilding success is to have as much of an understanding of muscle cell theory as possible. For example, if you know what the physiological function of a muscle is, then you will understand what former three-time IFBB Mr. Olympia Frank Zane meant when he stated on numerous occasions that "muscles don't have a brain, so they will be forced to respond, or react, when you jolt or surprise them while training." This is very good training advice. You will certainly shock your muscles to the maximum when you incorporate the following shock strategies individually, or in combination, into this one-set method. The beauty of these shock-training methods is knowing that you can't overtrain a muscle group by doing just one set of an exercise.

Primordial Muscle-Shock Strategies:
Use as heavy a weight as possible within the structure of the following advanced techniques, but not at the expense of continuous tension on the muscle cell.

The **four-component set:** This bodybuilding technique has been popularized over the years by such notable pro bodybuilders as Mike Mentzer, Tom Platz and Casey Viator, to name just a few. There are four stages of progression of the four-component set. The **first stage** consists of doing a set of conventional reps to positive failure. To clarify this in a little more detail: a set of conventional reps means maintaining a sustained intensity of effort for 40 to 70 seconds, during which there is a six-second (two seconds in the positive contraction phase and four seconds in the negative contraction) cadence per rep, for a total of from six to twelve reps. This is generally recognized as about right for the development of size and strength in the upper-body muscle groups. For the legs, the sustained effort of intensity varies somewhat in that a set may take from 70 seconds

(where a minimum of twelve reps are performed) to two-and-a-half minutes, where 25 or so reps can be completed. When training with a six-seconds-per-rep cadence your reps are neither fast nor slow, but moderate. To encourage the gain factor, it is always a good idea to use a holistic rep system whereby, after you have exhausted the muscle-stimulating effectiveness of, say, a set of six to eight reps, you might choose to go with eight to ten, or fifteen, or even up to thirty for a particular muscle group.

Rotation of the one-set-of-reps sequence will ensure that the three major components of the muscle cell (myofibrils, mitochondria, and sacroplasm) are stimulated at their optimum level of efficiency. The **percentage of max rep chart** listed in Chapter Nine will help you determine your rotation or maxi-reps. Also, within chapter two of our book *Mass!* (Contemporary Books, Inc., 1986) is explicit and detailed information on the science of reps.

Former boy wonder Casey Viator.

We mentioned previously that many body-builders have somewhat unique individual physiological variances within their muscle cells. This accounts for the transition point, where some bodybuilders can effectively stimulate their muscle myofibrils (a major muscle component which allows for sustained maximum contractions) for power and strength, using four to six power reps within a set, while another bodybuilder may find that he can stimulate this same muscle component to the max by beginning with the seven-to-ten maxi-pump range. One has only to read the training articles in the bodybuilding magazines by ten different champions regarding rep selection to find ten different answers. Bill Pearl, four-time Mr. Universe, has talked about the training topic of rep selection and this is what he had to say: "At least a dozen or more Mr. America winners have trained at my gyms over the years, and almost to a man they prefer between six and ten repetitions for muscle growth (and accompanying strength)."

As you can see, there are no absolutes in bodybuilding, nor are the bodybuilding publications trying to confuse you by printing articles on or by the champions relating to their sometimes totally unique, and sometimes complicated, training philosophies. All of the super-scientific training systems are, for the most part, based upon sound physiological concepts, and have been proven to work, one way or another, to create max results. Having said that, however, it's true that no one system of training is best for all muscle groups. For example: the Eastern Bloc Training System lends itself very well to the squat, bench press and deadlift, but more than likely it wouldn't be the preferred system to use for brutalizing the delts. Shoulders seem to have their own unique physiological personality. So, with this thought in mind, if you want to experience the thrill of achieving great gains, then you must be given the option to select the system of training which is best suited for your immediate and particular needs. The final judge of how well a system of training works or, in your case, how well "rep selection" works, is you. It is not how inviting it looks on paper, it is the results you are getting from actual workout application of it in the hardcore trenches of the gym.

Continuing our discussion on the value of the **four-component set**, when the effective-

Achim Albrecht

ness of a chosen rep selection begins to cease after being performed to momentary positive failure, here is what you must do: go on to **stage two, forced reps.** Assume that you have just completed eight hard, full reps to positive failure. You now begin to enter a new dimension of muscle burn by doing several (two to four) creative cheating or forced reps. This can be accomplished by numerous methods. The first is to have a training partner (if you are fortunate enough to have such a luxury) or spotter use a touch system where he places his hands under the bar and makes up the difference between your existing strength level and the actual weight of the barbell. This is done by the partner assisting (lifting) through the sticking point of positive failure. Most generally this type of assistance in terms of pounds lifted may amount to between 5 and 10 pounds on the first forced or double-failure rep, then 10 to 15 pounds on the second, and 15 to 20 pounds on the third creative-cheating rep. There are no pauses between those reps, to speak of, and if the spotter knows his business his assistance will never decrease the stress load (known as the resistance curve) on a muscle (strength curve) but, in fact, may increase it.

There is no denying the value in having a training partner or spotter assist you when it comes down to crunch time, and you need their help when doing the double-failure forced

Dave Fisher has shown great improvement in recent months.

◄ Edgar Fletcher and Nikki Fuller.

reps. The optimum safety factor here is most comforting. But suppose you don't have this option. What then? Well, the bottom line here, as you might have already guessed, is to do them solo or self-assisted. This is accomplished by initiating method two in the performance of the forced-reps modality. Upon completing your set of eight reps to momentary positive failure, take a very brief rest-pause of three to

as much as ten seconds, then grind out two to four more reps to positive failure. You may have to experiment with the rest-pause to find out where your critical threshold of recovery is so that you can nail those two to four forced reps. Some bodybuilders will take this up the ladder of progression by doing eight or more conventional reps (to momentary positive failure), rest for a few seconds, then do another conventional rep, rest again, do another conventional rep, and continuing on in this manner until they can't even get one more conventional rep without an extended rest. This is called interval minisets.

179

Lee Priest gives his version of a classic pose.

story of a lifter named George Irving Nathinson who would do 100 sub-maximal blast singles with a fixed poundage, rest-pausing one minute between each single. He would do this three times every two weeks and then take a complete one-week layoff from training.

Of all the blast-single concepts we have heard of probably the one we and many other bodybuilders favor the most is the one former IFBB Mr. World Chuck Sipes used to develop his rugged and granite-hard physique. His training concept consisted of doing heavy blast singles with a power movement, followed by maxi-pump reps with a shape-training exercise.

This is what one of his workout programs looked like:

No. 1 – performed twice weekly:
1. Behind-the-neck presses – *4 sets x 2 reps*
2. Front dumbell raises – *4 sets x 10 reps*
3. Supine bench presses – *4 sets x 1 rep*
4. Barbell straight-arm pullovers – *4 sets x 12 reps*
5. Barbell cheat curls – *4 sets x 1 rep*
6. Scott curls– *4 sets x 12 reps*
7. Conventional deadlifts – *5 sets x 2 reps*
8. Barbell good mornings – *5 sets x 12 reps*
9. Barbell bent-over rows – *4 sets x 2 reps*
10. Lat machine pulldowns – *4 sets x 15 reps*

Milos Sarcev and Mike Matarazzo.

Yet another giant step in this direction is to do a maximum triple power-rep set, and immediately start doing blast singles. (These are positive/negative single reps, usually done with 90 percent of a current unfatigued maximum single effort, and can be powered up with comparatively little stress.) Blast singles are performed by doing one rep, rest for ten seconds, do another rep, rest ten seconds, and on and on until six to eight singles to positive failure have been completed.

Another way to do blast singles is to implement the Brooks D. Kubic mathematical one-rep formula: Perform one blast single for each of the listed percentages of your current maximum single effort. Squats – 81 percent, 87 percent, 92 percent and 97 percent. Bench press and deadlift – 80 percent, 85 percent, 90 percent and 94 percent.

Sub-maximal blast singles should only be done every other week. This mode of training has been taken to some extremes in the past. *Powerlifting USA* author Don Pfeiffer tells the

Mike Matarazzo, Flex Wheeler and Lee Labrada.

No. 2 – performed twice weekly:

1. Lying (EZ-curl bar) French presses –
   5 sets x 2 reps
2. Triceps pushdowns – *5 sets x 15 reps*
3. Barbell full squats – *4 sets x 2 reps*
4. Leg extensions on machine –
   4 sets x 15 reps
5. Standing calf raises on machine –
   4 sets x 2 reps
6. One-legged calf raises (bodyweight only) –
   4 sets x 20 reps
7. Barbell shrugs – *4 sets x 8 reps*
8. Reverse barbell curls – *4 sets x 8 reps*
9. Incline situps – *4 sets x 20 reps*

Within the structure of this alternate twice-weekly workout program, a maxi-pump repetition set (any exercise where more than six repetitions are executed in all sets) immediately follows the double and/or blast single set for the same muscle group. (This does not apply to exercises 7, 8 and 9 in No. 2 above.)

With this in mind, Chuck Sipes suggests loading up the appropriate poundage on two pieces of exercise equipment applicable to the muscle group being trained at the time. This way you can move from one exercise to the next without hesitation. As you will notice, there are more double power-rep sets than blast single sets in the above workouts. The programs, therefore, do not represent a pure undiluted blast single/maxi-pump rep set in the truest sense of the word; but it does reveal some meaningful insight as to how you might upgrade your workout standard to that level.

There is a third method for doing double-failure forced reps and, much like the previous one (method two), it is also self-assisted. You have probably read and heard plenty about triple-drop sets or the multi-poundage power-pumping principle (also known as: four sets in one, breakdown training, railroading, and strip sets) from England. Triple-drop training simply described is the performance of four sets in one where, upon positive failure of multiple reps, the poundage is reduced by 7-1/2 to 10 percent each set without resting. With the absence of any type of rest, it appears that there is a combining of unrelated muscle fatigue within the strength equation. Both conflict! When the ultimate pump-out in a muscle is sought, this does not present too much of a problem. However, if maximum muscle mass and herculean strength is the primary objective, then most bodybuilders modify the triple-drop technique slightly. They take very brief rests within each of the poundage reductions. It is not, however, the same elapsed time for each muscle group. Depending on the current level of fitness, the following rest-pauses within the triple-drop technique are employed: quads 20 to 30 seconds, leg biceps 12 seconds, calves 10 seconds, back 10 seconds, chest 8 seconds, delts 8 seconds, and arms 5 seconds.

Your direction in training at this moment is not to do a triple-drop set, but to do two to three self-assisted double-failure forced reps. This can be accomplished most adequately by doing a single-drop set where, upon completion of the 8 conventional reps, you reduce your training poundage by 2.5 percent to 5 percent (or whatever is the amount necessary to get those two or three forced muscle-growth reps). Be sure that you not only have enough

Start...

...Finish

10-pound plates on your barbell, but also plenty of smaller ones in the 1.25, 2.5 and 5-pound range so that you won't lose time removing poundage.

Another very effective means of doing self-assisted forced reps is the alternate rebound principle. This is the fourth in a series of five methods for doing creative cheating or double-failure reps. It requires using two dozen or so 2-inch x 12-inch wooden boards, each precut to two feet in length, and four to six pieces of high-density rubber pads. The rubber pads should be one inch in thickness, and custom-cut to 2 x 12 inches. These rubber pads are very much like those that Richard Simons used for the "shock-rebounding" supine bench press technique in his *25 Pounds of Muscle in 21 Days* training concept (Monday workout program), mentioned in chapter six.

Once you have these items, have someone measure the vertical distance from the floor to where the bottom edge of the barbell or dumbell plates are when you are holding the bar in the negative prestretched position of the exercise. Once you have accurately determined what this distance is for a particular exercise, then it is just a matter of placing the precut boards, one on top of the other, in two stacks at the appropriate graduated height interval, capping the final two to three inches of each stack with the custom-cut rubber pads. If the positioning and height of the wooden stacks is done correctly, the bottom edge of the plates should strike the rubber surface of the pads when you are in the negative prestretch position. Now it is time to put the rebound principle into action.

We mentioned previously that the conventional eight reps was to be performed in a strict, full range of motion style. With the rebound principle in effect, we are gong to change our instruction. You will be asked to do the eight conventional reps in a strict controlled manner, but to stop each rep movement about one inch before where the bottom edge of the barbell or dumbell plates would strike the rubber surface of the rebound

Paul Jean-Guillaume is a great believer in correct form, regardless of whether he's using light or heavy weight.

Lee Priest displays a powerful most-muscular.

against rebounding of any type while doing forced reps in squatting-type movements. Performing the single-weight drop set, or better yet, using a Jesse Hoagland safety squat bar or a Frank Zane leg blaster would be better. Both of these state-of-the-art exercise pieces allow you the hand freedom needed to push on the tops of your thighs as a means of doing forced reps. The rebound principle when properly applied is one of the optimum forced-reps techniques which will help you overcome the stern law of gravity!

The fifth and final method of doing forced reps is called serial distortion. (Rick Valente, a superstar bodybuilder and a frequent co-host of ESPN's *Bodyshaping* program, calls this weight-tripping.) Serial distortion, as it applies to hardcore bodybuilding, is the momentary loss of the precision biomechanical integrity of the structured exercise movement. Don't worry, it sounds more complicated to say than it is to do.

What we are talking about here for putting two to three forced reps into orbit is doing little things like a twist of the wrist, pulling back the shoulders, tightening the abs when doing pulldowns, or raising the weight a little bit more forward than you would usually do.

On weight-resistance movements, such as all types of rowing, curling, vertical pressing and the various lateral or front raises, you will (in a rhythmic, rocking motion) bend forward slightly at the waist. Then, with a controlled thrust of your body, you get the weight moving through the sticking point as you then bend backward slightly. On heavy overhead triceps extensions you will reverse the order of the bending at the waist. (Lean back, body thrust lean forward.) On bench pressing, we have seen some bodybuilders do their cheating, or forced, reps by lowering the bar down to their abdominal region and, by simultaneously arching the back with a mighty thrust of abdominal power, put the barbell into orbit for two or three additional reps. We will agree that serial-distortion techniques in the manner described are, to the untrained eye, exaggerated body movements and, yes, they do give a milli-second of mechanical advantage, but never at the expense of decreasing maximum tension within the muscle cell structure.

stacks. Once you have completed these reps, and have reached the sticking or failure point, then push past it by allowing the weights to strike the rubber surface for two to three controlled, bouncing forced reps. Many of the top bodybuilders have found this rebound principle to work very well with pushing and pulling exercises. Rebounds can be done with deadlifts, bent-over and upright rows, flat bench presses, lying French presses, barbell bent-arm pullovers, dumbell flyes, lateral raises, and just about all combinations of curls. A couple of favorites we have seen are the rapid-pump kneeling rebound barbell curls and prone dumbell lateral raises. We know of some bodybuilders who do rebounding box squats, but we are not in favor of those because of their spine-jarring effect. We advise

The training tips that we have just given you are part of a complex system called tracking patterns or, as John Parrillo calls them, performance points. He is most definitely into this methodology in a big, big way. He covers dozens of performance points in books he's written with Maggie Greenwood Robinson – *High Performance Bodybuilding*, and John Parrillo's *50 Workout Secrets*.

These five sure-fire methods will help you tremendously in your quest to do two or three creative cheating or double-failure forced reps, either with a training partner or self-assisted. Again, exhaust the potential of this second stage (perhaps 8 to 10 workouts) and upon doing so, it is time to journey into **stage three** of the four-component set progression.

Immediately upon completion of the eight conventional reps and the two to four forced reps, you can do two or three negative failure reps. Though you have exhausted your positive strength reserves momentarily, your negative strength is still at a plus of between 15 and 40 percent on a single joint output. Each of the two negative reps should take 8 to 10 seconds to complete (up from the four-second phase requirement in the eight conventional reps, and the two to four forced reps mode). Some bodybuilders will go up to 30 seconds per negative rep, but in a most unusual and different way. Let us explain: The 30-second negative will utilize a 6 to 10 second isometric stop at three or four different positions, or levels, of the movement. This is done by lowering the loaded bar every three or four inches – stopping the descent and resisting the gravitational pull for from 6 to 10 seconds and, at the same time, mentally and physically tensing the muscles by squeezing. This procedure, as we have described it, involves stopping the bar in this manner at least three or four times during its descent.

As you may have noticed, we are back into a major dilemma in that a training partner or spotter is once again needed to assist with the negative failure reps. In the past not having spot assistance on the negatives could have put the skids on a trainer doing this third stage of **four-component set** progression – but not anymore. Strength and power champion Bob Kowalcyk has invented a new training tool

especially for those of you bodybuilders who desperately want to do stress-load negatives, but can't because you train alone. This training tool is a two-part device called weight release. We are including two detailed drawings of the weight release device in use. We feel these vivid drawings will be a most helpful visual aid as we describe its function.

The barbell bench press is the exercise depicted in the drawings, so we have elected, for the sake of simplicity, to base the description and use of the weight release on this popular exercise. Begin by calculating what your maximum single effort (MSE) is in this exercise. Let's assume that to be 300 pounds. Load up the long bar with 60 to 80 percent of that amount. If you choose to go with 80 percent of the 300-pound maximum single effort, the bar should be loaded to 240 pounds.

You will have a remaining 20 percent or 60 pounds, and this amount should be divided up and loaded equally onto each separate weight release. The total of the weight on the long bar and the combined amount on the two-part weight release now equals the 300-pound maximum single effort. You're not finished with the loading procedure on the weight release yet. As many of you probably know, one of the secrets to doing a maximal-mode negative is to use a poundage which is 20 percent and beyond your maximum single effort (MSE) in the conventional (negative/positive) style. So with this in mind load an additional 10 percent more poundage (30 pounds) onto each weight release. The 60-pound loaded release devices are hooked one over each end of the bench press bar. Now you are set to do the bench press. Do so by unracking the bar unassisted (this should not present a problem if your tendon and ligament strength levels are up from the previous tightrope or "support" training). Pause an extra second with the arms fully extended over your chest to minimize any sway or swing of the weight release device. Then, slowly lower the weight down to the sternum, and at the very instant the long bar touches your chest, the loaded weight release devices will disengage from it (provided the hooked bar

BARBELL BENCH PRESS USING WEIGHT RELEASE

DRAWING A

DRAWING B

and the base unit of each device has been properly adjusted to the correct length).

At the moment this takes place, you must immediately (and explosively) power the 240-pound barbell up, doing a complete positive-phase rep. Don't stop yet, but do an additional two or three more conventional reps (both negative and positive phases) with this

Dorian Yates in a regal pose.

poundage. Then rack the weight. Take a rest and, while doing so, hook each weight release device back on the long bar so they will be ready to work as you prepare for your second and final negative-mode rep.

The weight release device is versatile in that it can be used for the ultimate pump-out set. Using the same 80 percent of a maximum single effort, load the bar up to 180 pounds or 60 percent of your 300-pound maximum single effort. Now put 10 percent, or 30 pounds of resistance, on each weight release. Adjust the hook bar into the base of each device so that it is three to four inches shorter than the previous quick-release adjustment used for the maximal negative-mode rep. Attach the weight release to the bar.

Taking your normal grip on the bar, slowly lower down to your chest. Count slowly to 25 (one thousand one, one thousand two, etc.). Then press the bar back up and do a second rep In the manner described. A third rep is then begun by lowering the barbell (and attached weight release device) slowly down to the chest. Again, as with the previous two reps, hold this position for a slow count of 25. Now, rather than pressing the combined poundage of 240 pounds up to arms' length over the chest, rock, or tip, the bar ever so slightly (from one side then the other) just enough so that each 30-pound loaded weight release will disengage from the bar almost simultaneously.

Now pump out as many conventional reps as you can with the 180-pound barbell until your pecs look like a road map of blood-choked vascularity. Do a second set of three reps with the 25-count pause, but this time use only the 180-pound barbell. Your handspacing should now be three inches narrower than what you consider normal. Do a third and final set with the 180 pounds, and again adjust your handspacing to where it is another three inches closer than that of the second set (6 inches closer than normal). Try this three-set combination, using a cambered bench press bar rather than a straight long bar, and experience the ultimate in pec stretching.

The beauty of function of the weight release is that it can be adjusted for the one-shot, quick-release maximal-mode negative, or a set of conventional reps using a single weight-drop concept. Either way you go, the device is always just inches from the floor for instant disengagement. The strength athlete will find the device invaluable for doing the nonassisted negative. Just think, if a spotter **is** available, all he has to do is quickly attach the weight release back on the bar and it's an instant go for another negative rep or reps as the case may be.

The empirical hardcore bodybuilder will be thrilled at the number of options he has when using weight release for doing conventional reps in the squat, bench press, curls, upright rows and shrugs, etc. At the time of writing, weight release sells for an economical $64.95 plus $7.00 for shipping and handling. They are manufactured in two styles, for either an Olympic-style bar or a conventional one-inch bar, without sleeves. To order the weight release, or just to receive more information on this most revolutionary training tool, write or call (noncollect, please) Bob Kowalcyk at: Power Recruit, Inc., Rt. 1, Box 122C, Houtzdale, PA 16651, phone 814-378-7108.

Stage four is the final step in this particular version of the **four-component set**. Here you will be required to do four partial burn-pump reps. We have already discussed their function and importance as one part of many vital training techniques. Some bodybuilders will do these after completing stage three, others will modify these partial burnout reps (one-quarter, one-third and one-half movements) within the first stage of the conventional rep scheme. They will do two partial burnout reps to each conventional rep, and six at momentary failure on the last rep of the one set.

There are **other experimental variations** of the extended set. Two of the most result-producing when blitzing a select muscle group are the Dynamite Delt Blitz and the Ultimate Calf Blast Pump-Out. The following information will describe each system individually.

Ultimate Calf Blast Pump-Out:

This program works exceptionally well with the standing and donkey calf raise for maximizing development of the gastrocnemius muscle, but it works even better with the seated calf raise for pumping up the soleus.

Start

Many novice bodybuilders neglect calf development. Lee Labrada shows he is not a novice.

Finish

Darin Lannaghan points the way.

Select a poundage that will allow you to complete 15 maxi-pump repetitions in the exercise of your choice. Do 15 normal-speed reps, coming up on the ball of your feet and big toes, and make a conscious effort to stretch in the bottom position of each and every rep. When you have finished the last rep, lift one foot at a time off the calf block and shake one leg twice and then the other.

Now do eight more reps, but this time in super slow fashion, coming up on the lateral or outer edge of your foot. Shake each leg again as described. Perform another eight reps, but this time in super speed fashion, again coming up on the lateral edge of your foot. Repeat the leg shaking. Now do a final super slow eight reps, coming up on the balls of your feet and big toes, as before. This time around, instead of shaking your legs, do as many partial (almost bouncy) super speed, burn reps in the high one-quarter to one-third positive contraction range as you can. During these bounce reps, perform the calf roll. First shift your bodyweight to the outside edges of the balls of your feet, then roll the contraction to the inner edges. During the roll to the outer edge on the

Lee Priest

positive contraction, and the inner edge during the negative, the balls of your feet remain fully in contact with the surface of the calf block. Immediately upon completing these partial burnouts do the patented Vince Gironda alternate heel raise to absolute positive **and** negative failure. First raise the left heel up until the calf is fully contracted, then, at the top of the movement, shift the weight to the right leg and lower. Then raise up on the right leg and, at the top or contracted position, bend the knee and shift the weight to the left leg and lower, then up on the left leg, etc.

The above ultimate calf blast pump-out is considered to be one set, and should be performed without rest or pauses. If for some reason this program isn't enough of a saturation blast, then immediately begin doing a series of partial burnout reps – and alternate heel raises – to momentary failure.

Dynamic Delt Blitz:
On this program you will use the seated press behind the neck. Perform five slow, strict reps (with no cheating) using a poundage that you can handle properly. Immediately after you have done these, stand up and continue with two moderately fast reps in the behind-the-neck press, cheating only if necessary on the ninth and tenth reps. Now sit down and, with the help of a training partner, do ten negative reps (each one should take six to eight seconds). After these do five half presses behind the neck, pressing the bar to the top of your head and lowering the bar as far down behind your shoulders as you can. Now press the barbell from the top of your delts to eye level for three power reps. After this, grab an unloaded bar and, standing up, do five fast reps to help ease the lactic acid burn. This completes one continuous set, without any rest pauses whatsoever. The behind-the-neck press, when performed in the manner described, forces muscle growth in the delt width aspect. Seated front presses are a good substitute if you desire to create delt thickness when viewed from the side. If you are interested in using this as an only exercise in the primary phase of the total-body workout, then do a series of from five to seven sets, resting two to four minutes between each.

The 50-Rep Blitz:
This program is a one-set deal. Select a poundage that you can perform 20 to 25 conventional reps with while still holding good exercise form. When you complete the 20 to 25 reps, take a ten-second rest and continue on doing more reps – another rest of ten seconds, and some more reps. Continue on with this sequence until you have completed that magical 50 reps. There should be no more than five total rest-pauses during this single set.

This is an effective but limited three-week program which can be done on two alternate training days per week. Perhaps you might want to do a second 50-rep blitz in the primary phase of your total-body workout. This brief but super intense program works very well with such progressive-resistance exercises as squats, bench presses, stiff-legged deadlifts, upright rows, chinups and pullups, vertical dips (on the parallel bars), and various curl-type movements. Rest should be restricted to two or three minutes between exercises.

Compared to the instructions set forth in the **four-component set** program, the 50-rep blitz may seem like a walk in the park. In fact, you may be wondering if you can get anything more out of it than a vein-choked muscle pump. Well, as a matter of fact, this particular primordial muscle-shock technique is more than it appears to be because it uses a holistic rep-speed theory. The holistic rep theory is generally understood to mean that, within the scope of the 20 to 25 to 50 rep scheme, the speed of the reps will vary. Some of them will be performed at your normal speed, while other reps will be done at a super-slow speed. Still others will be done at a super-fast speed. Let's briefly examine each of these components as it relates to the holistic rep-speed theory.

Lee Labrada

Darin Lannaghan flashes his pair of big guns between sets.

Normal-Speed Reps (Eccentric/Concentric):

It is generally accepted that a normal rep speed for full-range-of-motion exercises uses a one-to-two muscle contraction ratio. If, for example, it takes two seconds to contract the muscle while moving the resistance (barbell or dumbell, etc.) through the positive (concentric) phase, then it should take four seconds in the negative (eccentric) phase, because of its overriding 20 percent to 40 percent reserve strength factor. The human body is, in a way, a lazy organism, and will only react and adapt to the progressive resistance stress put upon it. From then on, it is always looking for ways to coast. For example, if you continue to use the same exercises, sets, reps and poundages workout after workout, there is no added stimulus for the muscles to grow more massive.

So far we have shown you how to maintain a continuous muscle overload with major and

Chip Sigmon can look symmetrical or he can hit mass poses. No wonder this combination gives him the edge on the posing dais.

minor changes in training techniques, exercises, sets, reps and poundage selections. What we are attempting to do now is to show you a few of the options you have within the holistic rep-speed theory, and how, by uisng them, you can stimulate more muscle mass and strength gains.

While, as we said, the normal eccentric/concentric speed rep is two seconds in the positive contraction phase and four seconds in the negative contraction phase, many bodybuilders (both at the amateur and the pro levels) will experiment by mixing and matching different muscle contraction normal rep-speed ratios. There are four variations which seem to work quite well within the parameters of what is considered normal rep speed. They are:

Normal Rep Speed Ratios (Seconds):
1. **2-1-2** (equal time in the positive and negative phase)
2. **3-1-2** (slightly more time given in the positive phase)
3. **2-1-4** (this ratio allows for more time in the negative phase)
4. **3-1-4** (this unique rep-speed ratio incorporates the best of both 2 and 3 above)

An example which we like to use to illustrate the meaning of positive/isometric/negative phases of a rep is the body drag curl, which the Iron Guru, Vince Gironda, taught to one of his gym members in the premier issue of *MuscleMag's Video Magazine*. Vince has his students grip a loaded barbell just wider than shoulder width, elbows back, behind the plane of the upper torso and into the sides. Vince says that this elbow position is critical to the development of building the lateral – outside – of the biceps. From a standing position the bar is slowly curled all the way to the base of the neck, touching the front of the body constantly. This is what is called the positive or concentric phase of the rep. The moment the bar is curled into the neck, Vince demands that you tense and squeeze the biceps muscles for one or two seconds with as much muscle contraction as possible. This is called the isometric contraction phase. From here Vince has his students begin lowering the weight down slowly (keeping the elbows back and the bar touching the body) to an arms-extended position where the bar will rest, touching the front of the upper thighs. This slow descent of the weight is the negative aspect of the rep phase. Vince says that negatives are the easiest to do, so he makes it harder by having his student resist the bar's downward pull. The body-drag curl offers some unique variants. John Parrillo advises thrusting the chest forward and dropping the shoulders down as the bar is curled or pulled up to the low pec line and no further. Leo Costa Jr., on the other hand, takes it one step beyond by moving the elbows forward and upward to shoulder level (curling the bar into the neck).

Super Slow-Speed Reps (Contraction Control):

We remember former IFBB Mr. World Steve Davis of California expounding on his new breed of champion concepts of training. He said that if there was one training technique which helps a bodybuilder's potential for achieving raw muscularity, it would have to be the **12-count repetition technique.** He went on to say that a repetition done in this manner relies on maximal contraction of the muscle cells, with loss of momentum in the movement being the main factor. Going back to the Vince Gironda body-drag curl for a moment, a 12-count repetition (6-2-4) would be done in the following manner. It should take you a count of six seconds to curl the bar from

Steve Davis lets 'er rip!

191

Recipe: Take one Frank Zane, add in a full measure of lean mass, stir. Yield: one Lee Labrada.

pleasing symmetry, was enough to convince any hardcore bodybuilder that 12-count repetitions were worth doing. The evolution of this type of slow training has long enjoyed a quiet popularity among the hardcore bodybuilers. However, within the last year or two we have noticed slow-rep training literally explode into one of the most talked about (and used) training techniques.

We feel that much of this popularity on slow-rep training stems from the research of Ken Hutchins. He has refined the basic premise of the 12-count repetition into a technique he calls super slow. Super slow is a rep which requires a 10-second count in the positive-contraction phase, and, with smooth reversal of direction (called turnarounds), five seconds are taken to complete the negative-contraction phase.

As you may remember, we mentioned this super-slow method in the power four-rep/tri-pump system as one of the training-past-the-burn techniques (in Chapter Ten). Some bodybuilders will extend their super-slow reps to include stops at every two to three inches in the negative-contraction phase of every third rep in a set. The stops last only for a microsecond. Just long enough, in fact, to resist the gravitational force while, at the same time reversing your movement into a concentric (positive) muscle contraction, whereby you could (if you had to) actually move the resistance through a complete positive range of motion.

Some of the champions in our sport will do a slightly different version of super slow with momentary stop pauses in the rep by doing what is called the Schauer Stutter Rep. A stutter rep means pausing on both the positive and the negative movements of the rep. This separates the movement into three stages in the negative and four stages in the positive phase of the rep. We will use the bench press to show you how the actual stutter rep is accomplished.

Place an unloaded exercise bar on the upright rack supports of a flat bench and load 30 percent to 40 percent less poundage than you would normally use on the bar for a corresponding number of reps. Next, chalk your hands and lay down in a supine position

across the tops of the thighs to the neck. Then, at this contracted completion of the positive phase, you tense the muscle isometrically for two seconds, then you slowly lower the weight down to a count of four seconds. This completes one 12-count rep.

Davis went on to say that, by using the 12-second count, you are able to pump, burn and exhaust the muscle much faster, while using a much more moderate weight than you would if you did the reps at normal speed.

One look at the Davis physique, with its thick muscle density and high degree of muscularity and definition, coupled with a

on the bench. Your head should be positioned so that your eyes are approximately one inch past the upright rack supports (one inch nearer the end of the bench). Your back should be flat (not arched) against the bench surface as are your glutes. Elevate your legs so that your hips and knees both form right angles, and cross the lower legs at the ankles. Reach up and take what for you would be a wide handspacing, with your thumbs under and wrapped tightly around the bar. Your knuckles should be above the bar, with your hands straight and not bent backward at the wrist. The palms of your hands are facing forward. The purpose in keeping your hands straight and not bent backward is to allow the bar to be aligned down through the center of the arms rather than having the bar travel out of parallel with the arms as it does when the wrists are bent backward.

Inhale deeply and unrack the loaded barbell to an arms fully extended or locked out position. Your elbows should be directly over your shoulder joints. The barbell is motionless at this point, and aligned with your sternum – clavicular-pec junction. Tuck your chin down to your neck and keep it in this fixed position throughout the set. This little mechanical positioning of the head will take the lats out of this exercise, making for even more focused upper-pec isolation.

Now begin lowering the bar in stutter-rep fashion. Lower the bar three inches, do a momentary stop-pause, switch from a negative output to a positive output and press the bar back up two inches. Continue the procedure by lowering the bar back down four or five inches, stop-pause, press it back up a couple of inches. Lower it down further, stop-pause and press it back up another inch or so, and so on. Continue in this manner until you have done stutter-reps with three stop-pauses, and the bar is touching your chest. At this pont your elbows should be at 70 to 90 degrees perpendicular to the body. To place even more incredible stress on the upper aspect near the clavicles, turn your elbows out so that your upper arms are in line with the shoulders. The best way to accommodate this tracking pattern is by having the palms rotated so that the bar is positioned diagonally across the palms. A Smith machine is your best bet here.

Pause for two counts, then begin to press the bar up three to four inches, while keeping your elbows and upper arms directly under the bar and in line with your shoulder joints. Lower the bar back down one or two inches, stop-pause, press it back up three to four inches, lower it back down one to two inches, and so on. Continue in this manner until you have completed stutter reps with four stop-pauses, before locking the arms out hard.

Note: The preferred number of stutters in a rep seems to be between two and five. The originator of the stutter reps, Egan Schauer, suggests doing six reps on the first set, five reps on the second set and four reps for a third and final set of an exercise. Other practitioners

Roland Cziurlock

193

of stutter-rep philosophy find that doing an eight, seven and six-rep scheme worked equally as well. For our purposes, do only one set in the secondary phase.

Oxygen saturation is a key feature to the success of the stutter rep. Therefore, it is recommended that you inhale a fast, deep burst of air into your lungs at each momentary stop-pause and blow it out. There are two pretty good reasons for this. First, you will need all the oxygen saturation possible just to get through each stage of the stop sequence on each and every rep. Secondly, because of the elapsed work time in completing each rep, it is not a good idea to hold air in the lungs.

Remember when we discussed serial distortion for doing forced reps? Well, if you feel the need to do an extra forced rep or two after doing the stutter rep on this wide-grip bench press, just untuck your chin from your neck and lay your head back on the flat bench surface. Your lats will kick in and help for two more big forced reps. Another logical intensity

progression is to press the bar up from the neck six to eight inches and lower it again, continuing for four to six partial reps at the end of a full-reps set. Do these stutter reps in the manner just described and you'll feel an excruciating burn as you shape your muscles.

Ken Hutchins, whom we mentioned earlier as one of the individuals most responsible in the research and development of the super-slow rep, has written a manual titled *Super Slow: The Ultimate Exercise Protocol*. It goes far beyond anything previously written on the subject. Many bodybuilders worldwide have this manual as part of their bodybuilding library. It gives plenty of fresh instructional techniques for super slow rep training. The book can be purchased for $30.00 per copy from Media Support, P.O. Box 180154, Casselberry, FL 32718-0154. At this time prices include shipping and handling. Florida residents need to add 6% sales tax.

Paul Dillett eyes the competition.

Super Fast Speed Reps (Tantric Contraction):

The purpose behind the Super Fast Tantric Contraction Speed Rep is to get the maximum benefit from each and every rep before lactic acid buildup cuts the set short. In order to do this, many top bodybuilders like Serge Nubret and former IFBB Mr. Olympia Larry Scott will race the pump (or failure through fatigue point) by completing as many quality, controlled reps as possible within a set before lactic acid accumulates in the muscle.

One way to accomplish this is through a fixed work time interval of 40 to 70 seconds for upper-body exercises, and 70 to 150 seconds for the lower-body exercises (explained previously in the **four-component set**) while doing a regular number of reps. You will increase the number of reps by one or two within the same work time per set.

One of the most popular methods for beginning super fast speed reps is to go with a positive/isometric/negative ratio of 1-1-2. Work with this rep-speed ratio for a number of workouts, and then gradually change to a new ratio of one-and-a-half seconds in the positive contraction (while totally decreasing the isometric contraction) and decrease the negative-contraction phase by the same amount. Therefore, it is very important not to pause even slightly at any point in the rep-speed mode. This is 100 percent pure tantric contraction speed, where one muscle contraction is followed closely by another before the muscle cell can fully relax.

Each and every rep must be performed extremely fast. We have observed some of the top bodybuilders training at Gold's Gym in Venice, California and they are cranking out 24 to 40 reps in 60 seconds. This is usually accomplished, not with free weights, but with electro-magnetic machines, such as those manufactured by the Toro Company, or with weight-training machines which use hydraulics. These are some of the very best types of sophisticated training tools by which to generate resistance while eliminating the dangerous momentum and recoil forces that are normally associated with the use of free weights. Those using free weights, though, should use 60 percent of current unfatigued

Serge Nubret

10-rep maximum, and do 12 to 20 reps in a 20 to 30-second elapsed work time.

If you are looking for a fresh peak of training intensity, the speed reps are a good choice. Your motor nerve pathways to the muscles will be stimulated quite differently than would be the case with normal speed or super slow reps. This is because you will be performing these tantric reps with a burst of speed, as opposed to a slower dissipation of power. Your mental and physical powers will reach new optimum levels. Fast reps also burn less energy.

David Dearth

Pro Tip: Some of the champion bodybuilders will use a variable-speed rep mode within a select set. Using 35 percent of a 10-rep max do 10 super slow reps, then 10 super fast. These interval rep speeds are done continuously until 50 to 60 reps are completed for leg work. For upper-body exercises the intervals are five slow/five fast until 25 to 30 complete range of movement reps have been completed.

This concludes our discussion of the holistic rep speed theory and how you might apply it to the 50-rep blitz, or any other workouts you find appropriate for its use. We would suggest that you continue a private study of your own on the exciting science of reps. Some of the most comprehensive published studies we have read on the subject of reps and their training purpose have been written by Bernard Centralla, Jerry Robinson, Egan Schauer and Steve Wedan. In fact, we feel so strongly about these authors as a "must read," that we list the following sources:

Bernard Centrella:
"The Science of the Rep," *Ironman* magazine Volume 46, No. 2 (January 1987), No. 3 (March 1987), No. 4 (May 1987), No. 5 (July 1987), No. 6 (September 1987).
Volume 47, No. 1 (November 1987), No. 2 (January 1988), No. 3 (March 1988), No. 4 (April 1988), No. 5 (May 1988).

Jerry Robinson:
"The Rep and You," *Ironman* magazine Volume 50, No. 2 (February 1991), No. 3 (March 1991).

Egan Schauer:
"Change of Pace," *Ironman* magazine Volume 46, No. 4 (May 1987), "Less Is More," Volume 46, No. 5 (July 1987), "Stutter Reps," Volume 46, No. 6 (September 1987), "Beyond Stutter Reps," Volume 47, No. 3 (March 1988), "Wasted Reps," Volume 47, No. 4 (April 1988), and "Beyond Stutter Reps II," Volume 47, No. 8 (August 1988).

Steve Wedan:
"Total Reps," *Muscular Development* magazine, Volume 26, No. 4 (April 1989), No. 5 (May 1989), No. 6 (June 1989), No. 8 (August 1989).

You should not have any difficulty in obtaining back issues of the magazines in which the articles appeared. Simply write to the addresses where these magazines are published. Include the date, volume and number of the issue(s).

Continuing on with the discussion of The 50-Rep Blitz, in addition to using the holistic rep-speed components, there is also the available option of doing the 50 reps with the Asymmetrical Rest-Pause 5/20 Routine.

If you review most of the bodybuilding and strength-training programs of many of the champions in the iron game you will, for the most part, be struck by the fact that more than 90 percent of the exercises are performed in a bilateral manner. The meaning of bilateral is any two-limb exercise, such as a two-arm barbell or dumbell curl, press, row or two-legged barbell squat, etc. Many of the top bodybuilders realized a long time ago that, by continually doing two-limb exercises, one side of the muscle groups of the body automatically becomes more responsive and efficient at performing the exercise than the other. This creates an intra-muscular tension which, in turn, causes a size and strength imbalance on the muscle groups on the opposite side of the body. Vince Gironda was once reflecting on the subject of bilateral training, and he seemed to have found the answer to this problem when he said, "Pay attention to one-arm exercises and try and equalize the two body halves." Vince, smart bomb that he is, seemed to have a direct hit with his comment, or had he? Train asymetrically (or "uni-lateral") by doing one-limb exercises with one dumbell?

Vince then contradicted his statement by going on to say that he had personally worked with one-arm exercises and progressively worked his strength up in the one-dumbell bent-over rowing motion to where, at one point in his training, he could perform 20 reps with a 175-pound dumbell. However, he admitted that he could never "develop the left lat to match the right." The only way he was able to bring it up to a point of equalization, he said, was by using **both arms together** with the bent-over dumbell rowing exercise.

His training theory was that the legs, lats, pecs and arms must be worked together with dumbell exercises as opposed to that of a barbell, because of a mysterious nerve force or charge which emanates from the spine and travels around the body. After listening to Vince, one may begin to wonder about the rationale behind asymmetrical, one-side-at-a-time training, with one heavy dumbell.

Well, wonder no longer. Back in 1954 the late Paul Anderson, the strongest man of the century, inaugurated the concept of **asymmetrical training** into his workouts in

the form of one-arm heavy dumbell presses, either standing or lying on the bench. It started when he was trying to find an effective method of training overload to jack up his two-arm barbell press. He started out by pressing two dumbells together, but discovered that he was handling less total combined weight with the dumbells than he could press with two hands with a barbell. He then started lifting one dumbell at a time and found, to his amazement, that this gave his deltoids and triceps a maximum muscle overload which boosted his power in the press into orbit. The value of his asymmetrical training was always very evident at his public appearances, where he would

Paul Anderson

perform a one-arm dumbell press with as much as 300 pounds, not once, but for several reps!

Paul was always very innovative when it came to getting the maximum potential from exercises. In the case of the one-dumbell press overhead, he would find that as his exercise form began to fail, the dumbell would get out of the pressing groove either by floating out to the side or to the front. As a result of this, the set of reps would have to be terminated just short of completion. To overcome this problem of balance and control, he took two approaches. The first was to build a simple apparatus that would simulate the one-dumbell press overhead. He took a standard exercise bar and had a large hinge welded at one end. He then attached the hinged end of the bar to a sturdy wooden wall at shoulder height. Aproximately twelve inches in from the other end of the hinged bar, he attached another bar at a right angle, so as to extend vertically down to the floor. He would then load the free twelve inches of the horizontal hinged bar (which was not only attached to the wall but was supported on the ground by the other bar) and press away without fear of getting out of balance. One of the obvious advantages of this simplistic pressing device was the fact that he could vary his hand position on the horizontal bar. The closer he would move his hand to the hinged end of the bar, the heavier the resistance would become.

Tonya Knight

A second approach to ensuring balance and control of the one-dumbell lift is, of course, to grip a stationary object, such as a post, with the hand of the non-exercising arm, after getting the weight into the **get-set** position. Continue to hold onto the post for the duration of the set while you do your one-dumbell exercise with the opposite arm.

This approach lends itself to performing a one-arm dumbell bench press. It's a little awkward at first, but worth it. Get into position on the bench while holding a dumbell in one hand (close to the side of your chest) in the prestretch negative position and grasp one of the upright supports of the bench with the other hand. Once in a stable position on the bench, it is just a matter of pressing the single dumbell in a sort of modified flye-type motion, while exerting maximum muscle effort with pinpoint concentration. If you are training with a workout partner you can alternate the one-dumbell bench press first by pressing for a single rep with your right arm, and then – with

Ron Love is always a crowd pleaser.

the help of your training partner – pass the dumbell carefully over to your left hand and do a single rep. Continue on in this manner until you have completed your predetermined number of reps.

If you are training alone, it might be best to do a complete set of consecutive reps, first with one arm, then with the other. This will eliminate the problem of balance and jockeying for position that you would probably experience when alternating each arm rep for rep. Asymmetrical training, or doing one-limb exercises with one dumbell, adapts not only to the one-dumbell press and bench press but also to other exercises.

Now let's take a look at how the 5/20 routine blends in with the asymmetrical rest-pause. This routine requires two dumbells. One is loaded with a poundage that will allow you to do five maxi-power reps in asymmetrical style. The other dumbell is loaded with 50 to 60 percent less poundage (which is calculated to allow you to complete 20 maxi-pump reps).

Begin a 5/20 series by doing an asymmetrical one-limb exercise, such as the dumbell press (holding onto a pole or upright support with the hand of the non-exercising arm while leaning your torso away from the upright support), then press the dumbell moderately slow (eliminating momentum or swing) overhead. Lower and lightly touch the dumbell to your delt on each rep. Alternate arms (rep for rep). First press with the right arm for a rep, then the left, and back to the right, continuing on until you have completed five maxi-power reps. Immediately upon completion, take the lighter poundage dumbell and begin doing five consecutive reps, first with one arm then the other, back and forth until you have completed 20 maxi-pump reps with each arm. This is one series. Take a brief rest and do a second and final series as it applies to The 50-Rep Blitz. There are many other combinations that can be done within the structure of this training concept.

You could, for example, pick an exercise such as the one-dumbell deadlift (be sure to use a heavy-duty canvas wrist strap if you have trouble holding onto the bar), or dumbell power clean, etc. Again you will use the heavy and light system. But this time you will do five

consecutive power reps with the heaviest dumbell you can lift. Upon completion of the fifth and final rep, immediately take a lighter dumbell (50 to 60 percent less poundage) and blast out 20 consecutive maxi-pump reps. Work one side of the body independently of the other in the manner described. This too completes one series.

The hard and clearly defined muscular lines of natural bodybuilder John Hansen are revealed in this dramatic photo.

100 Percent-Plus Negative Training Sets:
There has been extensive research and analysis of the various training concepts we have been presenting to you. These systems are some of the very best ways to coax your body into very rapid muscle gains. Available training information literally abounds for the bodybuilder, but much of it is never put to use. We are amazed to see many bodybuilders

around the country who get locked into the conventional set and rep modality, where, day in and day out, they will take 80 percent of their maximum single-effort poundage and do 8 to 12 reps with it. Each rep is a 50/50 ratio consisting of a 2-to-4-second positive (concentric) and 4-to-8-second negative (eccentric) muscle-contraction movement.

A mistake we see with this combination (and many of the champions agree with us) is that, while there is maximum muscle stimulation in the positive contraction of the rep, the negative contraction is in a sub-maximal mode. One of the very best ways to increase your gain factor in negative, or eccentric strength, is by doing a 100 percent-plus negative training set. To do a maximal mode negative set, select a poundage which is 20 to 40 percent to as much as 60 percent over your best maximum conventional single effort. The idea is then to lower this poundage under control within a full range of the negative movement for one to six negative-only reps. Each pure negative-only rep should take four to eight or eight to ten seconds to complete. (Be sure to cycle your negative training set every few workouts by doing a negative-accentuated and/or a negative-emphasized set.)

A negative-accentuated set requires you to use a poundage which is 70 percent of your maximum single effort, both in the full positive and the negative range of an exercise that is done with two limbs. We'll use the leg extension on a machine for our hypothetical example, and assume that a poundage of 200 pounds can be extended in a positive contraction for one rep when using both legs. Seventy percent of this poundage is 140 pounds. The idea is to lift the weight by the power of the quadriceps muscles to the extended position with both legs, and then **slowly lower the weight** with one leg only. The weight is then extended with both legs again and lowered with the other leg, etc. You can do this with an exercise like a one-dumbell curl. If you can do a one-rep standing one-dumbell curl with 100 pounds, add 40 percent more poundage to the dumbell so that

it weighs 140. Now grasp the wrist of your curling arm and cheat the weight up to the top of the curl movement. Release the wrist of the curling arm, and slowly lower the weight down in full range of the negative-contraction movement. Switch the dumbell to the other hand and follow the curling procedure just described, alternating back and forth until you have done six pure negative-accentuated reps, or you can do them consecutively with one arm and then the other.

A set of six negative-emphasized reps is accomplished by selecting a poundage which is 40 percent of a conventional max single effort. Lift the weight through the positive phase of the movement, and then, with the help of a partner or spotter, press down on the bar with consistent but demanding pressure through the negative phase of the movement. These three possible styles of doing a negative set, for safety's sake, require a training partner for assistance, and a power rack. Don't attempt the maximal-mode negative set alone without using the weight-release device. We've read all the published training information that is available to the bodybuilder and strength athlete, and we know of only one specialized book which covers the topic of negative training in explicit detail. The name of the book is *Positive Results From Negative Training*, and it includes plenty of enlightening information on the correct procedures and testing for negative training. Best of all, the author, Robert Francis, includes a selection of 10 negative workouts which fit very nicely into the one-set-per-muscle-group training factor in the econo-time secondary phase of the total-body workout. This book can be purchased by sending $15.00 to Francis Strength/Medical, 300 Main Street, Suite 210, Huntington, New York 11743. This is the same company that invented the compound curl bar.

The training advantages of doing a 100 percent-plus negative training set are numerous. We can quickly think of two that work synergistically, or together, that will score some big muscle strength gains in muscle pump and positive (concentric) phase power. To begin with, there are many bodybuilders who have the muscle force capacity to back squat 400 pounds, supine bench press 300

Dorian Yates – "The Shadow knows…"

pounds and deadlift 500 pounds – but their respective lifts may only be 390 pounds, 285 pounds and 470 pounds. This problem, in part, can be caused by the sensitivity of a tiny defense mechanism in the muscles known as **golgi tendon organs.**

The golgi tendon organs are rather unique organelles which are located in the tendons of the muscles and are responsible for sensing stress and contraction tension levels within the muscle. For one reason or another, the golgi tendon organs may shut down the bodybuilder's genetic capacity to lift heavier poundages. The trigger for its activation seems to be an overstretched muscle. Bodybuilders can alter or set back the sensitivity threshold of the golgi tendon organs by doing negative-phase training, and its variations.

Arthur Jones, along with his Nautilus team of research experts, did some extensive studies on negatives (eccentrics), using training

poundages that were 20 to 40 percent in excess of those used in the positive phase. Conclusive results from the Nautilus and other

John Sherman

Legendary Dave Draper – "the world's oldest youth."

independent studies on negative-phase training proved two things: First, that training in a negative phase will alter the sensitivity threshold of the golgi tendon organ, and thereby improve muscle force (not only in the negative but also the positive power phase as well), but not at the expense of injury to the muscle.

Secondly, negative-phase training has the capacity to produce what is termed "elastic muscle energy" when the muscle is in a stretched position. Elastic energy has the capacity to generate muscle force in the positive phase of muscle contraction, but only when the time from the completion of the negative stretch position to the positive contraction is of a short duration (0.5 to 1 seconds). Any longer and this elastic muscle energy will escape and dissipate as heat energy.

Jeff Poulin shows off his ripped punch-proof abs.

To capture the advantage of elastic muscle energy when you are performing a positive/negative conventional set of training reps, it is critical that, upon completion of the negative stretch phase in each and every rep, there should be an instantaneous yet smooth reversal (turnaround) as you literally **explode** the

weight into orbit in the positive phase of the movement. The bottom line in rep strategy here is that there be absolutely no pause between the completion of the negative stretch phase and the beginning of the positive phase of the rep(s).

Well, there you have it – the ultimate training plateau breaker, the 100 percent-plus negative training set. This is a set which uses poundages in excess of what can be handled in the positive phase, resulting in a conditioning of the muscles to greater stretch stimulus which, in turn, sets back the sensitivity of the golgi tendon organ, and at the same time increases elastic muscle energy. Train in negative fashion from time to time, and experience the ultimate muscle and power pump, while breaking the training plateau.

Conclusion
(Omni-Resistance Muscle Pumping):

At certain specific angles within a rep of full range of movement, the resistance curve can vary dramatically. You experience this just about every time you do an exercise such as the two-hand barbell curl.

For example: Curling the barbell from your thighs to a range of positive movement (where your forearms are at right angles to your upper arms) can take a herculean effort on your part compared to the remaining range of positive movement which is done with comparative ease. While certain aspects of the muscle receive maximal tension, others get only limited range of continuous tension from the resistance.

To explain this in more detail: When you are performing a two-hand barbell curl with 150 pounds, the brachialis or lower sector of the long head of the biceps receives most of the tension and development. But because it is generally the weakest muscle aspect from the standpoint of strength, it limits the poundage, or resistance used to create maximum tension and development of the biceps belly. The muscle belly may need a hypothetical 20 percent more resistance in order to receive its share of maximal tension. Then there is the problem of developing the high peak. Actually, this training problem was solved back in the 1960s when Joe Weider and his research group developed and popularized the Triple-Range

203

Lee Priest and Chris Cormier. The mirror is an essential piece of equiptment, and here it is shown receiving heavy-duty use.

Training Principle. The basic concept behind this muscle-building principle was to select one correct exercise for each of the aspects of the muscle group, while performing the muscle contractions with limited-movement repetitions for 30 seconds of work time in the beginning, middle and ending range of the movement. One particular method of doing this that the champs seem to enjoy is the Three-Part Staggered Reps Principle. This is not to be confused with the 21s system that we discussed previously as a preferred training-past-the-burn technique. With that system, you used the exact same poundage for all three ranges of the movement within the same exercise.

The Three-Part Staggered Reps Principle is different in that you will be using three totally different exercises and the maximum poundage that each aspect of the muscle is capable of in order to create the absolute ultimate in tension and development within the muscle. Begin this system by working the brachialis (lower aspect of the biceps) by doing the two-hand barbell preacher curl off the 45-degree angled side of a Scott bench. Do half-measured movement curls, beginning from the bottom position of each rep. Be careful not to hyper-extend your elbow at this position. Curl for 30 seconds in this phase, and try to do seven of

these half-reps during that time. This will require slightly over four seconds per rep, which, if you were doing full range of movement style, would be less than a normal speed rep ratio, and would be just about dead even with super speed tantric contractions; but, since these are only half-reps, the speed might be considered slow.

Immediately upon completing the seventh half-rep, take an appropriate loaded poundage and begin doing seated barbell curls for another seven half-reps, curling the bar in a semi-circular motion, from where it is resting on your upper thighs, to the high contracted position at the neck. This 30 seconds of measured movements will develop the muscle belly. Remember to keep the bar about two inches from your abs and chest as you curl.

Upon completion of the final rep, and without any hesitation whatsoever, finish off the Three-Part Staggered Reps Principle by doing the two-dumbell curl on the 90-degree side of the Scott bench. Do seven half-measured movement curls from the top position where the forearm and biceps touch at approximately chin level and down to where your forearms are at right angles to your upper arms.

Thirty seconds in this phase will really enhance upper biceps peak and development. These three measured-movement exercises constitute one set. They also fit very nicely into the one-set-per-muscle-group situation we are into at the present time. For those of you bodybuilders who don't have a Scott bench but own an adjustable dual-purpose exercise bench, here are some adaptations to the above-described three-part exercises: Holding a barbell in your hands, step behind the raised seat back and place your elbows very close together on the bench – extending your arms down until the bar is resting on the inclined surface of the bench. While the angle of this exercise movement will work the brachialis and the biceps long head, you can get some additional training effect by the handspacing you choose to take. When the hands are three to four inches apart you will work the inner head aspect of the biceps, while an ultra-wide spacing of 24 inches will attack the outer aspect maximally. This exercise is an appropriate substitution for barbell preacher curls.

Most every bodybuilder will have no problem whatsoever finding a way to do seated barbell curls, although you could do them with a swingbell, which is a centrally loaded bar. The exercises here can be done in semi-cheat fashion, or very strict, using a Weider arm blaster for even more of a muscle belly isolationary effect.

Many bodybuilders may not have the specific angled bench to do the vertical curls, therefore we suggest that you use your flat exercise bench. Place two stable blocks of wood securely under the legs of the bench, to raise it 30 inches from the top of the flat bench surface to the floor. Lay maximally loaded dumbells on the floor at the high inclined end of the bench. Now you're ready to get into position for the prone bench and dumbell concentration curls. Simply lay face down on the flat bench. Position yourself so that your shoulders line up with the end of the bench, with your head and arms extending over the end. Reach down and grasp the dumbells and curl them up to your chin. You are now set to do the seven measured movement curls, described as the vertical curl, on the Scott bench.

Another sequence you might wish to use

Andreas Munzer brings new meaning to the term "onion skin."

would be: preacher curls, followed by body-drag curls, and finished off with dumbell supination curls (with a false grip).

To achieve maximum muscle growth benefits from this Three-Part Staggered Reps Principle, it is very important that you do not take a rest of any type whatsoever between each of the three measured movement exercises, but continue to the next movement without rest. In a sense you are getting some type of rest because you are shifting the work of each exercise you do to a different aspect of the muscle. Having said that, however, it is a good idea to have two barbells, and a set of dumbells, loaded and ready to go for each exercise. You can also have a barbell loaded

BARBELL UPRIGHT ROWS
THE JETTISON TECHNIQUE

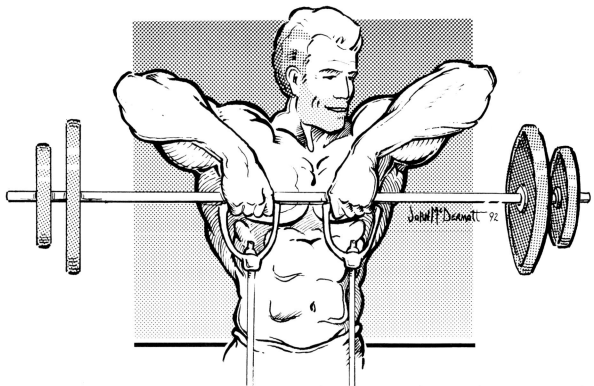

with correctly determined poundages which will accommodate a triple-drop. You are free to mix and match your barbells and dumbells for the exercises.

The Three-Part Staggered Reps Principle of training is one of the better options from the standpoint of producing consistent resistance over a full range of movement within the reps, which is relative to matching the strength curve of the muscle. The result of such training is a more uniform development of muscle size and strength, while eliminating the probability of muscle imbalance and injury caused by dramatic fluctuations in the resistance curve of most singular exercises.

Ideally, what needs to be done is to align the proper resistance of the barbell or dumbell(s) to match the strength curve of the muscle throughout its complete range of movement. The most obvious and immediate answer to solving this problem is to use certain types of exercise machines, such as Nautilus, to accomplish this – especially when you are only doing one set of a particular exercise for a muscle group. If you have this option, then go

for it when you are doing the econo-time secondary phase one-set-per-muscle-group exercises. However, we do realize that many bodybuilders are working out in a basement with only very basic weight-training equipment. With them in mind, we share with you three other rather unique ways that will improve the ratio of the resistance curve of the barbell/dumbell(s) to the strength curve of your muscles.

This way, basement trainers can progress equally with the bodybuilders who are fortunate enough to train in a fancy, well-equipped gym. The first way to improve the ratio of the resistance to the strength curve (anabolically stimulate the origins, insertions and the muscle belly) is to attach a very heavy chain to each end of a barbell or dumbell(s). This most effective training idea was revealed to bodybuilders back in 1970 by Arthur Jones, the famous pacesetting Nautilus exercise equipment inventor and bodybuilding expert. Mr. Jones proved that using heavy gauge chain when using a barbell, etc., will provide the necessary increasing variable resistance. As the bar rises, more and more of the heavy links are suspended in the air, making upward travel more and more difficult. The chain should be of such a length that there are four to five links on the floor upon completion of the positive (concentric) phase of the exercise movement. (Note: The chain should be of a very heavy duty variety, usually termed nautical stock.)

The second way to improve the resistance to strength curve ratio and shock the body into greater muscle growth is by using rubber expander cables. You can use rubber expander cable substitutes for most any of the upper-body exercises listed in this book. The beauty of expander cables is that they produce increased resistance on the muscles the further they are stretched through the full range of movement. Within pages 106 to 109 of our book *Mass!* (Contemporary Books, Inc., 1986), we wrote about a dynamic muscle-action principle called the Jettison Technique. We then felt (and still do) that a combination of free weights and rubber expanders is one of the most revolutionary training techniques for providing the muscle with maximal resistance and muscle tension, while at the same time increasing flexibility and usable strength.

At the time we also suggested the use of round rubber expander cables in conjunction with a barbell or dumbell combination. We found a couple of problems with using the conventional rubber expanders. First, the thickness of the handle on the expander cable, when combined with a barbell or dumbell handle of even greater thickness, made the unit extremely difficult to hold onto. Secondly, the number of exercises a bodybuilder could perform in the Jettison Technique was limited to upper-body exercises – in which the movements did not exceed a range of shoulder level height. The length of the expander cables simply was not adaptable to any type of overhead triceps extension or pressing movement.

Since that time we have modified the Jettison Technique to include the use of the Lifeline Gym power cables (these are the same ones that are used from time to time on ESPN's *Bodyshaping* program) as a replacement training tool to the rubber expander cables. The Lifeline Gym power cables consists of a superior progressive-resistance surgical rubber tubing that can instantly be adjusted in

DUMBELL CURL USING JETTISON TECHNIQUE WITH LIFELINE POWER CABLE

length and variable resistance (from 3 pounds to 350 pounds) by a minor adjustment of leg stance, or a quick flick of the wrist (if you are using the Lifeline lifting bar).

Another feature we really enjoy is the specially designed and ruggedly built stirrup handles attached to the rubber power cables that conform comfortably when used in combination with a barbell or dumbell(s). This feature alone is cause enough to switch over from the conventional rubber expander. Knowing that you can instantly adjust the resistance of the power cables to complement the corresponding poundage selection on the barbell or dumbell(s) to just the correct intensity level each and every rep, for the ultimate in muscle-pulverizing gains, will be enough to get you to switch over to Lifeline Gym. The retail price of Lifeline Gym power cables is $21.95 to $29.95 (depending on which of the 10 power cable units you might decide to purchase). plus $5.00 for shipping and handling. For more information on this versatile and most adaptable portable training tool call toll free: 1-800-553-6633, or fax: 608-251-1870. Wisconsin bodybuilders are asked to call 608-251-4778 for information on ordering the Lifeline Gym power cables. Tell them you are interested in its use with the Jettison Technique.

Ian Harrison and Aaron Baker.

The third and final way to improve your resistance-to-strength curve factor is by using iron teardrop plates. Iron teardrops are elongated-shaped plates which are designed to redistribute and relocate the center of gravity. This will act in direct relationship to the bodybuilder's strength curve (gravity versus progressive momentum) from the unique swaying action of the plates. The concept behind the iron teardrop plates is not some off-the-wall theory. It has been well-documented and tested by using a computer graphics system of digital tracking and image processing which shows the path of the bar, timing, key angles and velocities. Vince Gironda has, on occasion, said that bodybuilders sometimes seek the path of least resistance. Our observations have been that most bodybuilders are looking for the path of greatest resistance at all key angles of a full range of movement. The iron teardrops accomplish this purpose because they literally force maximum tension at angles previously of minimal tension. David Mayfield is the inventor of the revolutionary iron teardrops, and should you find this train-

ing concept fascinating and desire additional descriptive information, feel free to write or call him at Teardrops, Inc., 623 S. Maple, Staunton, IL 62088. Phone: 1-618-635-8060 (please call collect), or fax your inquiry to: 1-618-635-3793.

If you follow these dynamic ways of "omni-resistance muscle pumping" you can't help but increase your workout intensity.

This concludes our rather detailed explanation of the total-body workout concepts. You have plenty of information to guide you, which includes a model outline of a three-day "pack on the muscle mass" routine.

Each of the three-day, rotational anti-stress muscle grouping workouts contains an approximate total of 27, 33 and 36 sets respectively. This, in a sense, goes along with the training philosophy of Arthur Jones, the Nautilus guru. He once said, "Ninety sets for the total body may be too much and fifty sets or less is better."

As each of the three pacesetting total-body workouts should not last more than 75 to 90 minutes – or more than an elapsed total training time of 4-1/2 hours each week – this is excellent for maximizing blood testosterone stores.

The 75-to-90-minute blocks of workout time for each total-body workout will, of course, be dictated by the accumulated rest-pause time between consecutive reps (even micro-second pauses can add up after awhile). We are also very aware of the fact that some bodybuilders are, in fact, hardgainers, and lack the genetic profile necessary to accommodate the three-day rotational workout as described. For those of you who consider yourselves hardgainers, we suggest that you reduce the number of "base sets" for major and minor muscle groups from 8 to 10 and 5 to 7, respec-

Dorian Yates takes the lead.

tively to 6 to 8 for major and 3 to 5 for minor. You may also find it necessary to reduce the frequency of your workouts from three to two non-consecutive days per week. Try turning down the volume on one or the other to begin with, or both if necessary.

This will complicate your training protocol somewhat because some of the muscle-density techniques, etc., mentioned at the beginning of the book, and the 11 Training-Past-The-Burn Techniques will also have to be modified to meet your new training "base sets" and workout frequency structure.

Jerry Anderson seems to like adding variety to his workouts with the use of teardrop plates.

CHAPTER TWELVE

Super Muscle Specialization

There is one other training protocol that must be addressed and that is the topic of super muscle specialization. There are a couple of ways to accomplish this task. The first is to train the whole muscle group, or specific aspect of it, on one or two non-training days that are separate from the two or three rotational anabolic total-body workout days.

As space doesn't allow us to go into detail with regard to super muscle specialization, we suggest that those of you who would like to find out more follow the explicit and detailed guidelines set forth in chapter five, "Bodypart Specialization," in our book *Mass!*

Andreas Munzer

◄ Aaron Baker

The second way to specialize on a muscle group is to use a two-day anabolic total-body workout, but with a slightly radical training departure. Some of you bodybuilders who are quite observant may have noticed that we left the word *rotational* out of the descriptive title.

This word was deleted because you will not be rotating various major and minor muscle groups in and out of the primary phase of the

Aaron Baker and Robert Sherman

workouts. You will only train the muscle group assigned to the super specialization concept for two workouts a week. All remaining muscle groups are assigned to the secondary intra phase, and will utilize primordial muscle-shock strategies exclusively. This will last for a duration of four to six weeks.

The beauty of specializing on a muscle group, or aspect of it, is that any of the training options and training-past-the-burn bodybuilding techniques, etc., will adapt very nicely to the workout structure without modifications, as it applies to the two-day anabolic total-body workout. One of the all-time favorite muscle groups that many bodybuilders enjoy specializing on is legs. Why? Because, although leg training is brutally hard, the secondary effect of such training can spill over to produce worthwhile muscle gains in other select muscles. Some bodybuilders have gained as much as one inch on their upper arms, just from the secondary effect of leg training.

There are a number of result-producing workouts that you might consider when specializing on the legs twice per week. They are as follows:

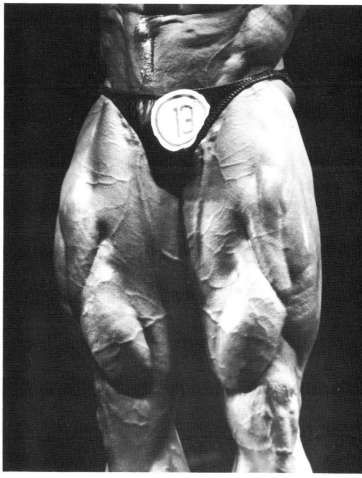

Mike Matarazzo

Start...

Shawn Ray performing lunges for ultimate cuts and separation in his quads.
...Finish

Super Circuit Leg Shaper:

The following eight progressive-resistance exercises are performed in the order of their listing in a non-stop circuit for 20 full range-of-motion repetitions each. Rests of one to two minutes are taken only after a circuit is completed. Do three circuits.

Alternate front leg lunges, Cory lunges (as described on page 196 of our book *Mass!),* single-leg calf raises, frog squats, leg extensions, leg curls, Olympic-style back squats, step-ups. (Step-ups are performed on a sturdy exercise bench or wooden box. The vertical measurement of the bench or wooden box should be in corresponding ratio to your physical height. If you are under 5 feet, use a box, etc., which is 12 inches in height. If you are 5'1'' to 5'3'', the box should be 14 inches, 5'4'' to 5'9'' – 16 inches, 5'10'' to 6 feet – 18 inches, and over 6 feet – a 20-inch box.)

The amount of progressive-resistance used on each exercise will vary depending on individual differences. Don't be deceived by the simplicity of this program. It is very demanding. One only has to ask the bodybuilders who followed six-time Ms. Olympia Cory Everson through the routine on an ESPN *Bodyshaping* segment some time ago, what they thought of it. This is an excellent program for men and women alike who are interested in shape-training the total leg, without acquiring additional muscle bulk and power.

Ultimate Leg-Training Secrets Program No. 1:

Barbell front squats – *3 sets x 8 reps*
*Duc leg presses – *4 sets x 8 reps*
Hack squats – *3 sets x 8 reps*
Prone leg curls – *2 sets x 20 reps*
Standing single-leg curls – *4 sets x 15 reps*
Donkey calf raises – *4 sets x 12, 15 or 20 reps*
Seated calf raises – *3 sets x 12 to 15 reps*

*The Duc exercise is performed on a vertical and/or a 45-degree leg press. Position your hips directly in alignment with the weight stack. The feet are placed 18 to 24 inches apart and rotated out at approximately 45 degrees from parallel on the foot platform. With your toes and balls of your feet off the platform, push with your heels only. This will stimulate hamstring and lower glute development, in addition to inner thighs, which are developed from the flaring motion of bringing the legs out to the sides as you lower the weight.

Changing positions by placing the feet close together and parallel will stimulate the quads maximally, especially if this time you push off the foot platform with the balls of your feet and not your heels.

The above workout program (No. 1) should be followed one training day per week.

Program No. 2:

Barbell back squats – *6 sets x 12, 10, 8, 6, 4, 4 reps*
Leg presses – *4 sets x 10, 8, 6, 4 reps*
Superset:
   Leg curls – *4 sets x 12 to 15 reps*
   Stiff-legged deadlifts – *4 sets x 10 to 12 reps*

The barbell squat and leg press should use the pyramid system of progression. This workout program should be performed on the second specialization training day of the week.

Paul DeMayo

Another popular way to train the legs is to split up the various aspects of the muscle groups. The quads, for example, could be worked on one training day. If you decided that you wanted to go for maximum in muscle separation and cuts, you could do five or so supersets of barbell front leg lunges, or front squats, using a Smith machine, or leg extensions using a 15, 20 or 30 maxi-pump rep selection. If, by chance, you would rather go for a ratio of muscle separation and quad power combined, then warm up with barbell front squats (barbell back squats Olympic-style is yet another option) and then proceed to do five to eight blast singles with 90 percent of your current max single effort.

After you have completed the blast singles, you will go on to do five sets (60 to 95 percent max) in the front squat.

Set No. 1 – *6-8 reps with 60 percent max*
Set No. 2 – *5 reps with 75 percent max*
Set No. 3 – *5 reps with 85 percent max*
Set No. 4 – *3-5 reps with 90 percent max*
Set No. 5 – *2-3 reps with 95 percent max*

This is the basis of your routine on quad-training days. On a second training day of the week you will train calves and hamstrings. Calves can be trained a number of ways. To begin with, you could use the ultimate calf blast pump-out, listed in the Primordial Muscle-Shock Strategies, doing three or four sets each.

A calf-jarring technique you can go with (and this really deviates from training this muscle twice per week), is to do compound pumpset one-leg calf raises every hour, on the hour, seven days per week. Do this with your bodyweight only to begin with, and do one set of 25 maxi-pump reps for each leg, then immediately do a second set of 20 reps for each leg. Bob Gajda, a former Mr. America and Mr. Universe, originated this method of training the calves back in 1966. He suggests that 10 compound sets of one-leg calf raises per day is the minimum. He says that the toes should be rotated out from parallel to work the

Kevin Levrone and Vince Taylor in the heat of the night.

inner aspect of the calf. When the number of reps becomes easy to perform, then and only then, should you consider using a dumbell for added resistance. However, this might not prove to be practical, especially if you are doing this exercise at work during your work breaks.

Another method to train the calves is to use the heavy, medium and light training principle. This is accomplished by performing the following three-in-one programs:

Scientific Calf Programs
No. 1 - Heavy:
Standing calf machine – *2-3 sets x 12-16 reps*
Seated calf machine – *2-3 sets x 12-18 reps*
Donkey calf raise – *2-3 sets x 16-24 reps*

Three trisets are to be performed on this program. Still another way to work the calves heavy is to select only one calf exercise and do a total of nine sets. Begin with a weight which will allow you to do 20 to 25 maxi-pump reps. Continue to add additional poundage each succeeding set. Depending upon the increased weight jump factor, and corresponding decrease in reps per set (due to the partial training effect of only resting 30 seconds between sets), you may be able to do only three heavy, slow and deliberate stretch-contraction reps, barely managing to raise your heels.

This is your heavy day calf workout.

No. 2 - Medium:
On this training day choose two exercises from the three listed in the above program. Perform three to four supersets while using a maxi-pump rep scheme of 35 throughout.

No. 3 - Light:
During this particular calf workout you are going to be asked to select one of your favorite calf exercises and do one set only. The number of reps is not the primary consideration here, but the constant time factor is. Do continuous circulation reps non-stop for one minute. This may seem easy the first time around, but the catch is that each time you perform this number three workout, you must increase the time factor by an additional 60 seconds! Try working up to a total of five minutes of a non-stop calf movement.

Again, you could select one of the exercises in the above two programs to accomplish

Mauro Sarni in "peak" shape.

this workout, but, for the sake of adding some needed variation within the structure of your program, you might instead go with the leg press calf raise. One very unusual exercise that can be used is the barbell heel-to-toe calf walk. This exercise is done by placing a barbell on the shoulders. From here a bodybuilder takes very short steps, rising high on his toes, and starting each step high on the tip (back edge) of the heel, rocking from heel to toe with each step. The knees are locked throughout, and the

215

steps are very close together. As previously advised, perform this exercise by the clock. Begin walking for two continuous minutes, gradually working up to five minutes. To increase your safety margin while doing this exercise, it might be a good idea to hold a dumbell in each hand, rather than using a barbell. Chalk your hands and use power wrist-straps to keep the dumbells from slipping from your grasp.

Yet another very good exercise variation is to do the dumbell front leg lunge, but, rather than keeping the foot on the front leg flat on the floor, rise up on the toes, mentally tensing the calf muscles as forcefully as possible. Relax and lower the heel to the floor. Repeat, tensing the calf hard and powerfully with both the mind and muscle link, for one minute. Massage the calf and repeat the sequence with the opposite leg. Some bodybuilders use a strength shoe when doing this unusual exercise.

This three-in-one program is a version of the one that Stoney Lee Grimes brought to the attention of bodybuilders in the February 1991 *Parrillo Performance Press* publication, and the February/March 1993 issue of *Muscle Media 2000.* He learned the original version of it from top bodybuilder James DeMelo.

While the three-in-one calf program virtually guarantees gigantic development, there are other programs that a bodybuilder can select also. For instance, one could select the super-flushing technique for calves mentioned at the beginning of this book, but rather than doing the high-volume of sets specifically outlined, do one or two cycles of the six exercises in giant-set fashion.

Another variation to the three-in-one calf program would be to do 10 sets of 8 to 10 reps for just one exercise on one training day. On another day do 5 sets of 30 reps on 3 different exercises. On a third day it could be donkeys for 3 sets of 10 reps, followed by the standing calf-machine heel thrust for 5 sets of 15 reps, and finish up with seated heel thrusts for 5 sets of 15 reps.

An article was published in the July 1989 issue of *MuscleMag International* titled "Six Weeks to Killer Calves." The author, Gunnar Sikk, listed six very detailed and systematic calf routines. Each routine is a varied combina-

tion of selected exercises, sets, and holistic reps modes, all of which are executed at both slow and fast speed within the full, and limited, range movements.

The particular back issue that this article appeared in can be purchased as a single copy. The cost is $5.00, including postage and handling. Those of you who are interested in obtaining the issue should send a check or postal money order to MuscleMag International, 6465 Airport Road, Mississauga, Ont., Canada L4V 1E4. Visa or MasterCard orders, call 905-678-2314.

We are now going to turn our attention to the development of the biceps femoris or the hamstrings. Dennis Tinerino, a former professional Mr. Universe and IFBB superstar, has said on numerous occasions that the leg biceps are "probably the single-most overlooked muscle in training and development." We are in total agreement with his statement. One has only to look through the pages of any of the bodybuilding publications to see that detailed information on hamstring building is lacking when compared to other muscle groups, such as the delts, biceps and chest, etc.

One of the most intense methods for the training and development of the hamstrings is to assign three exercises to that muscle aspect and do them in triset fashion, one after the other, without any type of rest. A rest can, however, be taken between each completed triset, but only for 30 to 45 seconds in duration. Three exercise selections which will balance and split the hamstrings when done with high repetitions are:

Standing single-leg curls – *2 to 3 sets x 18 reps*
Prone leg curls – *2 to 3 sets x 15 reps*
Stiff-leg deadlifts – *2 to 3 sets x 12 reps*

Do two or three trisets of the above three exercises. On the leg-curl movement, perform each and every rep slowly and deliberately, with a full stretch and contraction of the muscle. When this no longer proves to be effective, do the movements in hard, rapid succession, being careful not to cramp up the hamstrings.

Pro Tip: Perform a 6/12/40 double drop set on each of the 3 exercises listed above. Do 6 power reps with 89 to 80 percent maximum, then 12 max-pump reps with 69 to 60 percent

TENSILE CONTRACTION LEG CURL

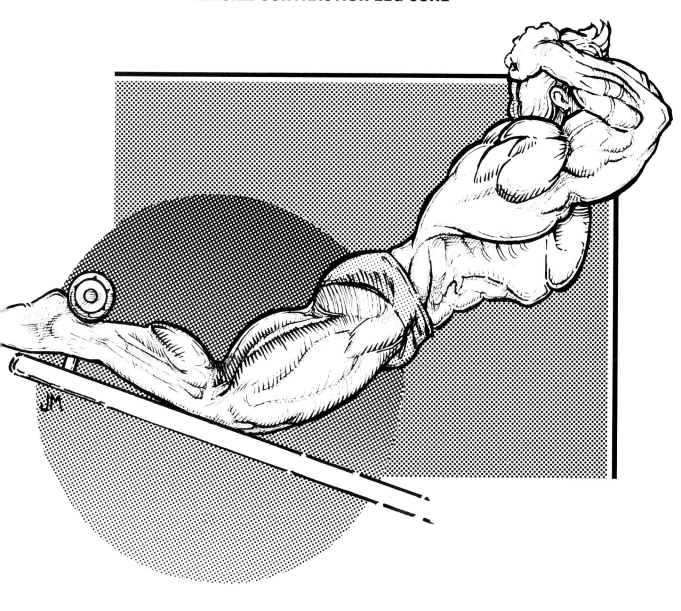

The fixed lower-leg position allows the knee to be in a straight line (or slightly behind) with the hip at all times. This allows for maximum leg biceps contraction.

of max, and finally 40 reps with 39 to 30 percent of maximum.

Another way to turn up the intensity on leg curls is to do forced reps, where a training partner assists you through the sticking point in the positive (concentric) phase. Also, within the negative (eccentric) phase of these forced reps, your training partner can apply manual resistance to the leg-curl machine or weight stack, pushing down as you slowly lower it to give added resistance. Do only four forced positive and negative reps per any given set.

If you do not have a training partner available, you can do the prone leg curl in a negative accentuated style by taking 70 percent of the poundage you normally use for a selected number of predetermined reps and curling the resistance up with both legs, then slowly lowering it with just one leg – alternating first the right then the left, etc., until the set is completed.

For those of you who don't have access to a leg-curl machine, and will need to improvise, we have a couple of suggestions that will help you. First, if you have an adjustable situp board, you're in business. A leg-curl exercise can be done by lying face down on the situp board with your feet strapped securely to the inclined end of the board. Once this is accomplished (usually with the help of a training partner), you then begin to curl your body up from the knees by pure hamstring strength alone. To begin with you may have to initiate each rep by pushing off with your hands, so it is a good idea not to adjust the incline of the board very much until you get the hang of the exercise. Near the completion of the positive phase of each rep you will assume what appears to be a kneeling, upright position.

Our second suggestion would be to do hanging dumbell leg curls. This is accomplished by placing a dumbell between your ankles while hanging from a pullup bar. With the dumbell pinched tightly between the ankles, flex your foot upward to further stabilize the dumbell, and begin curling your legs. Phil Hernon, a top bodybulder – who we feel has the potential to one day win the Mr. Olympia – devised this rather unique method of doing leg curls. The exercise doesn't require much weight at all, and some bodybuilders may find that even just wearing lead-filled neoprene or leather ankle weights will offer an incredible amount of stretch and contraction in the hamstrings.

Our third suggested alternate ham exercise is the stiff-legged deadlift. This can be done either while standing on the floor, or on a secured flat bench or wooden platform. Keep your back arched (never rounded), to help isolate hamstrings and be sure to pivot at the hip joint and not your lower back. At the lockout position, tighten the glutes and drive the hips forward. To keep constant tension on the hamstring muscles perform your reps in only the middle three-fifths range of the movement.

Pro Tip: To further stress the hams, the front of your feet should be raised slightly higher than heels (when doing deadlifts). Place a 2 x 4 under them prior to doing a set.

A method of training the calves and hamstrings that works equally well is the super rest-pause system. To correctly perform this technique, select a poundage which is 75 percent of your current unfatigued 10-rep maximum.

Begin the assigned exercise(s) by working down the rep ladder, doing 10 reps, resting 10 seconds, then 9 reps, resting 10 seconds, 8 reps, resting 10 seconds, etc., continuing on until you are down to one rep with a ten-second pause.

A reversal of the above procedure, with a variation in the rests, would be to do one rep, rest one second, two reps, rest two seconds, three reps, rest three seconds, continuing on until you have done 10 reps.

A terrific pump is attained with this system of constantly changing reps and rests. Some bodybuilders may experience a couple of training fluctuations within the first super rest-pause, down the rep ladder (10, 9, 8, 7, etc.), system. First, lactic acid burn (fatigue) may, in some cases, be so concentrated during the eighth or the seventh rep series that they can't continue. The solution here is to begin the program with a lower poundage. This problem almost reverses itself a few proceeding rep series later down the intensity ladder, where reps are done with ridiculous ease. This problem can be corrected by observing a more rigid performance within the tracking patterns of the exercise during those reps. The super slow rep(s) principle would apply here. When you are down to doing the one-rep series, don't be satisfied with stopping here. Squeeze out 1, 2, 3 or more reps on this final effort. The super rest-pause works great not only for calves and hamstrings, but for any muscle.

It is not uncommon to hear of gains in muscle size on the upper arms of half an inch in four weeks when using the super rest-pause system on biceps and triceps exercises.

John Carl Mese, former NPC secretary and bodybuilding champion from Miami, Florida, used the system to make this kind of gains. He did it by performing a total of five alternating triceps and biceps exercises, but working more on the triceps, since it is the largest contributor of muscle size.

He did one complete sequence (10, 9, 8, 7, etc.) of each of the following exercises, and no more.
1. Supine barbell (EZ-bar curl) French press
2. Two-hand barbell curl
3. Triceps pushdowns (on lat machine)
4. Supinated dumbell incline (45-50°) curls
5. Vertical dips on parallel bars

After his gains in upper-arm muscle size slowed, John changed from a super rest-pause down the rep ladder scheme to a system where he would use an appropriate poundage that would allow him to do six sets of 10 reps, resting **only** a constant 10 seconds between each set. He continued to use the same five exercises, and with the new training variation, he was able to add yet another 1/4 inch of muscle size to his upper arms in a further two-week period.

We agree that the total-body workout is a rather radical training approach, when its emphasis is directed toward a super muscle specialization effort (where only the same muscle group is assigned to the primary phase workout for a four to six week duration). This method of training specialization should never be used on and off during one training year. It will jump-start the gain factor in lagging muscles, but only when it is used once (or at the most twice) per year, and never back to back.

The remaining muscle groups which are assigned to the secondary intra phase of the workout will be continually stimulated with blow torch intensity when heavy-duty primordial muscle-shock strategies are used.

Therefore, there will be no loss or reverse in the functional capacity of any previous strength and muscle size gains. It is always a good idea to change your system of training each week within this training phase. On two training days per week, each muscle group has a different exercise assigned to it. Use the Vince Gironda "four sides to a muscle" concept here. For example: on the first training day of the week you might train the biceps with body-drag curls to stimulate the outer aspect of the biceps. The next workout day you might go with dumbell concentration curls, and work for a biceps peak. On the next you might opt for preacher curls for low biceps aspect training, etc.

Achim Albrecht

Also use primordial muscle-shock strategies on a rotational basis, perhaps doing the 50-rep blitz one workout, the **four-component set** the next, or the 100-percent-plus negative training set, etc. Many of these selections will be determined in part by whether you are going for more tendon strength or size, whatever the case may be. Use varying holistic rep schemes when applicable. By training in this manner your muscles will never fully adapt to the high-intensity training demands, and, as a result of this, your muscles will not reach an impasse training plateau. This way of training is one of the most effective approaches we know of for igniting muscle growth without using anabolic steroids.

CHAPTER THIRTEEN

Instinctive Knowledge

Instinctive training knowledge is knowing what works best for you. What not to do. When to up the intensity. When to utilize relaxed intensity. When to take a complete layoff from training. When your muscles have received adequate stimulation for continuous muscle gains. What to eat. How much sleep you need, etc.

Lee Priest

Sharon Bruneau – raise your hand if you're sure.

Your actual training days should be thought of as freestyle in nature. A day where, by instinctive knowledge, you will from time to time ask yourself certain questions:
1. Am I training at the proper intensity level?
2. Am I doing too much work with regard to the amount of volume training?
3. Am I getting enough recovery time both between workouts and during sleep?
4. What is my nutritional integrity like?
5. Am I bored? Motivated? Injured?
6. Is it time to make a minor (every couple of weeks) or major (every eight to ten weeks) change in my workout program?

To help you, let's answer at random two or three of these questions.

Question number three is an interesting one. Recovery and restoration must always precede muscle growth; therefore, we suggest that you review the tables of variables affecting recovery time. If you come into a scheduled workout and you have not gotten enough rest, then by all means use the 24-hour float method previously discussed. Try and get between 7-1/2 and 9 hours of sleep each night. If your everyday schedule of events allows you two to

Mike Matarazzo

Lee Haney

three hours of total relaxation, then go for it. Many bodybulders agree that two or three hours of total relaxation is equivalent to a full night's sleep. Ted Arcidi, the world's foremost heavyweight bench-press champion, used to take 1-1/2 hour naps every day when he was on his world-record shattering crusades in the bench press. His reasoning behind taking the naps was that, if the body is tired, it will stop growing in size and strength. Ted's naps, in addition to sound sleep, kept his body growing.

Also it is a good idea to meditate for 20 uninterrupted minutes prior to your scheduled workout. Larry Scott used to meditate prior to his super intense Mr. Olympia workouts.

Questions five and six could be combined. Perhaps you are bored simply because your motor pathways (nerves from the brain to the muscle) have become so ingrained that exercise has become a rather automatic series of continuous repetition sets, with the end result being a slowdown or halt to the training gain process. This is not unique among bodybuilders, and if this is a symptom of your training, then it is time for you to make some necessary changes to vaporize this plateau effect from your workouts.

These changes could include: varying the speed of the rep cadence (has been discussed in detail already), or changing the precision exercise technique. This can be done in the following way:

Bar Placement and Stance:
Power-style versus Olympic-style squatting techniques will illustrate the difference a bar placement, or stance, can make regarding the effectiveness of the exercise. The power-style squat requires that the bar be positioned low across the back of the trapezius, and the feet are at least shoulder-width apart; sometimes wider. These two actions alone will create maximum leverages and strength output from the muscles of the hips, quads and lower back.

By changing the bar placement, where it rests higher on the traps, and moving the foot stance to less than shoulder-width, you have the classic Olympic-style squatting technique – one which, while taking certain leverage and muscle contributions into account (e.g. the hips and lower back) maximizes total frontal thigh development and strength.

Hand Orientation
No. 1 – Science of Parallel-Bar Dips
Vince Gironda once did an exhaustive study of the various widths of handspacing and elbow positions on the parallel-dip bar, and their relationship to specific areas of upper-body muscle development. Other master bodybuilding trainers too did some research into the science of parallel-bar dips. In the process they came up with an interesting conclusion on hand orientation as it relates to this exercise.

They discovered that a simple rotation of the hands on the parallel-dip bar can, in fact, change the stress angle on the triceps for a new and rather refreshing kinetic muscle action. This can be accomplished by doing what is called triceps double dip. It is best performed on a dip bar which is no wider than 26 inches.

Begin the triceps dips by grasping the bars in such a way that the palms and heels of the hands are pointed outward. The thumbs are to the rear and the knuckles of each hand facing one another. (We are assuming that the actual dipping movement is understood, so do as many reps as possible in cumulative rep style, referred to in pages 81 to 83 of our book *Mass!)*

This movement will maximally stress the outer aspect of the triceps head. Upon completion of the cumulative reps, and without hesitation, turn your hands to a neutral or suitcase position (palms and heels of the hands facing one another), and pump out more vertical dips on the parallel bar to failure.

Hand Orientation
No. 2 – Secret of Pressing Power
Load a barbell to within 60 percent of your current unfatigued maximum single effort in the overhead press. Assume a handspacing on the bar (thumbless or false grip) which is 12 inches wider than you normally use. Perform five presses over the head. When the bar is completely extended and the arms locked out overhead on the fifth rep, "rock" the bar in such a way that you can shift each hand inwards on the bar to your normal handspacing and perform another five reps. At the conclusion of these five reps (which will be your 10th consecutive total rep), while the bar is locked out overhead, again move your hand position in on the bar until your thumbs are only nine inches apart. Perform five more presses from as low a position on the sternum as possible (dead under the neck). This completes one series of what could be termed an **extended** set. Stop here if you are going to use this technique in "econo-time." If, on the other hand, this is your primary phase exercise technique, then perform two more series, resting only a short time (perhaps 1-1/2 to 2 minutes) between each series. After you have completed the three series in which 45 reps have been completed, reduce your poundage down an additional 15 to 20 percent, and after a suitable rest, perform another three series of 15 reps each, using the three different hand positions described.

The object of this program is to keep the entire pressing structure of the deltoids and triceps under continuous tension and contraction for as long as possible in order to promote maximum muscle growth.

Another way bodybuilders make variable changes in their training programs is to drastically alter the number of reps per set that they are doing. This is achieved by doing sets of 15 maxi-pump reps for two to three weeks, then dramatically reducing reps to 10s or even triple power reps. This will really vary the intensity (question 1) and shock the muscles into greater adaptation.

Some bodybuilders have been known to scrap the entire workout program they were currently following in favor of the sure-fire golden 6 x 6 x 6 system. This program consists of using six basic and proven exercises. They are, parallel barbell back squats, supine barbell bench presses, wide pronated-grip pullups (or lat machine pulldowns), behind-the-neck-presses, barbell curls and concemetric doubleups (or hanging leg raises while using Ab-Originals or power straps. These items will increase your ability to hang from the pullup/chinning bar). The exercises are performed in order of their listings, working from the largest muscle group down to the smallest.

Eddie Robinson – "Major Guns" loaded and ready to pose.

223

Gary Strydom

This allows him to use a maximum poundage for his final six power-rep set. He feels that with this method of pyramiding poundages bodybuilders can control their own destiny by creating an acceptance in their own mind each succeeding set. This method of weight-jump progression develops a graduated conditioning of the muscles.

The 6 x 6 x 6 system is very much like a workout program that Arnold Schwarzenegger used to train members of his bodybuilding gym in Munich, Germany years ago.

One thing that Arnold taught his students, when following one of his workout programs, was to learn how to perform an exercise with their own specific variation(s), so that they will instinctively get the most training benefit from it. This is training advice well worth taking.

The 6 x 6 x 6 system can be followed two to three times per week (depending on existing recovery and gain theory factors), on alternate

Kim Chizevsky

Work into the 6 x 6 x 6 system gradually, doing four sets of six power reps during the first four weeks of training. Then jump to five sets of six power reps during the next 30 days, and finally six sets of six power reps are to be done on each of the first five exercises. Rest two to three minutes between each and every one of these sets. On the abdominal exercise, do six sets of 20 maxi-pump reps while resting only 20 seconds between each set. Many bodybuilders will use the same weight for each of the six sets for a particular exercise, whereas, when Ted Arcidi is doing sets of six power reps, he will begin with a weight which is 30 to 40 pounds under his best workout set. Depending on the number of sets he is doing, he will use a weight-jump factor of between five and ten pounds when moving from one set to the next.

days. A bodybuilder could employ the stagger-ed volume training (SVT) technique within the structure of this workout as a means of decreasing the accumulated rest time between sets on the first five exercises.

It is very important to remember when following the above workout program (or many of the others – plus the advanced training techniques mentioned in this book) that you must use as heavy a weight as possible in ratio to your rep factor (unless otherwise instructed) but never at the expense of continuous tension on the muscles. In other words, don't focus all your attention just on trying to get the weight up, unless you are training for brute power and unreal superhuman strength.

One of the very best ways to follow through with the advice just suggested, is to use the flash point training concept. It is a sys-tem where you train at the lowest intensity allowable that will still accommodate the muscle-gain theory. We would very much like to tell you that, by following the detailed training advice in this book, you will produce continuous gains in strength and dynamic muscle growth, but unfortunately it has been our experience that no continuous gains are *ever* made. You can form a graph of slow rises, a leveling off, a slight drop, another small gain, another leveling off, and so on. As a matter of fact, one can see just how valid this is by observing nature. In this sense training echoes nature that we see all around us.

A Final Comment...

Without a doubt you can expect increases in metabolic muscle mass and strength, coupled with vascularity, when using the advanced bodybuilding training techniques and pro-grams which utilize less than 12 to 15 sets per muscle group. Perhaps, in certain select situations, some genetic superior bodybuilders – with their hyper recovery ability – may have to go back onto an anabolic high-volume train-ing system of 12 to 15 and 8 to 10 sets for each of the major and minor muscle groups respec-tively in order to exceed their previous peak in revolutionary muscle growth without the use of anabolic steroids, but we doubt it.

"Dr. Squat" Fred C. Hatfield once said, "Bodybuilders, in order to achieve the tremen-dous musculature that they possess, have to

Nasser El Sonbaty

do slow movements, fast movements, light and heavy poundages, and everything in between, thereby increasing the efficiency of the mechanisms of the muscle structure."

This is indeed the basis to achieving muscle gains, and we feel very confident that we have shared with you some of the very best training information that will help you accom-plish this purpose. In any case, we sincerely hope that the information in this rather extensive book is of some value to you, and we look forward to hearing from you as to the training results you make from it. Remember, knowledge creates possibilities and therefore **applied knowledge is power!** Experiment, adopt and gain herculean size and strength. Good luck, future bodybuilding champion.

Highly Recommended Reading...

Evolutionary Training by Atletika Sports International.
Phone: 800-621-2602

In the highly competitive field of athletics, a well-conceived training and restoration program can separate those who actually succeed from those who merely envision success. The following explains the basic tenets of Evolutionary Training. When followed religiously, and coupled with a sound diet – plus supplementation – *Evolutionary Training* is prepared for those bodybuilders who have a desire to elevate their ability to the advanced level.

Evolutionary Training is the progressive realization of those physical qualities necessary to master the skills in the bodybuilder's chosen sport. The levels of mastery are assessed and maintained on an individual basis; thus, the difference between those bodybuilders who wish to compete and those who want to reach their full genetic potential without participating in competition is reviewed.

The *Evolutionary Training* program involves the development and integration of four essential training characteristics: strength, speed strength, strength endurance, and flexibility. This program emphasizes the development of strength throughout the entire range of motion (ROM) of an exercise, which allows the bodybuilder to execute at peak performance levels with a lesser chance of injury during periods of fatigue. The above training characteristics, at the appropriate levels, integrate for peak performance.

Evolutionary Training is the long-term organization of four interrelated actions. These actions, when used as a system, are far more potent than any single one by itself.

1. Evaluation: The bodybuilder first completes a series of tests specific to his sport. The results are used to determine his level of fitness, including strong and weak links. The bodybuilder is then placed in his individual ability level and given the proper program for that level.

2. Program Design: Beginner programs (from 1 to 3) each cover one full block lasting two months. Intermediate-level bodybuilders progress from Class I through Class III. Each class lasts six months and includes blocks lasting two months (three blocks in each class). The advanced levels (Candidate Master of Sport and Master of Sport) each last one year. The advanced-level training blocks last from one to two months, depending on the needs of the bodybuilder.

At each level of the program (each student is tested and retested to determine his level), the bodybuilder will be supplied with specific training tips that include the workout plans, exercises, and restoration means. After the bodybuilder has completed his current block of training, he retests to determine improvements and to pinpoint changes in his strong and weak points. If he has made sufficient progress, he will graduate to the next level and be given those training plans appropriate to that level. If, for some reason, he has not improved, his weaknesses are targeted and are corrected in the next training block or blocks. The bodybuilder will not be given the programs for the next level until his test results indicate that this is the best step.

While the bodybuilder may at times appear to be "held back" using this method, the format will best serve his long-range ability to make gains. It is only after the major weak links of a person are corrected that he will be able to make significant gains toward the advanced level.

3. Base and specialized exercises: Each bodybuilder will perform a series of exercises that will best benefit him at a particular fitness level. These exercises can be used as a reference point to use within the individualized training plans.

4. Restoration: The Evolutionary System will address, in a very comprehensive manner, a variety of restorative means which can improve the recovery of a bodybuilder from hard training. These means will be recommended in general form depending on the level of the bodybuilder, as well as more specific in cases of eliminating weak links. Restoration will include base nutritional integrity, supplementation, physical means (massage, hydro therapy, sauna, trigger-point therapy, EMS, muscle balancing, chiropractic, and others).

We feel that **The Evolutionary Training Program** is a comprehensive and quite synergistic system which focuses on bodybuilding (mass) and powerlifting (maximal strength).

Magazines, Newsletters Audio Cassettes, VHS Videos Thoughtfully Suggested For The Bodybuilder and Strength Athlete

Magazines:

Hardgainer
P.O. Box 8186, CY 2091, Nicosia, Cyprus
6 issues – $25.00

Muscle Media 2000
P.O. Box 277, Golden, CO 80402
12 issues – $59.40
All major credit card orders
call 1-800-615-8500

Powerlifting USA
Box 467, Camarillo, CA 93011
12 issues – $31.95

Newsletters:

H.I.T.
P.O. Box 19446, Cincinnati, OH 45219
4 issues – $10.00

Master Trainer
c/o Ageless Athlete
Suite 221, Memorial Building,
610 N. Main St., Blackburg, VA 24060
6 issues – $20.00/Foreign $26.00

Serious Growth Newsletter
2945 South Mooney Blvd., Visalia, CA 93277
12 issues – $69.00 per year
    When subscribing to any of the above magazines or newsletters payments should be made in US funds only. Allow six to eight weeks for delivery of the first issue.

Audio Cassettes

Training secrets revealed on audio cassette Top strength giants (Ted Arcidi, Ken Lain, etc.) and best in the world bodybuilders like Bill Pearl, Chuck Sipes talk about strength training, nutrition, contest preparation, and much more. For information and prices on these audio interviews and seminars, write to: Dennis B. Weis, P.O. Box 9485, Ketchikan, Alaska 99901.

VHS Videos

Health For Life
8033 Sunset Blvd., Suite 483
Los Angeles, CA 90046
Tape I (back, biceps, delts) –
$39.95 plus $2.00 for shipping
    This video is titled *Secrets of Advanced Bodybuilders* just like their best-selling book. It features live-action exercise demonstrations as only the **Health For Life** research team can do. The bottom line? It will help you reach a new supercharged level of training experience. Credit card orders call 1-800-874-5339

Chris Cormier

Optimum Training Systems
2945 South Mooney Blvd., Visalia, CA 93277
Vol. I and II – $99.00 plus $6.50 shipping
and handling

    The authors (Leo Costa Jr., Dr. Russ Horine) of the "Serious Growth" system and their associates produced this two-volume video package titled: *Advanced Training Techniques*. The comprehensive demonstration and explanation of the most effective bodybuilding exercises known will help you pack on rock-hard muscle mass, fast. Credit card orders call 1-800-582-2083

Larry Scott and Associates
P.O. Box 540162, N. Salt Lake, UT 84054-0162
4-volume set – $79.95 plus $5.00 shipping
    This *Hidden Secrets* video package is literally jam-packed with Larry Scott's useful, fascinating, inspiring and rather unique ways of doing exercises. It's like having Larry Scott step out of the pages of a *MuscleMag* and into the gym as your very own one-on-one personal trainer. Credit card orders call 1-800-225-9752

Graphic Art and Photography
John McDermott
626 Anderson Drive, Ketchikan, Alaska 99901
    Commercial art and illustration (including logo and letterhead design), and photography. John is a contributing consultant to *MuscleMag International,* and is a biographee of record in Marquis's *Who's Who in the World* and *Who's Who in the West.*

Designed Foods of the '90s
MET-Rx – The Protein Pump:

We are continually amazed at the growing number of today's bodybuilders who recognize the importance of correct nutrition – and it's no wonder. Every bodybuilding magazine in the world, it seems, is full of information concerning the use of ergogenic nutritional substances as a means of achieving peak bodybuilding gains, without the use of anabolic drugs. You just can't avoid seeing the facts every time you pick up one of the bodybuilding magazines.

One thing that causes us great concern, though, is all the pseudo-scientific/intellectual junk that is being written about, either in an article or advertisement format, which makes reference to natural "anabolic steroid replacement" nutrition formulas. There will always be many who actually believe this to exist but this is simply not true.

Anabolic drugs interact with specific cellular receptors and hormone response elements in the genetic site of the muscle cell. There is no known natural nutrient which is capable of interacting with the androgen and anti-catabolic hormone receptors in the body as anabolic steroids do. Therefore, such advertised substitutes are absolutely incapable of reproducing or exerting an anabolic steroid-like effect.

Basically, what some of the legitimate so-called "anabolic steroid replacement" nutrient formulas do is support the physiological adaptations which occur naturally in association with an effective high-intensity bodybuilding program. The problem, as we see it, is trying to determine which pill, capsule or powder or combinations will produce that almost miraculous muscle gain beyond anyone's fondest hopes.

Unless you are bank-rolled like H. Ross Perot, it will become a huge financial burden trying the literally dozens upon dozens of food supplements available to the bodybuilding public. It takes an average of from four to six weeks for the biological system in the body to become receptive to a product – so you can pretty much determine that you're going to be in for the long haul.

There are five non-biased, objective guidelines for determining which food supplements will accelerate and help extend your bodybuilding potential. The supplementation plan should produce the following:

1. Maintain and increase muscle mass size
2. Maintain and increase strength
3. Decrease intercellular bodyfat
4. Keep energy levels at an optimum high for high-intensity bodybuilding workouts
5. Not cause additional, or abnormal hunger

If the product meets all five criterion then you're in the ballpark, so to speak. To get to home base you must also ask yourself these three questions:

1. Do I appear physically as if I am getting the right results from my nutritional plan and structured workout program?
2. Do I, in all honesty, feel that I am getting the results I desire from the supplementation techniques?
3. Does the supplement program give me a good nutritional return?

If your present supplementation technique does not meet the demands of either of the first five guidelines above, or if you had to answer "no" to any of the second

Mauro Sarni

three questions posed, then perhaps it is time to seek out one which does.

We have interviewed many competitive amateur and pro bodybuilders regarding supplementation, and they universally agreed that, "yes," there are some products out on the market which give an apparent surge of strength and energy but none like the surge experienced from an engineered food called **MET-Rx.**

As you may have noticed, MET-Rx is called a food and not a supplement, and there is indeed a vast difference between the two. A supplement implies that there is some unique ingredient within its formulation which will ignite an energy release, or muscle mass gain.

MET-Rx, on the other hand, is an array of substrates in specific amounts which upgrade a bodybuilder's biological system to burn fat by as much as 350 percent, and increase lean muscle tissue mass by 500 percent when compared to non-engineered food supplements. MET-Rx can best be described as the diet with food as a supplement.

Kevin Levrone

MET-Rx is being characterized by those who study contemporary orthomolecular biochemistry as possibly the most advanced result-producing bodybuilding nutritional program in existence today. Don't think for one moment that, if MET-Rx didn't deliver superior results, Marjo Selin, the uncrowned Ms. Olympia and one of bodybuilding's most educated and respected champions, would put her signature of endorsement on it, or Jeff Everson, for that matter.

Top bodybuilders like Marjo and Jeff are interested in just one thing – results! If they weren't getting it from the MET-Rx products, they wouldn't have anything to do with it. This isn't just an isolated example of two top bodybuilders using the products, because many, many top physiques all over the country and the world, for that matter, are on the MET-Rx bodybuilding program. We have confirmed this not only by seeing documented proof, but more importantly by talking to the bodybuilders themselves. We plan to talk to many more as time goes on.

One thing is very apparent when talking to these bodybuilders – they are not on any exotic products reserved just for them so they can make super muscle gains. They consume exactly the same Met-Rx individual serving packets that MET-Rx USA Inc., Irvine, California would ship to any bodybuilder.

We are using the MET-Rx Engineered Foods ourselves, and we are absolutely thrilled with the efficacy of it. Not only is it helping us achieve our genetic bodybuilding

potential, but, as an added feature, it serves as a pleasant drink which is easy to mix (no lumps or chunks here), absolutely delicious (no gagging or running for the porcelain), and it digests and assimilates easily.

Some bodybuilders mix MET-Rx with water, ice and a bit of apple juice, but one of our all-time favorites is to simply blend 16 ounces of skim milk together with a handful of frozen strawberries and, of course, one MET-Rx individual serving packet. Not only is this liquid food shake absolutely delicious, but it contains virtually no fat, no sugar, and is loaded with nutrients, including a proprietary blend of substrates which have the power to partition nutrients toward lean muscle tissue mass and away from fat storage.

Dr. Scott Connelly, M.D., the inventor and pioneer of the popular MET-Rx movement will stay "numero uno" in the field of designed or engineered foods, in spite of any feeble attempts by others to duplicate his product's unique blend of ingredients or substrates.

There is no doubt in our minds that the MET-Rx powders are designed for the hardcore bodybuilder (powerlifters too) who wants to improve his or her muscle mass and strength.

If you are seriously interested in learning more about the **MET-Rx Engineered Foods,** then take the initiative and call the sincere and enthusiastic people at MET-Rx USA for more information. The number is: 1-800-546-3879.

Gary Strydom

INDEX

PHOTO INDEX